FAVORITE BRAND NAME™

CHINESE

Publications International, Ltd.

Favorite Brand Name Recipes at www.fbnr.com

Some of the products listed in this publication may be in limited distribution.

Front cover photography by Chris Cassidy Photography Inc.

Pictured on the front cover *(clockwise from top left):* Green Beans and Shiitake Mushrooms *(page 290),* Asparagus Chicken with Black Bean Sauce *(page 155),* Honey-Glazed Spareribs *(page 120),* Apricot-Chicken Pot Stickers *(page 22),* Barbecued Pork *(page 30)* and Hunan Chili Beef *(page 78).*

Pictured on the jacket flaps: Sesame Chicken and Vegetable Stir-Fry *(page 330)* and Ginger Wonton Soup *(page 328).*

Pictured on the back cover *(clockwise from top):* Stir-Fried Tofu and Vegetables *(page 178),* Oriental Shrimp & Steak Kabobs *(page 226),* Braised Cornish Hen *(page 144)* and Mu Shu Vegetables *(page 186).*

ISBN-13: 978-1-4127-2995-6
ISBN-10: 1-4127-2995-5

Manufactured in China.

8 7 6 5 4 3 2 1

Nutritional Analysis: The nutritional information that appears with some recipes was submitted in part by the participating companies and associations. Every effort has been made to check the accuracy of these numbers. However, because numerous variables account for a wide range of values for certain foods, nutritive analyses in this book should be considered approximate.

CONTENTS

Introduction   4

Tasty Appetizers & Snacks   8

Hearty Beef & Lamb   38

Sensational Pork   84

Perfect Poultry   126

Meatless Pleasures   176

Splendid Seafood   206

Satisfying Salads   244

Comforting Soups   268

Delicious Side Dishes   288

Lean Delights   324

Acknowledgments   375

Index   376

INTRODUCTION

Everyone loves Asian cuisine. From the sharp peppery flavor of fresh ginger and the fiery impact of Chinese chili sauce, to the delicate richness of oyster sauce, the authentic tastes of Chinese cuisine are captivating. As a special bonus, this exciting cookbook includes recipes from several other Asian cuisines. Imagine the spicy zing of Thai cooking, the wonderful mysteries of Indian dishes and the exotic appeal of Vietnamese foods. You'll quickly discover just how easy it is to add Asian specialties to your culinary repertoire.

Recipes for Asian dishes may contain some unfamiliar ingredients. Always check the glossary on the following pages for a brief description before looking for these items in the ethnic section of your supermarket or in a local Asian market.

BEAN PASTE: Also known as brown or yellow bean sauce and miso in Japan, bean paste is a thick sauce made from fermented soybeans, flour, water and salt. It may be smooth or contain whole beans. Hot bean paste, which gets its heat from chilies, is also available. Bean paste may be purchased in Asian markets and some supermarkets.

BEAN SPROUTS: Small white shoots of the mung bean, bean sprouts are available fresh and canned. They are one of the few sprouts that are sturdy enough to stand up to cooking. Both fresh and canned bean sprouts should be thoroughly rinsed in cold water and drained before using.

BEAN THREADS: Also called transparent or cellophane noodles, these dry, fine white noodles are made from powdered mung beans. They have little flavor, but readily absorb the flavors of other foods. Bean threads are available in packets or bundles.

BOK CHOY: A member of the cabbage family, bok choy has 8- to 10-inch-long white or greenish-white stalks and large dark green leaves. Both the stalks and leaves are used in cooking, but they are usually cooked separately.

CARDAMOM: Cardamom seeds grow in pods, about 15 seeds to a pod. An aromatic spice often used in Indian cooking, cardamom is available most often as seeds or ground into a powder, but the edible seed-filled pods are sometimes found in some markets.

CHILI OIL: This reddish-colored oil is made from peanut oil infused with dried red chili peppers. Use it sparingly as it is blazing hot.

CHILI PASTE: Chili paste and garlic chili paste are used extensively in Chinese, Thai, Vietnamese and other Asian cuisines. Made from mashed chili peppers, soy beans, vinegar, seasonings and often garlic, chili paste is extremely hot.

CHILI PEPPERS: A wide variety of chili peppers are used throughout Asia. Green and red Thai chili peppers, which are 1 to 1½ inches long and very narrow, are available in some supermarkets. Jalapeño and serrano chili peppers may be substituted for most other Asian chili peppers.

CHINESE CHILI SAUCE: A thick, fiery sauce of ground chilies and salt, Chinese chili sauce should be used sparingly.

CHUTNEY: A spicy fruit-based relish served as a refreshing accompaniment to certain Indian dishes, chutney can be raw or cooked. Prepared chutneys can be purchased in most supermarkets.

COCONUT MILK/COCONUT CREAM: A creamy unsweetened liquid made from the grated meat of mature coconuts, coconut milk should not be confused with the thin liquid that is drained from a fresh coconut. A richer coconut cream is also available. Both coconut milk and coconut cream are readily available in most supermarkets.

CORIANDER SEEDS: This aromatic spice comes from the parsleylike plant of the same name. Many Americans know the green leaves of the coriander plant as cilantro. The seeds are used in Indian cooking. The leaves are used in Thai, Vietnamese and Indian cuisines as well as in Latin and Caribbean cooking.

CORN, BABY: The edible cobs of baby corn are 2 to 3 inches long with rows of tiny yellow kernels. They are slightly sweet and crunchy. Available in cans or jars packed in salted water, baby corn should be drained and rinsed with cold water to remove brine before using.

DAIKON: This long, white radish with a sweet flavor is used extensively in Japan. Daikons are most often grated and eaten raw as a condiment. They are also cooked in some simmered or braised dishes. Slender white icicle radishes may be substituted.

EGG NOODLES, CHINESE-STYLE: Made of flour, eggs, water and salt, Chinese egg noodles can be purchased fresh, frozen or dried.

EGG ROLL WRAPPERS: These thin sheets of noodlelike dough are available in 7- and 8-inch squares or circles. Wonton wrappers are also available, but are cut into 3- and 4-inch squares. Both are sold refrigerated or frozen. Keep wrappers tightly wrapped in plastic to prevent drying during storage.

FERMENTED, SALTED BLACK BEANS: These pungent, salty black soybeans are used in Chinese cooking. Fermented black beans are available in Asian markets. They need to be rinsed under cold running water before using to reduce their saltiness.

FISH SAUCE: A salty brown liquid extract of fermented fish, fish sauce is used as a flavoring in several Southeast Asian cuisines. It is called nuoc nam in Vietnam, nam pla in Thailand and shottsuru in Japan. In American supermarkets it is most often labeled as fish sauce. The strong aroma disappears during cooking.

FIVE-SPICE POWDER: This blend of five ground spices has a pungent, slightly sweet flavor. Generally made of anise seed, fennel, cloves, cinnamon and ginger or pepper, five-spice powder is readily available in most supermarkets.

GARAM MASALA: A blend of roasted ground spices, garam masala is used often in the cooking of northern India. For the freshest flavor, Indian cooks grind whole spices as needed. American cooks will find it easy to prepare.

GINGER, CRYSTALLIZED: Crystallized ginger is gingerroot that has been cooked in a sugar syrup to preserve it and then coated with coarse sugar. Also know as candied ginger, it is used most often as an ingredient in desserts.

GINGER, FRESH: This knobby root with light brown skin is available fresh in the produce section. Always remove the tough outer skin before using ginger. Wrapped in plastic, ginger will keep for several weeks in the refrigerator. Peeled ginger can also be kept in salted water or dry sherry in the refrigerator for several months.

HOISIN SAUCE: This dark brown sauce is made of soybeans, flour, sugar, spices, garlic, chilies and salt. It has a sweet, spicy flavor and is used in many Chinese recipes. Once opened, canned hoisin sauce should be transferred to a glass container, sealed and refrigerated.

KIMCHEE: Kimchee, or kimchi, is a hot and spicy pickled vegetable mixture served as a condiment with many Korean meals. It is most often made of cabbage. Available in jars in the produce sections of some supermarkets and in Asian markets, kimchee must be kept refrigerated.

LEMONGRASS: A stiff, pale green grasslike plant, lemongrass is an essential part of Southeast Asian cooking. It has a lemony aroma. To use, remove the outer leaves and chop or slice it across the stem from the base up to where the leaves begin to separate. It is available in some supermarkets and Asian markets.

MUSHROOMS, DRIED ASIAN: Dehydrated black or brown mushrooms from Asia are available packaged or by the ounce. They are often labeled as Chinese or Asian mushrooms. Dried mushrooms must be soaked in warm or hot water until they are softened.

MUSHROOMS, SHIITAKE: These wild Japanese mushrooms are now cultivated and are readily available both fresh and dried in most supermarkets.

MUSHROOMS, STRAW: These small mushrooms with a deep umbrella shape are most commonly found canned. Used in Chinese cuisine, they have a mild flavor.

NAPA CABBAGE: Also known as Chinese cabbage, napa is a loosely packed elongated head of light green stalks that are slightly crinkled. It has a mild flavor.

OYSTER SAUCE: This thick, brown Chinese sauce is made from oysters that have been boiled with soy sauce and seasonings and then strained. Oyster sauce adds a surprisingly delicate taste to meat and vegetable dishes. Its salty, fishy flavor disappears when cooked.

RICE, JASMINE: A long-grain aromatic rice, jasmine rice is grown in Thailand. It has a subtle aroma and a slightly nutty taste.

RICE, SWEET/GLUTINOUS: This short-grain rice is almost round in shape. It has a higher starch content than long-grain varieties, which causes the grains to stick together when cooked.

RICE STICKS: Also called rice noodles, these dried flat noodles are made from rice flour. They are available in several widths. Soften the noodles in warm water before using, unless frying them in oil.

RICE VERMICELLI: Available in several widths in packets or small bundles, rice vermicelli are dried round noodles made from rice flour. They look similar to bean threads.

RICE VINEGAR: Mellow and tangy in flavor, this vinegar is made from fermented rice. Chinese rice vinegar is pale yellow in color and is generally more readily available than the almost colorless Japanese rice vinegar.

RICE WINE: Made from fermented rice, rice wines are sweet and usually low in alcohol. Japanese versions are sake and mirin.

SESAME OIL: Dark or Oriental sesame oil is an amber-colored oil pressed from toasted sesame seeds. It has a strong nutty taste that if used sparingly adds a unique flavor to Asian dishes. Do not confuse it with the pale-colored sesame oil made from untoasted sesame seeds.

SOBA: Grayish brown in color, Japanese soba noodles are made of buckwheat flour. Unlike other dried noodles, soba must be used within two or three months.

SOY SAUCE: This dark, salty liquid is made from fermented soy beans and wheat or barley. Although there are different varieties available, such as dark and light, the major brands found in supermarkets are all-purpose. A reduced-sodium version is available as well.

TAMARI: A dark liquid made from soybeans, tamari is similar to soy sauce but is thicker and stronger in flavor.

TOFU: Also known as bean curd, tofu is made from soy milk. It is white or creamy in color with a smooth texture. Tofu, which is high in protein, has a bland, slightly nutty flavor but readily takes on the flavor of foods it is cooked with. Firm and extra-firm tofu can be cut into pieces and used in cooking. Tofu is available fresh in the refrigerated section of some supermarkets. It is also found in aseptic packages (a form of vacuum packaging); store these packages at room temperature.

WATER CHESTNUTS: Water chestnuts are the fruit of an Asian aquatic plant. They add crunchiness to stir-fries, salads and rice dishes. Water chestnuts are readily available canned, both whole and sliced.

WONTON WRAPPERS: see Eggroll Wrappers.

WOOD EARS: Also known as cloud ears, these dried Asian mushrooms have a mild flavor. They will absorb the flavors of the other ingredients they are cooked with. Wood ears must be rehydrated in warm water before use.

TASTY APPETIZERS & SNACKS

⅓ cup reduced sodium soy sauce

2 teaspoons minced garlic

1 teaspoon dark sesame oil

½ teaspoon ground ginger

1 pound boneless, skinless chicken breasts, cut into 4×½-inch strips

6 ounces (1 carton) ALPINE LACE® Fat Free Cream Cheese with Garlic & Herbs

2 tablespoons finely chopped green onions

2 tablespoons sesame seeds, toasted

1 tablespoon extra virgin olive oil

CHICKEN SESAME WITH ORIENTAL CRÈME

Makes 24 appetizer servings

1. In a small bowl, whisk the first four ingredients. Reserve 2 tablespoons; pour the remaining marinade into a self-sealing plastic bag. Add the chicken and seal the bag. Refrigerate for 2 hours, turning occasionally.

2. To make the Oriental Crème: In a bowl, place the cream cheese. Stir in the reserved 2 tablespoons of marinade. Stir in the onions. Cover and refrigerate.

3. Remove the chicken from the marinade. Spread the sesame seeds on a plate and roll the chicken in them. In a large nonstick skillet, heat the olive oil over medium-high heat. Add the chicken and stir-fry for 6 minutes or until golden brown and the juices run clear. Serve with the Oriental Crème.

CHICKEN SESAME WITH ORIENTAL CRÈME

½ cup lime juice
⅓ cup reduced-sodium soy sauce
¼ cup packed brown sugar
4 cloves garlic, minced
¼ teaspoon ground red pepper
3 boneless skinless chicken breast halves (about 1¼ pounds)
¼ cup chunky or creamy peanut butter
¼ cup thick unsweetened coconut milk* or Thick Coconut Milk Substitute (recipe follows)
¼ cup finely chopped onion
1 teaspoon paprika
1 tablespoon finely chopped cilantro

Coconut milk separates in the can, with thick cream (consistency may be soft like yogurt or firm like shortening) floating to the top over thin, watery milk. Spoon thick cream from top after opening can. If less than 1/4 cup, make up difference with remaining coconut milk.

Chicken Satay with Peanut Sauce

Makes 6 servings

1. Stir lime juice, soy sauce, brown sugar, garlic and red pepper in medium bowl until sugar dissolves. Set ⅓ cup marinade aside.

2. Slice chicken lengthwise into ⅓-inch-thick strips. Add to marinade in bowl and stir to coat evenly. Cover and set aside at room temperature 30 minutes or cover and refrigerate up to 12 hours.

3. Cover 18 wooden skewers (10 to 12 inches long) with cold water for 20 minutes to prevent them from burning; drain.

4. Place peanut butter in medium bowl. Stir in ⅓ cup reserved marinade, 1 tablespoon at a time, until smooth. Stir in coconut milk, onion and paprika. Transfer sauce to small serving bowl; set aside.

5. Drain chicken; discard marinade. Weave 1 or 2 slices chicken onto each skewer.

6. Grill skewers over hot coals or broil 2 to 3 minutes per side or until chicken is no longer pink in center. Transfer to serving platter.

7. Sprinkle sauce with cilantro; serve with skewers. Garnish as desired.

THICK COCONUT MILK SUBSTITUTE

⅓ cup milk
1 teaspoon cornstarch
½ teaspoon coconut extract

Combine milk and cornstarch in small saucepan. Stir constantly over high heat until mixture boils and thickens. Immediately pour into small bowl; stir in extract.

CHICKEN SATAY WITH PEANUT SAUCE

Vietnamese Dipping Sauce
(recipe follows)
8 ounces medium shrimp,
peeled and deveined
3½ ounces very thin dry rice
vermicelli
12 rice paper wrappers,*
6½ inches in diameter
36 whole cilantro leaves
4 ounces roasted pork or
beef, sliced ⅛ inch thick
1 tablespoon chopped
peanuts
Lime peel for garnish

*Available at specialty stores or
Asian markets.

VIETNAMESE SUMMER ROLLS

Makes 12 summer rolls

1. Prepare Vietnamese Dipping Sauce; set aside.

2. Fill large saucepan ¾ full of water; bring to a boil over high heat. Add shrimp; simmer 1 to 2 minutes or until shrimp turn pink and opaque. Transfer shrimp with slotted spoon to small bowl.

3. Add rice vermicelli to saucepan. Cook according to package directions until tender but still firm, about 3 minutes. Drain and rinse under cold running water to stop cooking; drain again.

4. Slice shrimp in half lengthwise with utility knife.

5. To form summer rolls, soften 1 rice paper wrapper in large bowl of water 30 to 40 seconds. Drain; place wrapper on cutting board. Arrange 3 cilantro leaves upside down in center of wrapper. Layer 2 shrimp halves, flat side up, on cilantro leaves. Top with layer of pork and ¼ cup vermicelli.

6. To form summer rolls, fold bottom of wrapper up over filling; fold in each side. Roll up toward top of wrapper. Place on platter with leaf design on top. Repeat with remaining wrappers and fillings. Sprinkle summer rolls with peanuts. Serve with Vietnamese Dipping Sauce. Garnish, if desired.

VIETNAMESE DIPPING SAUCE
½ cup water
¼ cup fish sauce
2 tablespoons lime juice
1 tablespoon sugar
1 clove garlic, minced
¼ teaspoon chili oil

Combine all ingredients in small bowl; mix well.

Makes about 1 cup

VIETNAMESE SUMMER ROLLS

ASIAN DRUMS

Makes about 48 appetizers

3 packages (about
  1¾ pounds each)
  PERDUE® Fresh Chicken
  Wingettes
1 bottle (5 ounces) teriyaki
  sauce
¼ cup peanut or vegetable
  oil
¼ cup honey
1 tablespoon white vinegar
1 teaspoon ground ginger
2 cups lightly toasted, finely
  chopped peanuts or
  pecans

To make mini-drums from wing sections, use a small, sharp knife to cut around the narrower end of wing to loosen meat. Then use knife blade to gently scrape meat down toward the larger, knobby end of bone, turning meat inside out. On sections with two bones, pull out and discard smaller bone, detaching with knife if necessary.

In large bowl, combine teriyaki sauce, oil, honey, vinegar and ginger; mix well. Add chicken pieces, stirring to coat well. Cover and marinate overnight in refrigerator.

Preheat oven to 375°F. Grease 2 large jelly-roll pans; arrange chicken on pans. Bake 35 minutes or until tender. Remove mini-drums and roll in chopped nuts. Serve hot or at room temperature.

STIR-FRIED SHRIMP APPETIZERS

Makes 8 servings

¼ cup KIKKOMAN® Soy
  Sauce
¼ cup dry white wine
¼ cup chopped green onions
1 clove garlic, pressed
1 teaspoon ground ginger
1 pound medium-size raw
  shrimp, peeled and
  deveined
3 tablespoons vegetable oil

Combine soy sauce, wine, green onions, garlic and ginger; stir in shrimp and let stand 15 minutes. Heat oil in hot wok or large skillet over medium-high heat. Drain shrimp and add to pan. Discard marinade. Stir-fry 1 to 2 minutes, or until shrimp are pink. Serve immediately.

¼ cup soy sauce
2 tablespoons dry sherry
4 teaspoons cornstarch
  Peanut or vegetable oil
6 cups chopped or shredded
  cabbage *or* preshredded
  coleslaw mix or cabbage
  (about 12 ounces)
1 cup chopped mushrooms
⅔ cup thinly sliced green
  onions
½ pound ground beef, pork
  or turkey
3 cloves garlic, minced
¼ teaspoon crushed red
  pepper
12 egg roll wrappers *or*
  64 wonton wrappers
  Sweet and sour sauce for
  dipping
  Chinese hot mustard
  (optional)

EGG ROLLS

Makes about 12 egg rolls or 64 mini egg rolls

1. Blend soy sauce and sherry into cornstarch in cup until smooth.

2. Heat wok or large skillet over medium-high heat. Add 1 tablespoon oil; heat until hot. Add cabbage, mushrooms and green onions; stir-fry 2 minutes (cabbage will still be crisp). Remove; set aside.

3. Add beef, garlic and crushed red pepper to wok; cook until beef is no longer pink, stirring to separate. Spoon off fat.

4. Stir soy sauce mixture and add to wok. Stir-fry 2 minutes or until sauce boils and thickens. Return cabbage mixture to wok; heat through, mixing well.*

5. Place each egg roll wrapper with one point toward edge of counter. Spoon filling across and just below center of wrapper; use heaping ⅓ cup filling for each egg roll wrapper or 1 tablespoon filling for each wonton wrapper.

6. To form egg roll, fold bottom point of wrapper up over filling. Fold side points over filling, forming an envelope shape. Moisten inside edges of top point with water and roll egg roll toward that point, pressing firmly to seal. Repeat with remaining wrappers and filling.

7. Pour ½ inch oil into large skillet. Heat oil to 375°F. Fry egg rolls, 2 or 3 at a time, or mini-egg rolls, 6 to 8 at time, 2 minutes per side or until crisp and golden brown. Drain on paper towels. Serve with sweet and sour sauce and hot mustard, if desired.

Egg roll filling may be made ahead to this point; cover and refrigerate up to 24 hours. When ready to use, heat mixture until hot. Proceed as directed in step 5.

12 chicken wings (about
        2½ pounds)
3 cloves garlic, divided
2 tablespoons soy sauce
2 tablespoons dry sherry
1 tablespoon sugar
1 tablespoon cornstarch
1 teaspoon crushed red
        pepper
1 tablespoon sesame seeds
2 tablespoons vegetable oil
3 green onions with tops,
        cut into 1-inch pieces
¼ cup chicken broth
1 teaspoon dark sesame oil
        Elderberries and mixed
        greens for garnish

Soy-Braised Chicken Wings

Makes 2 dozen appetizers

1. Cut off wing tip from each chicken wing; discard or use for soup or stock. Cut wings in half between remaining joint to make 2 pieces; set aside. Mince 2 garlic cloves.

2. For marinade, combine soy sauce, sherry, sugar, cornstarch, minced garlic and crushed red pepper in large bowl; mix well. Stir in wing pieces; cover and marinate overnight in refrigerator, turning once or twice.

3. To toast sesame seeds, heat wok over medium-high heat about 30 seconds or until hot. Add sesame seeds; cook and stir about 45 seconds or until golden brown. Remove seeds to small bowl; set aside.

4. Drain chicken wings, reserving marinade. Heat wok over high heat 1 minute or until hot. Add vegetable oil and heat 30 seconds. Add ½ of wings; cook 10 to 15 minutes until wings brown on all sides, turning occasionally with tongs. Remove with slotted spoon to bowl; set aside. Reheat oil in wok 30 seconds and repeat with remaining wings. Reduce heat to medium. Pour off any remaining oil.

5. Mince remaining garlic clove. Add garlic and green onions to wok; cook and stir 30 seconds. Add wings and broth. Cover and cook 5 minutes or until wings are tender and no longer pink, stirring occasionally to prevent wings from sticking to bottom of wok.

6. Add reserved marinade and stir-fry wings until glazed with marinade. Add sesame oil; mix well. Transfer wings to serving platter; sprinkle with sesame seeds. Garnish, if desired. Serve immediately.

SOY-BRAISED CHICKEN WINGS

3 cups finely shredded cabbage
1 egg white, lightly beaten
1 tablespoon reduced-sodium soy sauce
¼ teaspoon plus ⅛ teaspoon crushed red pepper, divided
1 tablespoon minced fresh ginger
4 green onions with tops, finely chopped
¼ pound ground chicken breast, cooked and drained
24 wonton wrappers, at room temperature
  Cornstarch
½ cup water
1 tablespoon oyster sauce
2 teaspoons grated lemon peel
½ teaspoon honey
1 tablespoon peanut oil

GINGERED CHICKEN POT STICKERS

Makes 24 pot stickers

1. Steam cabbage 5 minutes, then cool to room temperature. Squeeze out any excess moisture; set aside. To prepare filling, combine egg white, soy sauce, ¼ teaspoon crushed red pepper, ginger and green onions in large bowl; blend well. Stir in cabbage and chicken.

2. To prepare pot stickers, place 1 tablespoon filling in center of 1 wonton wrapper. Gather edges around filling, pressing firmly at top to seal. Repeat with remaining wrappers and filling.

3. Place pot stickers on large baking sheet dusted with cornstarch. Refrigerate 1 hour or until cold. Meanwhile, to prepare sauce, combine water, oyster sauce, lemon peel, honey and remaining ⅛ teaspoon crushed red pepper in small bowl; mix well. Set aside.

4. Heat oil in large nonstick skillet over high heat. Add pot stickers and cook until bottoms are golden brown. Pour sauce over top. Cover and cook 3 minutes. Uncover and cook until all liquid is absorbed. Serve warm on tray as finger food or on small plates with chopsticks as first course.

GINGERED CHICKEN POT STICKERS

½ cup sweet (glutinous) rice
2 to 3 drops yellow food
   coloring (optional)
3 large dried black Asian
   mushrooms
   Boiling water
½ pound lean ground pork
   or beef
1 small egg white, lightly
   beaten
1 tablespoon minced green
   onion, white part only
1½ teaspoons soy sauce
1½ teaspoons rice wine
½ teaspoon minced fresh
   ginger
½ teaspoon sugar
¼ teaspoon salt
   Pinch black pepper
1½ teaspoons cornstarch

GARLIC-SOY SAUCE
3 tablespoons soy sauce
1½ tablespoons white vinegar
¼ teaspoon minced garlic
⅛ teaspoon sugar

PEARL-RICE BALLS

Makes about 18 balls

1. To prepare pearl-rice balls, place rice in medium bowl of cold water. Comb through rice with fingers several times; drain. Repeat until water remains clear. Return rice to bowl; fill with warm tap water. Stir in food coloring. Soak rice 3 to 4 hours, or refrigerate, covered, overnight. Drain.

2. Place mushrooms in bowl and cover with boiling water. Let stand 30 minutes. Drain. Remove and discard stems; squeeze out excess water. Mince mushrooms. Combine with pork, egg white, green onion, soy sauce, rice wine, ginger, sugar, salt and pepper in bowl; mix well. Stir in cornstarch.

3. Shape meat mixture into 1-inch balls; mixture will be fairly soft. Roll each ball in rice to coat completely; press lightly between hands to make rice adhere.*

4. Place 12-inch bamboo steamer in wok. Add water to ½ inch below steamer. (Water should not touch steamer.) Remove steamer. Bring water to a boil over high heat.

5. Place pearl-rice balls in single layer in steamer lined with wet cloth, leaving about ½-inch space between balls; cover. Place steamer in wok. Steam, covered, over high heat 40 minutes until rice is tender, adding boiling water as needed to maintain level.

6. To prepare Garlic-Soy Sauce, mix ingredients in small bowl.

7. Transfer pearl-rice balls from steamer to serving dish. Serve with Garlic-Soy Sauce.

Pearl-Rice Balls can be made through Step 3 up to 8 hours ahead. Refrigerate, covered with plastic wrap; uncover and let stand at room temperature 15 to 20 minutes before steaming. Recipe can be doubled if you have 2 steamer baskets.

1 can (20 ounces) crushed pineapple in juice, undrained
¼ cup firmly packed brown sugar
2 tablespoons cornstarch
Dash of ground ginger
1 cup water
2 tablespoons margarine
1 pound finely chopped, cooked, skinned turkey or chicken or cooked lean ground turkey
¾ cup QUAKER® Oat Bran hot cereal, uncooked
⅓ cup plain low-fat yogurt
⅓ cup finely chopped water chestnuts, drained
⅓ cup sliced green onions
2 tablespoons lite soy sauce
1 egg white, slightly beaten
1 teaspoon ground ginger
½ teaspoon salt (optional)
Red and green bell pepper pieces, fresh pineapple wedges and whole water chestnuts (optional)

SHANGHAI PARTY PLEASERS

Makes 2 dozen appetizers

Drain crushed pineapple, reserving juice. In medium saucepan, combine brown sugar, cornstarch and dash of ginger; mix well. Add combined pineapple juice, water, ¼ cup crushed pineapple and margarine; mix well. Bring to a boil over medium-high heat; reduce heat to low. Simmer about 1 minute, stirring frequently or until sauce is thick and clear. Set aside.

Heat oven to 400°F. Lightly spray 13×9-inch metal baking pan with nonstick cooking spray, or oil lightly. Combine turkey, oat bran, yogurt, water chestnuts, onions, soy sauce, egg white, 1 teaspoon ginger, salt and remaining crushed pineapple; mix well. Shape into 1-inch balls. Place in prepared pan. Bake 20 to 25 minutes or until light golden brown. If desired, alternately thread meatballs, bell pepper pieces, pineapple wedges and water chestnuts onto skewers to serve. Serve with pineapple sauce.

Spicy Sweet & Sour Sauce
(page 24, optional)
2 small boneless skinless
chicken breasts (about
8 ounces)
2 cups finely chopped
cabbage
½ cup all-fruit apricot
spread
2 green onions with tops,
finely chopped
2 teaspoons soy sauce
½ teaspoon grated fresh
ginger
⅛ teaspoon black pepper
30 (3-inch) wonton wrappers

APRICOT-CHICKEN POT STICKERS

Makes 10 servings

1. Prepare Spicy Sweet & Sour Sauce, if desired; set aside.

2. Bring 2 cups water to a boil in medium saucepan. Add chicken. Reduce heat to low; cover. Simmer 10 minutes or until chicken is no longer pink in center. Remove from saucepan; discard water.

3. Add cabbage and 1 tablespoon water to saucepan. Cook over high heat 1 to 2 minutes or until water cooks off, stirring occasionally. Remove from heat. Cool slightly.

4. Finely chop chicken. Add to saucepan along with fruit spread, green onions, soy sauce, ginger and pepper; mix well.

5. To assemble pot stickers, remove 3 wonton wrappers at a time from package. Spoon slightly rounded tablespoonful of chicken mixture onto center of each wrapper; brush edges with water. Bring 4 corners together; press to seal. Repeat with remaining wrappers and filling.

6. Spray steamer with nonstick cooking spray. Assemble steamer so that water is ½ inch below steamer. Fill steamer basket with pot stickers, leaving enough space between each to prevent sticking. Cover; steam 5 minutes. Transfer pot stickers to serving plate. Serve with Spicy Sweet & Sour Sauce and garnish, if desired.

continued on page 24

APRICOT-CHICKEN POT STICKERS

Apricot-Chicken Pot Stickers,
continued

SPICY SWEET & SOUR SAUCE

1 green onion with top
1 tablespoon cornstarch
2 tablespoons rice vinegar
¼ cup packed brown sugar
½ teaspoon crushed red pepper
2 tablespoons finely grated turnip

1. Finely chop white part of green onion; cut green portion into thin, 1-inch strips. Reserve green strips for garnish.

2. Combine cornstarch and vinegar in small bowl; mix well. Set aside.

3. Combine ¾ cup water, brown sugar, crushed red pepper and chopped green onion in small saucepan; bring to a boil. Stir in cornstarch mixture. Return to a boil; cook 1 minute or until sauce is clear and thickened. Cool. Sprinkle with turnip and reserved green onion strips just before serving.

1 cup preshredded cabbage
**   or coleslaw mix**
½ cup finely chopped
**   cooked ham**
¼ cup finely chopped water
**   chestnuts**
¼ cup sliced green onions
3 tablespoons plum sauce,
**   divided**
1 teaspoon dark sesame oil
3 flour tortillas (6 to 7
**   inches in diameter)**

SPRING ROLLS

Makes 12 appetizers

1. Combine cabbage, ham, water chestnuts, green onions, 2 tablespoons plum sauce and oil in medium bowl. Mix well.

2. Spread remaining 1 tablespoon plum sauce evenly on tortillas. Spread about ½ cup cabbage mixture on each tortilla to within ¼ inch of edge; roll up.

3. Wrap each tortilla tightly in plastic wrap. Refrigerate at least 1 hour or up to 24 hours before serving.

4. Cut each tortilla into 4 pieces.

SPRING ROLLS

Spicy Sweet & Sour Sauce
(page 24)
3 ounces rice stick noodles
4 ounces large or medium
shrimp, deveined
1 large bunch green leaf
lettuce or Boston
lettuce
1 medium cucumber,
peeled, seeded and cut
into matchstick-size
pieces
½ cup cilantro leaves
½ cup mint leaves

THAI SALAD ROLLS WITH SPICY SWEET & SOUR SAUCE

Makes 6 servings

1. Prepare Spicy Sweet & Sour Sauce; set aside.

2. Soak noodles in hot water 10 minutes to soften. Rinse under cold running water to cool; drain.

3. Meanwhile, fill medium saucepan with water. Bring to a boil. Add shrimp; return to a boil. Cook 3 to 5 minutes or until shrimp turn pink; drain. Rinse under cold running water to cool. Split each shrimp lengthwise in half.

4. Select the 12 best and largest leaves of lettuce. Rinse under cold running water; pat dry.

5. To assemble rolls, place lettuce leaf, dark, glossy side down, on work surface. Arrange shrimp, noodles, cucumber, cilantro and mint lengthwise along center rib of leaf. Roll up leaves as tightly as possible, taking care not to split leaves; secure with wooden toothpicks. Remove toothpicks before eating. Serve with Spicy Sweet & Sour Sauce. Garnish, if desired.

THAI SALAD ROLLS WITH SPICY SWEET & SOUR SAUCE

GROUND TURKEY SPRING ROLLS

Makes 16 spring rolls

1 pound Ground Turkey
1 large clove garlic, minced
1 ½ teaspoons minced fresh ginger
2 cups thinly sliced bok choy
½ cup thinly sliced green onions
2 tablespoons reduced-sodium soy sauce
1 teaspoon dry sherry or rice wine
1 teaspoon dark sesame oil
8 sheets phyllo pastry
Nonstick cooking spray
Chinese mustard (optional)
Hoisin sauce (optional)
Additional reduced-sodium soy sauce (optional)

Preheat oven to 400°F. In medium nonstick skillet, over medium-high heat, cook and stir turkey, garlic and ginger 4 to 5 minutes or until turkey is no longer pink. Drain thoroughly.

In medium bowl combine turkey mixture, bok choy, green onions, soy sauce, sherry and oil.

On clean, dry counter, layer phyllo sheets into a stack and cut into 2 (18×7-inch) rectangles. Work with one rectangle of phyllo at a time. (Keep remaining phyllo covered with a damp cloth following package instructions.)

Coat 1 rectangle of phyllo with nonstick cooking spray. On counter, arrange phyllo sheet so 7-inch side is parallel to counter edge. Place ¼ cup of turkey mixture in 5-inch strip, 1 inch away from bottom and side edges of phyllo. Fold 1-inch of bottom edge of phyllo over filling and fold longer edges of phyllo toward center; roll up, jelly-roll style. Phyllo may break during rolling, but will hold filling once the roll is completed.

Repeat process with remaining rectangles of phyllo and filling to make remaining spring rolls. Place rolls, seam side down, on 2 (10×15-inch) cookie sheets coated with nonstick cooking spray. Coat tops of rolls with nonstick cooking spray. Bake 14 to 16 minutes or until all surfaces of rolls are golden brown.

Serve immediately with Chinese mustard, hoisin sauce and additional soy sauce, if desired.

Favorite recipe from **NATIONAL TURKEY FEDERATION**

3 pounds lamb breast riblets, cut into serving-size pieces
Water
⅓ cup KIKKOMAN® Teriyaki Marinade & Sauce

TERIYAKI LAMB RIBLET APPETIZERS

Makes 8 servings

Place riblets in large saucepan. Add enough water to cover. Bring to boil over high heat. Reduce heat to low; cover. Simmer 20 minutes. Remove riblets from saucepan; discard water. Pat riblets dry with paper towels. Place riblets on grill 4 to 5 inches from hot coals; brush thoroughly with teriyaki sauce. Cook 8 minutes, turning over and brushing frequently with remaining teriyaki sauce. (Or, place on rack of broiler pan; brush with teriyaki sauce. Broil 4 inches from heat 4 minutes on each side, brushing frequently with remaining teriyaki sauce.)

1 tablespoon soy sauce
2 teaspoons peanut or vegetable oil
½ teaspoon sugar
¼ teaspoon garlic salt
12 wonton wrappers

EASY WONTON CHIPS

Makes 2 dozen chips

1. Preheat oven to 375°F.

2. Combine soy sauce, oil, sugar and garlic salt in small bowl; mix well.

3. Cut each wonton wrapper diagonally in half. Place wonton wrappers on 15×10-inch jelly-roll pan coated with nonstick cooking spray. Brush soy sauce mixture lightly but evenly over both sides of each wonton wrapper.

4. Bake 4 to 6 minutes or until crisp and lightly browned, turning after 3 minutes. Transfer to cooling rack; cool completely.

1/4 cup soy sauce
1 green onion with top, cut in half
2 tablespoons dry red wine
1 tablespoon brown sugar
1 tablespoon honey
2 teaspoons red food coloring (optional)
1 clove garlic, minced
1/2 teaspoon ground cinnamon
2 whole pork tenderloins (about 12 ounces each), trimmed
Green Onion Curls (recipe follows), for garnish

BARBECUED PORK

Makes about 8 appetizer servings

1. Combine soy sauce, green onion, wine, sugar, honey, food coloring, garlic and cinnamon in large bowl. Add meat; turn to coat completely. Cover and refrigerate 1 hour or overnight, turning meat occasionally.

2. Preheat oven to 350°F. Drain meat, reserving marinade. Place meat on wire rack over baking pan. Bake 45 minutes or until no longer pink in center, turning and basting frequently with reserved marinade.

3. Remove meat from oven; cool. Cut into diagonal slices. Garnish with Green Onion Curls, if desired.

GREEN ONION CURLS

6 to 8 medium green onions with tops
Cold water
10 to 12 ice cubes

1. Cut green onions into 4-inch lengths, leaving about 2 inches of both white onion and green top.

2. Using sharp scissors, cut each section of green stems lengthwise into very thin strips almost down to beginning of stems, cutting 6 to 8 strips in each stem section.

3. Fill large bowl about half full with cold water. Add green onions and ice cubes. Refrigerate 1 hour or until onions curl; drain.

BARBECUED PORK

12 dried Asian mushrooms
(1 ounce)
1 large carrot, cut into
julienned strips
2 teaspoons sugar, divided
Hoisin Peanut Dipping
Sauce (page 34)
3 cups plus 2 tablespoons
vegetable oil, divided
1 medium yellow onion, cut
in half and sliced
1 clove garlic, minced
1 tablespoon soy sauce
1 teaspoon dark sesame oil
1½ cups fresh bean sprouts
(about 4 ounces), rinsed
and drained
14 egg roll wrappers
(7 inches in diameter)
1 egg, beaten
1 bunch fresh mint sprigs or
basil leaves (optional)
14 large lettuce leaves
(optional)

Vietnamese Vegetarian Spring Rolls

Makes 14 rolls

1. Place mushrooms in bowl; cover with hot water. Let stand 30 minutes. Place carrot strips in small bowl. Add 1 teaspoon sugar and toss until mixed. Let stand 15 minutes, tossing occasionally.

2. Meanwhile, prepare Hoisin Peanut Dipping Sauce; set aside.

3. Drain mushrooms, reserving ½ cup liquid. Squeeze out excess water. Remove and discard stems from mushrooms. Cut caps into thin slices; set aside.

4. Heat wok over medium-high heat. Drizzle 2 tablespoons vegetable oil into wok and heat 30 seconds. Add onion; stir-fry 1 minute. Stir in mushrooms, garlic and reserved liquid. Reduce heat to medium. Cover and cook 3 minutes or until mushrooms are tender. Add soy sauce, sesame oil and remaining 1 teaspoon sugar. Cook and stir mushroom mixture 3 to 5 minutes more until all liquid has evaporated. Remove mixture to medium bowl; cool slightly.

5. Add carrot and bean sprouts to mushroom mixture; toss lightly. Place 1 wrapper on work surface with one corner toward edge of counter, keeping remaining wrappers covered. Drain mushroom mixture; place 3 tablespoons mixture on bottom third of wrapper. Brush edges of wrapper with some beaten egg.

6. To form spring rolls, fold bottom corner of wrapper up over filling. Fold in right and left corners to form 3½-inch-wide log. Roll up filling and cover spring roll with plastic wrap. Repeat with remaining wrappers and filling.

continued on page 34

VIETNAMESE VEGETARIAN SPRING ROLLS

Vietnamese Vegetarian Spring Rolls,
contintued

7. Heat remaining 3 cups vegetable oil in wok over high heat until oil registers 375°F on deep-fry thermometer. Fry 4 rolls 2 to 3 minutes until golden brown, turning once with tongs. Repeat with remaining rolls, reheating oil between batches. Drain on paper towels. Arrange on serving plate with bowl of Hoisin Peanut Dipping Sauce. Garnish as desired. To serve, wrap mint and lettuce around rolls, if desired, then dip into sauce.

HOISIN PEANUT DIPPING SAUCE

2 tablespoons creamy peanut butter
2 tablespoons water
1 tablespoon soy sauce
⅓ cup hoisin sauce
½ teaspoon dark sesame oil
1 clove garlic, minced
   Dash hot pepper sauce

Combine peanut butter, water and soy sauce in small bowl until smooth. Stir in remaining ingredients. Pour into serving bowl.   *Makes about ½ cup*

1 cup water
½ cup dry white wine
2 tablespoons reduced-sodium soy sauce
½ teaspoon Szechuan or black peppercorns
1 pound raw large shrimp, peeled, deveined
¼ cup prepared sweet and sour sauce
2 teaspoons hot Chinese mustard

CHILLED SHRIMP IN CHINESE MUSTARD SAUCE

Makes 6 servings

1. Combine water, wine, soy sauce and peppercorns in medium saucepan. Bring to a boil over high heat. Add shrimp; reduce heat to medium. Cover and simmer 2 to 3 minutes until shrimp are opaque. Drain well. Cover and refrigerate until chilled.

2. Combine sweet and sour sauce and mustard in small bowl; mix well. Serve as a dipping sauce for shrimp.

CHILLED SHRIMP IN CHINESE MUSTARD SAUCE

1 pound frozen white bread dough
12 ounces Barbecued Pork Tenderloin, chopped (recipe follows)
4 dried black Asian mushrooms
1 tablespoon peanut oil
¼ cup chopped green onions
1 tablespoon minced fresh ginger
1 tablespoon brown sugar
1 tablespoon soy sauce
1 tablespoon hoisin sauce
1½ teaspoons cornstarch
Plum Sauce (recipe follows)
1 egg
1 tablespoon water
1 tablespoon black and ivory sesame seeds

DIM SUM PORK BUNS

Makes 16 buns

1. Follow manufacturer's directions for thawing frozen bread dough.

2. Prepare Barbecued Pork Tenderloin.

3. To prepare filling, place mushrooms in small bowl. Cover with warm water; let stand 30 minutes. Rinse well and drain, squeezing out excess water. Cut off and discard stems. Cut caps into thin slices.

4. Heat oil in large skillet over medium heat. Add pork, mushrooms, green onions and ginger; cook and stir 2 minutes. Add sugar, soy sauce, hoisin sauce and cornstarch; cook and stir until thickened. Cool slightly.

5. Cut parchment paper or waxed paper into 16 (4-inch) squares. Place 1 inch apart on baking sheets.

6. Punch dough down. Divide dough in half; cover one half with plastic wrap. Cut remaining dough into 8 equal pieces. Shape each piece of dough to form disc. Pinch edge of disc between thumb and forefinger, working disc in circular motion to form a circle 4 inches in diameter. Center should be thicker than edge.

7. Place disc flat on work surface. Place 1 heaping tablespoon filling in center. At 3 or 4 places gently lift edge of dough up around filling; pinch dough together to seal. Repeat with remaining dough and filling.

8. Place buns, seam side down, on parchment paper squares. Cover with towel; let rise in warm place 45 minutes or until doubled in bulk.

9. Prepare Plum Sauce.

10. To bake buns,* preheat oven to 375°F. Beat egg and water until well blended; gently brush onto tops of buns. Sprinkle with sesame seeds. Bake 14 to 18 minutes or

until buns are golden brown and sound hollow when tapped. Serve warm with Plum Sauce.

*To steam buns, place 12-inch bamboo steamer in wok. Add water to ½ inch below steamer. (Water should not touch steamer.) Remove steamer. Bring water to a boil over high heat. Arrange 4 buns at a time in steamer, using parchment paper to lift. Place steamer over boiling water; reduce heat to medium. Cover and steam buns 15 minutes. To prevent splitting, turn off heat and let buns stand, covered, 5 minutes.

BARBECUED PORK TENDERLOIN

- **1 tablespoon soy sauce**
- **1 tablespoon hoisin sauce**
- **2 teaspoons brown sugar**
- **1 clove garlic, minced**
- **½ teaspoon Chinese 5-spice powder**
- **1 whole pork tenderloin (about 12 ounces)**

1. Combine all ingredients except pork in large glass bowl. Add pork; turn to coat. Cover and refrigerate at least 1 hour or overnight, turning occasionally.

2. Preheat oven to 350°F. Place meat on meat rack in shallow foil-lined baking pan. Insert meat thermometer in center of meat. Bake 30 minutes or until meat registers 160°F. Remove meat from oven; cool slightly.

PLUM SAUCE

- **1 cup plum preserves**
- **½ cup prepared chutney, chopped**
- **2 cloves garlic, minced**
- **2 tablespoons brown sugar**
- **2 tablespoons lemon juice**
- **2 teaspoons soy sauce**
- **2 teaspoons minced fresh ginger**

Combine all ingredients in small saucepan. Cook and stir over medium heat until preserves melt.

Makes 1 cup

HEARTY BEEF & LAMB

BEEF & BROCCOLI STIR-FRY

Makes 6 servings

⅔ cup A.1. THICK & HEARTY® Steak Sauce
⅓ cup soy sauce
2 cloves garlic, minced
1 tablespoon cornstarch
¼ teaspoon crushed red pepper flakes
1 (1½-pound) beef flank steak, thinly sliced across grain
1 tablespoon Oriental sesame oil
1 (16-ounce) bag frozen broccoli, red peppers, bamboo shoots & mushrooms, thawed (Oriental mixture)
Hot cooked rice
2 tablespoons sesame seed, toasted

In large nonmetal bowl, combine steak sauce, soy sauce, garlic, cornstarch and pepper flakes; add steak, stirring to coat. Cover; refrigerate 30 minutes, stirring occasionally.

Remove steak from marinade; reserve marinade. In 12-inch skillet, over medium-high heat, stir-fry steak in oil 3 to 4 minutes or until steak is no longer pink. Using slotted spoon, remove steak to large bowl; keep warm.

In same skillet, heat reserved marinade and vegetables to a boil; reduce heat. Cover; simmer 5 minutes. Stir in warm steak. Serve over rice; sprinkle with sesame seed. Garnish as desired.

BEEF & BROCCOLI STIR-FRY

1 beef flank steak (1¼ to
    1½ pounds)
¼ cup seasoned rice vinegar
¼ cup soy sauce
2 tablespoons dark sesame
    oil
4 cloves garlic, minced
2 teaspoons fresh ginger
½ teaspoon crushed red
    pepper
2 to 3 teaspoons sesame
    seeds
¼ cup water
½ cup thinly sliced green
    onions
    Hot cooked rice (optional)

Szechuan Grilled Flank Steak

Makes 4 to 6 servings

1. Place steak in large resealable plastic food storage bag. Combine vinegar, soy sauce, oil, garlic, ginger and crushed red pepper in cup; pour over steak. Seal bag; turn to coat. Marinate in refrigerator 3 hours, turning once.

2. Prepare grill for direct cooking.

3. Drain steak, reserving marinade in small saucepan. Place steak on grid. Grill, on covered grill, over medium-hot coals 14 to 18 minutes for medium or to desired doneness, turning steak halfway through grilling time.

4. Meanwhile to toast sesame seeds, spread seeds in large, dry skillet. Shake skillet over medium-low heat about 3 minutes or until seeds begin to pop and turn golden. Remove to small bowl; set aside.

5. Add water to reserved marinade. Bring to a boil over high heat. Reduce heat to low; simmer 5 minutes.

6. Transfer steak to carving board. Slice steak diagonally across grain into thin slices.

7. Drizzle steak with boiled marinade. Sprinkle with green onions and sesame seeds. Serve with rice, if desired.

SZECHUAN GRILLED FLANK STEAK

1 pound beef round tip steaks, cut ⅛ to ¼ inch thick

1 to 2 jalapeño peppers,* minced

2 cloves garlic, minced

2 tablespoons Oriental sesame oil, divided

1 (3-ounce) package beef-flavored instant ramen noodles

1 cup diagonally sliced carrots

½ cup chopped green onions

½ cup A.1. THICK & HEARTY® Steak Sauce

¼ cup water

¼ cup PLANTERS® Unsalted Peanuts, chopped

2 tablespoons chopped fresh cilantro or parsley

*Remove interior ribs and seeds if a milder flavor is desired.

Thai Beef and Noodle Toss

Makes 4 servings

Cut steaks crosswise into 1-inch-wide strips; cut each strip in half. In large bowl, toss steaks, jalapeños and garlic with 1 tablespoon oil; set aside.

Break noodles into 3 or 4 pieces; set aside seasoning packet. Cook noodles according to package directions; drain and rinse. Meanwhile, heat large skillet or wok over medium-high heat; stir-fry reserved steak mixture in batches 30 to 60 seconds or until steak is desired doneness. Remove steak mixture from skillet; keep warm.

In same skillet, in remaining 1 tablespoon oil, stir-fry carrots and green onions until tender. Add cooked noodles, steak sauce, water, peanuts and cilantro; sprinkle with reserved seasoning packet. Heat mixture until hot, stirring occasionally. Return warm steak mixture to skillet; mix lightly. Serve immediately.

THAI BEEF AND NOODLE TOSS

1 can (15¼ ounces)
   DEL MONTE® *FreshCut*™
   Sliced Pineapple In Its
   Own Juice, undrained
¼ **cup teriyaki sauce**
2 **tablespoons honey**
1 **pound flank steak**

Marinated Flank Steak with Pineapple

Makes 4 servings

1. Drain pineapple, reserving 2 tablespoons juice. Set aside pineapple for later use.

2. In shallow 2-quart dish, combine reserved juice, teriyaki sauce and honey; mix well. Add meat; turn to coat. Cover and refrigerate at least 30 minutes or overnight.

3. Remove meat from marinade, reserving marinade. Grill meat over hot coals (or broil), brushing occasionally with reserved marinade. Cook about 4 minutes on each side for rare; about 5 minutes on each side for medium; or about 6 minutes on each side for well done. During last 4 minutes of cooking, brush pineapple slices with marinade; grill until heated through.

4. Slice meat across grain; serve with pineapple. Garnish, if desired.

Prep & Marinate Time: 35 minutes
Cook Time: 10 minutes

Tip: Marinade that has come into contact with raw meat must be discarded or boiled for several minutes before serving with cooked food.

1½ teaspoons dry mustard
½ teaspoon water
3 pounds beef short ribs,
  about 2½ inches long
½ cup KIKKOMAN® Teriyaki
  Baste & Glaze
2 cloves garlic, pressed
¼ teaspoon ground red
  pepper (cayenne)

SPICY GLAZED SHORT RIBS

Makes 4 servings

Combine mustard with water to make a smooth paste; cover. Let stand 10 minutes. Meanwhile, score meaty side of ribs, opposite bone, ½ inch apart, ½ inch deep, both lengthwise and crosswise. Combine teriyaki baste & glaze, garlic, red pepper and mustard mixture. Place ribs on grill 5 to 7 inches from hot coals; brush thoroughly with baste & glaze mixture. Cook 15 minutes, or until ribs are brown and crispy, turning over and brushing frequently with remaining baste & glaze mixture. (Or, place ribs, scored side up, on rack of broiler pan; brush thoroughly with baste & glaze mixture. Broil 4 to 5 inches from heat 13 minutes, or until ribs are brown and crispy, turning over and brushing frequently with remaining baste & glaze mixture.)

⅓ cup vegetable oil
3 pounds round steak, cut
  into 2×½×⅛-inch strips
2 cans (4 ounces each)
  sliced mushrooms,
  drained
2 red bell peppers, cut into
  2×½-inch strips
1 tablespoon
  MCCORMICK®/
  SCHILLING® Chinese
  Five Spice
3 tablespoons soy sauce
2 tablespoons cornstarch
⅓ cup cold water
  Hot cooked rice (optional)

SIZZLING FIVE-SPICE BEEF

Makes 12 servings

1. Heat oil in large skillet or wok over high heat. Add beef and stir-fry 3 to 4 minutes.

2. Add mushrooms, bell peppers, and Chinese five spice. Cook, stirring, 1 minute.

3. Place soy sauce, cornstarch, and water in small bowl or cup measure and mix well. Pour over meat and cook, stirring, until sauce is clear and thickened. Serve, sizzling hot, over hot cooked rice, if desired.

¼ cup Masaman Curry Paste
(page 48) or ½ cup
canned Masaman curry
paste
2 pounds boiling potatoes
4 tablespoons vegetable oil,
divided
1 medium onion, cut into
¼-inch strips
1½ pounds boneless beef
chuck or round, cut into
1-inch pieces
2 cans (about 14 ounces
each) unsweetened
coconut milk
3 tablespoons fish sauce
1 large red bell pepper, cut
into strips
½ cup roasted peanuts,
chopped
2 tablespoons lime juice
¼ cup slivered fresh basil
leaves or chopped
cilantro
Hot cooked rice or
noodles (optional)
Lime wedges for garnish

Masaman Curry Beef

Makes 6 servings

1. Prepare Masaman Curry Paste; set aside.

2. Peel potatoes and cut into 1½-inch pieces. Place in bowl with cold water to cover; set aside.

3. Heat 1 tablespoon oil in wok or large skillet over medium-high heat. Add onion; stir-fry 6 to 8 minutes or until golden. Transfer onion to bowl with slotted spoon.

4. Add 1 tablespoon oil to wok. Increase heat to high. Add half the beef; stir-fry 2 to 3 minutes until browned on all sides.

5. Transfer beef to another bowl; set aside. Repeat with remaining beef, adding 1 tablespoon oil to prevent sticking if necessary.

6. Reduce heat to medium. Add remaining 1 tablespoon oil and curry paste to wok; cook and stir 1 to 2 minutes or until very fragrant. Add coconut milk and fish sauce; stir to scrape bits of cooked meat and spices from bottom of wok.

7. Return beef to wok. Increase heat to high and bring to a boil. Reduce heat to low; cover and simmer 45 minutes or until meat is fork-tender.

8. Drain potatoes; add to wok with onions. Cook 20 to 30 minutes more or until potatoes are fork-tender. Stir in bell pepper; cook 1 to 2 minutes more or until pepper is heated through.

9. Stir in peanuts and lime juice. Pour into serving bowl and sprinkle with basil. Serve with rice or noodles and garnish, if desired.

continued on page 48

MASAMAN CURRY BEEF

Masaman Curry Beef, continued

MASAMAN CURRY PASTE

Grated peel of 2 lemons
6 tablespoons coarsely chopped ginger
3 tablespoons coarsely chopped garlic (10 to 12 cloves)
2 tablespoons ground cumin
4 teaspoons packed brown sugar
1 tablespoon ground mace or nutmeg
2 teaspoons ground cinnamon
1 to 3 teaspoons ground red pepper*
2 teaspoons paprika
2 teaspoons black pepper
2 teaspoons anchovy paste
1 teaspoon ground turmeric
1 teaspoon ground cloves

Use 1 teaspoon ground red pepper for mild paste and up to 3 teaspoons for very hot paste.

Place all ingredients in food processor; process until mixture forms dry paste.   *Makes about ½ cup*

¾ pound sirloin tip steak, cut into thin strips
½ cup teriyaki sauce
¼ cup water
1 tablespoon cornstarch
1 teaspoon sugar
1 bag (16 ounces) BIRDS EYE® frozen Farm Fresh Mixtures Broccoli, Carrots and Water Chestnuts

TERIYAKI BEEF

Makes 4 to 6 servings

■ Spray large skillet with nonstick cooking spray; cook beef strips over medium-high heat 7 to 8 minutes, stirring occasionally.

■ Combine teriyaki sauce, water, cornstarch and sugar; mix well.

■ Add teriyaki sauce mixture and vegetables to beef. Bring to a boil; quickly reduce heat to medium.

■ Cook 7 to 10 minutes or until broccoli is heated through, stirring occasionally.

PREP TIME: 5 to 10 minutes
COOK TIME: 20 minutes

TERIYAKI BEEF

1 pound boneless beef top
  sirloin steak, 1 inch
  thick
¼ cup hoisin sauce
2 tablespoons reduced-
  sodium soy sauce
1 tablespoon water
2 teaspoons dark sesame
  oil
2 cloves garlic, crushed
⅛ to ¼ teaspoon crushed
  red pepper
4 ounces uncooked
  vermicelli or thin
  spaghetti
1 package (10 ounces) fresh
  spinach leaves, rinsed,
  stemmed and thinly
  sliced
1 cup fresh bean sprouts,
  rinsed and drained
¼ cup sliced green onions

Stir-Fried Sirloin & Spinach with Noodles

Makes 4 (1½-cup) servings

1. Trim fat from beef steak. Cut steak lengthwise in half and then crosswise into ⅛-inch-thick strips. Combine hoisin sauce, soy sauce, water, oil, garlic and crushed red pepper; pour half over beef. Cover and marinate in refrigerator 10 minutes. Reserve remaining marinade.

2. Meanwhile, cook vermicelli according to package directions; drain.

3. Remove beef from marinade; discard marinade. Heat large nonstick skillet over medium-high heat until hot. Add beef (½ at a time) and stir-fry 1 to 2 minutes or until surface is no longer pink. (Do not overcook.) Remove from skillet with slotted spoon; keep warm.

4. In same skillet, combine vermicelli, spinach, bean sprouts, green onions and reserved marinade; cook until spinach is wilted and mixture is heated through, stirring occasionally. Return beef to skillet; mix lightly. Serve immediately.

PREP AND COOK TIME: 30 minutes

Favorite recipe from **NORTH DAKOTA BEEF COMMISSION**

4 tablespoons vegetable oil, divided
3 pounds beef stew meat, cut into 1¼-inch chunks
12 shallots, peeled
2 medium onions, chopped
4 cloves garlic, minced
3 cups water
2 tablespoons sugar
1½ teaspoons salt
1 teaspoon anise seeds
¼ teaspoon ground cinnamon
¼ teaspoon black pepper
2 bay leaves
1 pound carrots, peeled
1 pound white turnips (3 or 4) *or* 1 icicle radish or Japanese daikon
3 strips (2×½-inch) lemon peel
1 can (6 ounces) tomato paste
Japanese daikon sprouts tied together with green onion top for garnish
French bread slices (optional)

AROMATIC ASIAN BEEF STEW

Makes 6 to 8 servings

1. Heat wok over high heat 1 minute or until hot. Drizzle 1 tablespoon oil into wok and heat 30 seconds. Add ½ of beef and stir-fry about 5 minutes or until browned. Remove beef to bowl. Repeat with 1 tablespoon oil and remaining beef. Remove beef to same bowl and set aside. Reduce heat to medium.

2. Add 1 tablespoon oil to wok and heat 30 seconds. Add shallots; stir-fry about 3 minutes or until lightly browned. Remove to small bowl; set aside. Add remaining 1 tablespoon oil to wok and heat 30 seconds. Add onions and garlic; stir-fry 2 minutes.

3. Return beef and all juices to wok. Add water, sugar, salt, anise, cinnamon, pepper and bay leaves. Cover and bring to a boil over high heat. Reduce heat to low and simmer 1¼ hours or until meat is almost tender.

4. Meanwhile, cut carrots into 1½-inch chunks. Peel turnips or radish. Cut each turnip into 8 wedges or cut radish into 2-inch lengths, then into wedges.

5. Add carrots, turnips, shallots and lemon peel to beef mixture. Cover and cook 30 minutes more or until meat is tender, stirring occasionally.

6. Remove and discard bay leaves and lemon peel. Stir tomato paste into stew. Cook and stir until sauce boils and thickens. Transfer to serving bowl. Garnish and serve with bread, if desired.

1 package (about 4 ounces)
  bean thread noodles
1 pound beef tenderloin or
  sirloin
½ pound firm tofu
12 fresh shiitake or button
  mushrooms (about
  6 ounces)
½ cup beef broth
½ cup teriyaki sauce
¼ cup sake, rice wine or dry
  sherry
1 tablespoon sugar
2 tablespoons vegetable oil,
  divided
6 green onions with tops,
  cut diagonally into
  2-inch pieces
½ pound fresh spinach,
  washed, stemmed and
  dried
  Hot cooked rice (optional)

WOK SUKIYAKI

Makes 4 servings

1. Place noodles in bowl; cover with cold water. Let stand 30 minutes or until softened; drain. Cut into 4-inch lengths; set aside.

2. Slice beef across the grain into ¼-inch-thick strips; set aside.

3. Drain tofu on paper towels. Cut into 1-inch cubes; set aside.

4. Cut off mushroom stems; discard. Cut out decorative cross in center of each mushroom cap with small paring knife; set aside.

5. Combine broth, teriyaki sauce, sake and sugar in small bowl; mix well. Set aside.

6. Heat wok over high heat 1 minute or until hot. Drizzle 1 tablespoon oil into wok and heat 30 seconds. Add half of beef; stir-fry 3 minutes or until browned. Remove from wok to bowl; set aside. Repeat with remaining 1 tablespoon oil and beef.

7. Reduce heat to medium. Add mushrooms to wok; stir-fry 1 minute and move to one side of wok. Add tofu to bottom of wok; stir-fry 1 minute, stirring gently. Move to another side of wok. Add green onions to bottom of wok. Add broth mixture and bring to a boil. Move onions up side of wok.

8. Add noodles and spinach, keeping each in separate piles and stirring gently to soften in teriyaki sauce. Push up side of wok. Add beef and any juices; heat through.

9. Place wok on table over wok ring stand or trivet. Serve with rice, if desired.

WOK SUKIYAKI

1 tablespoon sesame seeds
2½ pounds flanken-style beef
    short ribs, cut ⅜ to
    ½ inch thick*
¼ cup chopped green onions
¼ cup soy sauce
¼ cup water
1 tablespoon sugar
2 teaspoons dark sesame
    oil
2 teaspoons grated fresh
    ginger
2 cloves garlic, minced
½ teaspoon black pepper

*Flanken-style ribs may be ordered
from your meat retailer. They are
cross-cut short ribs sawed through
the bones, ⅜ to ½ inch thick.*

KOREAN BEEF SHORT RIBS

Makes 4 to 6 servings

1. To toast sesame seeds, spread seeds in large, dry skillet. Shake skillet over medium-low heat until seeds begin to pop and turn golden, about 3 minutes.

2. Place ribs in large resealable plastic food storage bag. Combine green onions, soy sauce, water, sugar, oil, ginger, garlic and pepper in small bowl; pour over ribs. Seal bag tightly, turning to coat. Marinate in refrigerator at least 4 hours or up to 24 hours, turning occasionally.

3. Prepare grill for direct cooking.

4. Drain ribs; reserve marinade. Place ribs on grid. Grill ribs, on covered grill, over medium-hot coals 5 minutes. Brush tops lightly with reserved marinade; turn and brush again. Discard remaining marinade. Continue to grill, covered, 5 to 6 minutes for medium or until desired doneness. Sprinkle with sesame seeds.

1 pound beef flank steak
2 tablespoons reduced-
    sodium soy sauce
4 teaspoons dark sesame
    oil, divided
1½ teaspoons sugar
1 teaspoon cornstarch
2 cloves garlic, crushed
1 tablespoon minced fresh
    ginger
¼ teaspoon crushed red
    pepper
1 small red bell pepper, cut
    into 1-inch pieces
1 package (8 ounces) frozen
    baby corn, thawed
¼ pound pea pods, julienned

SZECHWAN BEEF STIR-FRY

4 servings

Cut steak lengthwise into 2 strips; slice across the grain into ⅛-inch strips. Combine soy sauce, 2 teaspoons oil, sugar and cornstarch; stir into strips. Heat remaining 2 teaspoons oil in large skillet over medium-high heat. Add garlic, ginger and crushed red pepper; cook 30 seconds. Add bell pepper and corn; stir-fry 1½ minutes. Add pea pods; stir-fry 30 seconds. Remove vegetables. Stir-fry beef strips (½ at a time) 2 to 3 minutes. Return vegetables and beef to skillet; heat through.

PREP TIME: 30 minutes

***Serving Suggestion:** Serve with hot cooked rice.*

Favorite recipe from **NORTH DAKOTA BEEF COMMISSION**

KOREAN BEEF SHORT RIBS

1 boneless beef top sirloin
  or tenderloin steak,
  1 inch thick (about
  1 pound)
2 teaspoons minced fresh
  ginger
2 cloves garlic, minced
1 tablespoon peanut or
  vegetable oil
3 cups broccoli florets
¼ cup water
⅓ cup stir-fry sauce
  Hot cooked white rice
  (optional)

BEEF AND BROCCOLI

Makes 4 servings

1. Cut beef across the grain into ⅛-inch slices; cut each slice into 1½-inch pieces. Toss beef with ginger and garlic in medium bowl.

2. Heat wok or large skillet over medium-high heat. Add oil; heat until hot. Add beef mixture; stir-fry 3 to 4 minutes until beef is barely pink in center. Remove and set aside.

3. Add broccoli and water to wok; cover and steam 3 to 5 minutes until broccoli is crisp-tender.

4. Return beef along with any accumulated juices to wok. Add stir-fry sauce. Cook until heated through. Serve over rice, if desired.

½ cup LAWRY'S® Thai Ginger
  Marinade with Lime
  Juice
1 pound flank steak, cut
  into thin strips
1 tablespoon vegetable oil
2 cups broccoli florets
1 red bell pepper, chopped
2 tablespoons soy sauce
1 teaspoon cornstarch
1 teaspoon LAWRY'S® Garlic
  Powder with Parsley
1 package (8 ounces)
  vermicelli pasta or
  Japanese-style noodles,
  prepared according to
  package directions

GINGER BEEF & NOODLE STIR-FRY

Makes 4 servings

In large resealable plastic bag combine Thai Ginger Marinade and beef. Marinate in refrigerator 30 minutes. Remove beef from marinade. In large skillet, heat oil. Add broccoli and bell pepper; stir-fry over high heat 2 minutes. Set aside. In same skillet, add beef; stir-fry over high heat about 5 to 7 minutes. In small bowl, combine soy sauce, cornstarch and Garlic Powder with Parsley; mix well. Add to beef; cook over medium heat until sauce is thickened. Stir in broccoli and bell pepper; heat through. Spoon over noodles.

Serving Suggestion: *Serve as a one-dish meal with fresh tropical fruit on the side.*

BEEF AND BROCCOLI

SESAME SAUCE
>1 tablespoon sesame seeds
>¼ cup soy sauce
>1 green onion with top,
> finely chopped
>1 tablespoon dry sherry
>1 tablespoon red wine
> vinegar
>1½ teaspoons sugar
>1 clove garlic, minced
>½ teaspoon sesame oil

LAMB
>1 pound boneless lean
> lamb* (leg or shoulder)
>2 small leeks, cut into
> 2-inch-long slivers
>4 green onions with tops,
> cut into 2-inch-long
> slivers
>4 tablespoons vegetable oil,
> divided
>4 slices peeled fresh ginger
> Chili oil (optional)
>2 medium carrots, shredded
>1 medium zucchini,
> shredded
>1 each green and red
> pepper, cut into
> matchstick-size pieces
>½ small head napa cabbage,
> thinly sliced
>1 cup bean sprouts, rinsed
> and drained

*Or, substitute boneless lean pork
or beef flank steak for the lamb.*

MONGOLIAN LAMB

Makes 4 servings

1. For sauce, place sesame seeds in small skillet. Carefully shake over medium heat until seeds begin to pop and turn golden brown, about 2 minutes; let cool.

2. Crush seeds with mortar and pestle (or place between paper towels and crush with rolling pin); scrape up sesame paste with knife and transfer to small serving bowl. Add remaining sauce ingredients; mix well.

3. Slice meat across grain into 2×¼-inch strips. Arrange meat and all vegetables on large platter. Have Sesame Sauce, vegetable oil, ginger and chili oil near cooking area.

4. At serving time, heat wok or electric griddle to 350°F. Cook one serving at a time. For each serving, heat 1 tablespoon vegetable oil. Add one slice ginger; cook and stir 30 seconds. Discard ginger. Add ½ cup meat strips; stir-fry until lightly browned, about 1 minute. Add 2 cups assorted vegetables; stir-fry 1 minute. Drizzle with 2 tablespoons Sesame Sauce; stir-fry 30 seconds. Season with a few drops chili oil. Repeat with remaining ingredients.

3 tablespoons soy sauce
1 tablespoon minced fresh
   ginger
2 cloves garlic, minced
1/4 teaspoon crushed red
   pepper
1 beef tenderloin or
   boneless beef sirloin
   steak, 1 inch thick
   (about 1 pound)
3/4 cup beef or chicken broth
3 1/2 teaspoons cornstarch
2 tablespoons peanut or
   vegetable oil, divided
1 large yellow or sweet
   onion, cut into thin
   wedges
1/2 teaspoon sugar
   Hot cooked white rice
   (optional)
1/4 cup coarsely chopped
   cilantro or sliced green
   onions for garnish

Ginger Beef

Makes 4 servings

1. Combine soy sauce, ginger, garlic and crushed red pepper in medium bowl. Cut beef across the grain into 1/8-inch slices; cut each slice into 1 1/2-inch pieces. Toss beef with soy sauce mixture. Marinate at room temperature 20 minutes or cover and refrigerate up to 4 hours.

2. Blend broth into cornstarch in cup until smooth. Set aside.

3. Heat wok or large skillet over medium heat. Add 1 tablespoon oil; heat until hot. Add onion; stir-fry 5 minutes. Sprinkle sugar over onion; cook 5 minutes more or until onion is light golden brown, stirring occasionally. Remove and set aside.

4. Heat remaining 1 tablespoon oil in wok over medium-high heat until hot. Drain beef; reserve marinade. Add beef to wok; stir-fry until beef is barely pink in center. Return onion to wok. Stir broth mixture and add to wok along with reserved marinade. Stir-fry 1 minute or until sauce boils and thickens. Serve over rice, if desired. Garnish with cilantro.

1 (8-ounce) can sliced pineapple in its own juice, drained (reserve juice)
½ cup A.1. THICK & HEARTY® Steak Sauce
3 tablespoons teriyaki sauce
1 teaspoon ground ginger
1 (1½-pound) beef flank or top round steak, lightly scored

PINEAPPLE TERIYAKI MARINATED STEAK

Makes 6 servings

In small bowl, combine reserved juice, steak sauce, teriyaki sauce and ginger. Place steak in nonmetal dish; coat with steak sauce mixture. Cover; refrigerate 1 hour, turning occasionally.

Remove steak from marinade; reserve marinade. Grill steak over medium-high heat or broil 4 inches from heat source 15 to 20 minutes or to desired doneness, turning and basting with marinade occasionally. Grill or broil pineapple slices 1 minute, turning once. In small saucepan, over high heat, heat reserved marinade to a boil; simmer 5 minutes or until thickened. Slice steak across grain; serve with pineapple slices and warm sauce. Garnish as desired.

¾ pound extra-lean (90% lean) ground beef
1 clove garlic, minced
1 teaspoon vegetable oil
6 ounces snow peas, halved lengthwise
1 red bell pepper, cut into strips
1 (15-ounce) can baby corn, rinsed and drained
1 tablespoon soy sauce
1 teaspoon dark sesame oil
Salt and freshly ground black pepper
2 cups hot cooked rice

BEEF WITH SNOW PEAS & BABY CORN

Makes 4 servings

Brown ground beef in wok or large skillet. Drain. Add garlic; cook until garlic is tender. Remove beef mixture from wok. Wipe out wok with paper towel.

Heat vegetable oil in wok over medium-high heat. Add snow peas and bell pepper; stir-fry 2 to 3 minutes or until vegetables are crisp-tender. Stir in ground beef mixture, corn, soy sauce and sesame oil. Season with salt and black pepper to taste. Serve over rice.

PINEAPPLE TERIYAKI MARINATED STEAK

4 thin slices beef top round
  steak (7 to 8 ounces
  each)
2 medium carrots, peeled
  and halved
2 medium parsnips, peeled
  and halved
8 small green beans, halved
  lengthwise
4 tablespoons vegetable oil,
  divided
1 can (13¾ ounces) beef
  broth, divided
1 piece fresh ginger (about
  1½ inches long), peeled
  and cut into 6 (¼-inch-
  thick) slices
¼ teaspoon ground red
  pepper
1 small ripe tomato, cut
  into 6 wedges
1 tablespoon rice wine or
  dry sherry
1 tablespoon soy sauce
1 teaspoon sugar
1 teaspoon cornstarch
1 teaspoon dark sesame oil
  Lettuce leaves or
  Japanese mizuna*
  Kimchee (optional)

*Mizuna is a leafy salad green. It is
occasionally found in produce
markets.

SEOUL ROLLED BEEF WITH VEGETABLES

Makes 4 servings

1. Cut each beef slice crosswise into 2 pieces (about 4 to 5 inches in length). Cut carrots and parsnips lengthwise into pencil-thick strips.

2. Place ⅛ of carrots, ⅛ of parsnips and 2 green bean halves on each piece of beef along one short end. Starting with short end, roll up beef, jelly-roll fashion, to enclose vegetables; secure with short skewers.

3. Heat wok over high heat 1 minute. Drizzle 2 tablespoons vegetable oil into wok; add 4 beef rolls. Cook rolls 2½ to 3 minutes until browned on all sides, turning occasionally. Transfer to bowl. Repeat with remaining 2 tablespoons vegetable oil and 4 beef rolls.

4. Return all rolls to wok. Add 1 cup broth, ginger and red pepper. Cover; bring to a boil. Reduce heat to low; simmer rolls 1 hour or until beef is fork-tender, turning rolls to cook evenly.

5. From pointed tip of each tomato wedge, cut skin from pulp halfway down length of wedge. Gently bend back skins away from wedges to form "petals." Set aside.

6. Transfer cooked rolls to cutting board. Pour liquid from wok into glass measuring cup. Discard ginger. Add enough broth or water to make ⅔ cup liquid; return to wok and bring to a boil. Meanwhile, combine wine, soy sauce, sugar, cornstarch and sesame oil in small bowl; mix well and add to wok. Cook and stir until liquid boils and thickens.

7. Remove skewers from beef rolls. Cut rolls in half. Arrange over lettuce-lined platter. Garnish with tomato wedge "petals." Serve with sauce and kimchee, if desired.

SEOUL ROLLED BEEF WITH VEGETABLES

2 tablespoons dried cloud ears or wood ears or other Asian mushrooms
2 tablespoons Sesame Salt (page 66)
5 ounces fresh spinach, washed and stemmed
4 ounces Chinese-style egg vermicelli or mung bean noodles
2 tablespoons soy sauce, divided
1 teaspoon dark sesame oil
2 tablespoons vegetable oil, divided
1 cup matchstick-size carrots strips
1 medium onion, cut into halves and thinly sliced
1 piece fresh ginger (about 1 inch square), finely chopped
1 teaspoon minced garlic
8 ounces flank steak, cut into 2-inch-long pieces
1 teaspoon sugar
⅛ teaspoon black pepper
Additional soy sauce
Chives and chive blossom for garnish

MIXED VEGETABLES WITH NOODLES AND BEEF (CHAP CH'AE)

Makes 4 servings

1. Place mushrooms in bowl; cover with hot water. Let stand 30 minutes or until caps are soft. Drain mushrooms; squeeze out excess water. Remove and discard stems. Cut caps into thin slices.

2. Meanwhile, prepare Sesame Salt; set aside. Bring 1 quart lightly salted water to a boil in medium saucepan over high heat. Add spinach; return to a boil. Cook 2 to 3 minutes. Drain spinach; immediately plunge into cold water to stop cooking. Place in colander to drain. Let stand until cool enough to handle. Squeeze spinach to remove excess moisture; chop finely.

3. Bring 2 quarts water to a boil in large saucepan over high heat. Add noodles; cook 2 minutes or according to package directions. Drain and immediately run cold water over noodles. Cut noodles into short strands. Return noodles to saucepan. Stir in 1 tablespoon soy sauce and sesame oil; toss to coat. Set aside and keep warm.

4. Heat 1 tablespoon vegetable oil in wok over medium-high heat. Add carrots; stir-fry 5 minutes or until crisp-tender. Add mushrooms and onion; stir-fry 2 minutes or just until soft. Remove vegetables from wok.

5. Heat wok over high heat 1 minute or until hot. Drizzle remaining 1 tablespoon vegetable oil into wok; heat 30 seconds. Add ginger and garlic; stir-fry 30 seconds or until fragrant.

6. Add beef to wok; stir-fry 3 to 5 minutes or until lightly browned. Remove wok from heat; stir in Sesame Salt, sugar, pepper and remaining 1 tablespoon soy sauce.

continued on page 66

MIXED VEGETABLES WITH NOODLES AND BEEF (CHAP CH'AE)

Mixed Vegetables with Noodles and Beef (Chap Ch'ae), continued

7. Return vegetables and noodles to wok; cook and stir until heated through. Add additional soy sauce to taste. Garnish with chives and chive blossom.

SESAME SALT
½ cup sesame seeds
¼ teaspoon salt

1. Heat sesame seeds in large skillet over medium-low heat, stirring or shaking pan frequently until seeds begin to pop and turn golden, about 4 to 6 minutes. Set aside to cool.

2. Crush toasted sesame seeds and salt with mortar and pestle or process in spice grinder. Refrigerate in covered glass jar. *Makes ½ cup*

---

1 package (3¾ ounces) bean threads
1 boneless beef sirloin steak, 1 inch thick (about 1 pound)
2 cloves garlic, minced
1 teaspoon minced fresh ginger
1 tablespoon peanut or vegetable oil
½ cup beef or chicken broth
2 tablespoons oyster sauce
2 cups coarsely chopped napa cabbage

BEEF WITH BEAN THREADS AND CABBAGE

Makes 4 servings

1. Place bean threads in medium bowl; cover with warm water. Soak 15 minutes to soften; drain well. Cut into 2-inch lengths.

2. Cut beef across grain into ⅛-inch slices; cut each slice into 2-inch pieces. Toss beef with garlic and ginger in medium bowl.

3. Heat wok or large skillet over medium-high heat. Add oil; heat until hot. Add beef mixture; stir-fry 2 to 3 minutes until beef is barely pink in center. Add broth, oyster sauce and cabbage; stir-fry 1 minute. Add bean threads; stir-fry 1 to 2 minutes until liquid is absorbed.

HOT AND SPICY ONION BEEF

Makes about 4 servings

2 tablespoons soy sauce, divided

3 teaspoons cornstarch, divided

¾ pound flank steak, thinly sliced across the grain

2 tablespoons dry sherry

1 teaspoon dark sesame oil

1 teaspoon chili paste (optional)

2 tablespoons vegetable oil

1 large onion (12 to 14 ounces), sliced vertically

1 teaspoon minced garlic

Dried whole red chili peppers to taste

1 tablespoon water

Combine 1 tablespoon soy sauce and 1 teaspoon cornstarch in medium bowl. Add beef; stir to coat. Let stand 30 minutes. Combine remaining 1 tablespoon soy sauce, the sherry, sesame oil and chili paste, if desired, in small bowl; set aside. Heat wok or large skillet over high heat. Add vegetable oil, swirling to coat sides. Add onion, garlic and chili peppers; cook and stir until onion is tender. Add beef; stir-fry 2 minutes or until lightly browned. Add soy sauce mixture and mix well. Combine remaining 2 teaspoons cornstarch and the water; mix into onion mixture. Cook and stir until sauce boils and thickens.

Favorite recipe from **NATIONAL ONION ASSOCIATION**

ORIENTAL BEEF & NOODLE TOSS

Makes 4 servings

1 pound lean ground beef

2 packages (3 ounces each) Oriental-flavor instant ramen noodles, divided

2 cups water

2 cups frozen Oriental vegetable mixture

⅛ teaspoon ground ginger

2 tablespoons thinly sliced green onion

1. In large nonstick skillet, brown ground beef over medium heat 8 to 10 minutes or until beef is no longer pink. Remove with slotted spoon; pour off drippings. Season beef with one seasoning packet from noodles; set aside.

2. In same skillet, combine water, vegetables, noodles, ginger and remaining seasoning packet. Bring to a boil; reduce heat. Cover; simmer 3 minutes or until noodles are tender, stirring occasionally.

3. Return beef to skillet; heat through. Stir in green onion before serving.

Favorite recipe from **NATIONAL CATTLEMEN'S BEEF ASSOCIATION**

1 pound boneless beef top
　round or flank steak
3 tablespoons reduced-
　sodium soy sauce
1 tablespoon cornstarch
1 tablespoon brown sugar
1½ teaspoons dark sesame
　oil
¼ teaspoon crushed red
　pepper
3 tablespoons vegetable oil,
　divided
1 small green bell pepper,
　cut into strips
1 small red bell pepper, cut
　into strips
1 small yellow bell pepper,
　cut into strips
1 medium onion, cut into
　1-inch pieces
2 cloves garlic, minced
　Hot cooked rice

THREE-PEPPER STEAK

Makes 4 servings

■ Cut beef across grain into ¼-inch-thick slices.
Combine soy sauce, cornstarch, brown sugar, sesame
oil and crushed red pepper in medium bowl; stir until
smooth. Add beef and toss to coat; set aside.

■ Heat wok over high heat about 1 minute or until hot.
Drizzle 1 tablespoon vegetable oil into wok and heat 30
seconds. Add pepper strips; stir-fry until crisp-tender.
Remove to large bowl. Add 1 tablespoon vegetable oil
and heat 30 seconds. Add half the beef mixture to wok;
stir-fry until well browned. Remove beef to bowl with
peppers. Repeat with remaining 1 tablespoon vegetable
oil and beef mixture. Reduce heat to medium.

■ Add onion; stir-fry about 3 minutes or until softened.
Add garlic; stir-fry 30 seconds. Return peppers, beef and
any accumulated juices to wok; cook until heated
through. Serve over rice.

1 boneless beef sirloin or
　tenderloin steak, 1 inch
　thick (about 1 pound)
2 cloves garlic, minced
1 teaspoon grated fresh
　orange peel
2 tablespoons orange juice
2 tablespoons soy sauce
1 tablespoon dry sherry
1 tablespoon cornstarch
1 tablespoon peanut or
　vegetable oil
2 cups hot cooked white
　rice (optional)
　Orange slices for garnish

ORANGE BEEF

Makes 4 servings

1. Cut beef across the grain into ⅛-inch slices; cut each
slice into 2-inch pieces. Toss with garlic and orange peel
in medium bowl.

2. Blend orange juice, soy sauce and sherry into
cornstarch in cup until smooth.

3. Heat wok or large skillet over medium-high heat. Add
oil; heat until hot. Add beef mixture; stir-fry 2 to 3
minutes or until beef is barely pink in center. Stir orange
juice mixture and add to wok. Stir-fry 30 seconds or
until sauce boils and thickens. Serve over rice, if
desired. Garnish with orange slices.

THREE-PEPPER STEAK

½ cup A.1. ORIGINAL® or
A.1.® Bold & Spicy Steak
Sauce
2 tablespoons soy sauce
2 tablespoons firmly packed
light brown sugar
2 cloves garlic, minced
1 teaspoon grated fresh
ginger
1 (1-pound) boneless beef
sirloin steak, about
1 inch thick, thinly
sliced
2 cups broccoli flowerettes,
blanched
2 cups fresh mushroom
caps (about
16 mushrooms)
1 cup pineapple chunks
2 tablespoons sesame seed,
toasted

TERIYAKI STEAK STRIP KABOBS

Makes 4 servings

Soak 8 (10-inch) wooden skewers in water at least 30 minutes.

In small bowl, combine steak sauce, soy sauce, sugar, garlic and ginger. Place steak in nonmetal dish; coat with steak sauce mixture. Cover; refrigerate 1 hour, stirring occasionally.

Remove steak from marinade; discard marinade. Alternately thread steak, broccoli, mushrooms and pineapple onto skewers. Grill kabobs over medium heat or broil 6 inches from heat source 5 to 8 minutes or until steak is desired doneness, turning occasionally. Sprinkle kabobs with sesame seed. Serve immediately over hot cooked rice. Garnish as desired.

½ cup WISH-BONE® Italian
Dressing
2 tablespoons firmly packed
brown sugar
2 tablespoons soy sauce
½ teaspoon ground ginger
(optional)
1 (1- to 1½-pound) flank or
top round steak

ORIENTAL FLANK STEAK

Makes 6 servings

In large, shallow nonaluminum baking dish or plastic bag, combine all ingredients except steak. Add steak; turn to coat.

Cover, or close bag, and marinate in refrigerator, turning occasionally, 3 to 24 hours.

Remove steak, reserving marinade. Grill or broil steak, turning once, until steak is done.

Meanwhile, in small saucepan, bring reserved marinade to a boil and continue boiling 1 minute. Pour over steak.

Note: *Also terrific with WISH-BONE® Robusto Italian or Lite Italian Dressing.*

TERIYAKI STEAK STRIP KABOBS

2 teaspoons Garam Masala (page 149)
1½ pounds ground lamb or ground round
2 eggs
1½ cups finely chopped onions, divided
½ cup chopped cilantro
2 cloves garlic, minced
1½ teaspoons salt, divided
1 teaspoon minced fresh ginger
24 whole blanched almonds
1 tablespoon peanut oil
1 teaspoon ground coriander
1 teaspoon ground cumin
1 teaspoon chili powder
½ teaspoon turmeric
2 tomatoes, peeled, seeded and chopped
½ cup water
1 cup plain yogurt
Fresh cilantro and chilies for garnish

KOFTAS (LAMB MEATBALLS IN SPICY GRAVY)

Makes 6 servings

1. Prepare Garam Masala. Place 2 teaspoons in medium bowl. Add lamb, eggs, ½ cup onion, cilantro, garlic, ½ teaspoon salt and ginger; mix well. Cover and refrigerate at least 1 hour or overnight.

2. Divide mixture into 24 portions. Shape into ovals or balls; insert 1 almond into center of each meatball.

3. Heat oil in large skillet over medium-high heat until hot. Add half the meatballs; cook 8 minutes or until brown, turning frequently. Remove meatballs from skillet. Repeat with remaining meatballs.

4. Reduce heat to medium. Add remaining 1 cup onion. Cook and stir 6 to 8 minutes or until browned. Stir in remaining 1 teaspoon salt, coriander, cumin, chili powder and turmeric. Add tomatoes. Cook 5 minutes or until tomatoes are tender.

5. Add water; bring mixture to a boil over high heat. Add meatballs. Reduce heat to medium-low. Simmer 15 minutes or until thoroughly cooked. Remove meatballs from skillet to serving platter; keep warm.

6. Remove skillet from heat; place yogurt in small bowl. Stir in several spoonfuls hot mixture. Stir yogurt mixture into sauce in skillet. Cook over medium-low heat until sauce thickens. *Do not boil.* Pour sauce over meatballs. Garnish, if desired.

Curried Beef Kabobs

Makes 4 servings

1 cup A.1. ORIGINAL® or
   A.1.® Bold & Spicy Steak
   Sauce
1½ teaspoons curry powder
1 (1-pound) beef top round
   steak, thinly sliced
2 medium onions, cut into
   wedges
1 green bell pepper, cut into
   squares
8 pineapple chunks
⅓ cup low fat lemon yogurt
   Hot cooked rice or
   noodles

Soak 8 (10-inch) wooden skewers in water at least 30 minutes.

In small bowl, combine steak sauce and curry. Place steak strips, onions and pepper in nonmetal dish; coat with steak sauce mixture. Cover; refrigerate 1 hour, stirring occasionally.

Remove steak, onions and pepper from marinade; reserve marinade. Alternately thread steak (accordion style), onions, pepper and pineapple onto skewers. Grill kabobs over medium heat or broil 6 inches from heat source 8 to 10 minutes or until steak is desired doneness, turning occasionally.

Meanwhile, in small saucepan, over high heat, heat reserved marinade to a boil; simmer 5 minutes or until thickened. Remove from heat; stir in yogurt. Serve kabobs immediately with warm sauce and rice.

BEEF BENIHANA

Makes 4 servings

1 tablespoon sesame seeds
2 tablespoons vegetable oil, divided
1 pound boneless beef sirloin, cut into ¼-inch strips
½ pound mushrooms, sliced
2 medium zucchini, cut into thin strips
1 large onion, cut in half and thinly sliced
3 tablespoons teriyaki sauce
1 teaspoon sugar
½ teaspoon salt
¼ teaspoon black pepper
Hot cooked rice

■ Heat wok over high heat about 1 minute or until hot. Add sesame seeds; cook and stir until lightly browned. Remove to small bowl.

■ Drizzle 1 tablespoon oil into wok and heat 30 seconds. Add beef; stir-fry about 2 minutes or until well browned on outside and rare on inside. Remove beef to large bowl. Reduce heat to medium.

■ Add remaining 1 tablespoon oil to wok and heat 30 seconds. Add mushrooms, zucchini and onion; stir-fry about 5 minutes or until vegetables are crisp-tender. Stir in teriyaki sauce, sugar, salt and pepper. Return beef and any accumulated juices to wok; cook until heated through. Spoon rice onto serving plate; top with beef mixture. Sprinkle with sesame seeds.

SPICY BEEF AND BROCCOLI STIR-FRY

Makes 4 (1-cup) servings

½ cup HEINZ® Chili Sauce
3 tablespoons water
2 tablespoons soy sauce
1 tablespoon cornstarch
½ teaspoon ground ginger
¼ to ½ teaspoon crushed red pepper
1 pound boneless sirloin steak, cut into ½-inch strips
2 tablespoons vegetable oil, divided
1½ cups broccoli flowerets
1 small green or red bell pepper, cut into strips
1 small onion, sliced
1 can (8 ounces) sliced water chestnuts, drained

Combine chili sauce, water, soy sauce, cornstarch, ginger and crushed red pepper in small bowl; set aside. In preheated large skillet or wok, stir-fry beef strips in 1 tablespoon oil about 3 minutes or until browned. Remove and set aside. Add remaining 1 tablespoon oil to wok; stir-fry broccoli, bell pepper, onion and water chestnuts 3 to 4 minutes or until vegetables are tender-crisp. Stir in reserved chili sauce mixture; cook until thickened. Stir in browned beef strips and heat 1 to 2 minutes or until hot. Serve over hot cooked rice.

BEEF BENIHANA

1 beef flank steak (about
     1½ pounds)
  Grated peel and juice of
     2 lemons
6 tablespoons sugar,
     divided
2 tablespoons dark sesame
     oil
1¼ teaspoons salt, divided
½ teaspoon black pepper
¼ cup water
¼ cup rice vinegar
½ teaspoon crushed red
     pepper
6 (8-inch) flour tortillas
6 red leaf lettuce leaves
⅓ cup lightly packed fresh
     mint leaves
⅓ cup lightly packed fresh
     cilantro leaves
  Star fruit slices
  Red bell pepper strips
  Orange peel strips

Vietnamese Grilled Steak Wraps

Makes 6 wraps

Cut beef across the grain into thin slices. Combine lemon peel, juice, 2 tablespoons sugar, sesame oil, 1 teaspoon salt and black pepper in medium bowl. Add beef; toss to coat. Cover and refrigerate at least 30 minutes. Combine water, vinegar, remaining 4 tablespoons sugar and ¼ teaspoon salt in small saucepan; bring to a boil. Boil 5 minutes without stirring until syrupy. Stir in crushed red pepper; set aside.

Remove beef from marinade; discard marinade. Thread beef onto metal or wooden skewers. (Soak wooden skewers in hot water 30 minutes to prevent burning.) Grill beef over medium-hot KINGSFORD® briquets about 3 minutes per side until cooked through. Grill tortillas until hot. Place lettuce, beef, mint and cilantro on tortillas; drizzle with vinegar mixture. Roll tortillas to enclose filling. Garnish with star fruit, bell pepper and orange peel strips.

VIETNAMESE GRILLED STEAK WRAP

1 pound beef flank steak
3 tablespoons reduced-
  sodium soy sauce
3 tablespoons vegetable oil,
  divided
1 tablespoon rice wine or
  dry sherry
1 tablespoon cornstarch
2 teaspoons brown sugar
1 cup drained canned baby
  corn
3 green onions with tops,
  cut into 1-inch pieces
1 piece fresh ginger (1-inch
  square), peeled and
  minced
2 cloves garlic, minced
1 jalapeño pepper,*
  stemmed, seeded and
  cut into thin strips
¼ small red bell pepper, cut
  into thin strips
1 teaspoon hot chili oil
  Hot cooked rice

*Jalapeños can sting and irritate the skin; wear rubber gloves when handling peppers and do not touch eyes. Wash hands after handling.

Hunan Chili Beef

Makes 4 servings

■ Cut beef across grain into 2×¼-inch slices. Combine soy sauce, 1 tablespoon vegetable oil, wine, cornstarch and brown sugar in medium bowl. Add beef; toss to coat. Set aside.

■ Heat wok over high heat 1 minute or until hot. Drizzle 1 tablespoon vegetable oil into wok; heat 30 seconds. Add half of beef mixture; stir-fry until well browned. Remove to large bowl. Repeat with remaining 1 tablespoon vegetable oil and beef mixture. Reduce heat to medium.

■ Add corn, green onions, ginger and garlic to wok; stir-fry 1 minute. Add jalapeño pepper and bell pepper; stir-fry 1 minute.

■ Return beef and any accumulated juices to wok; add chili oil. Toss to combine; cook until heated through. Serve with rice.

HUNAN CHILI BEEF

1 beef flank steak (about
   1 ¼ pounds)
2 tablespoons soy sauce
2 tablespoons hoisin sauce
1 tablespoon dark sesame
   oil
2 cloves garlic, minced

SESAME-GARLIC FLANK STEAK

Makes 4 servings

1. Score steak lightly with a sharp knife in a diamond pattern on both sides; place in large plastic bag.

2. Combine remaining ingredients in small bowl; pour over steak. Close bag securely; turn to coat. Marinate in refrigerator at least 2 hours or up to 24 hours, turning once.

3. Drain steak; reserve marinade. Brush steak with some of the marinade. Grill or broil 5 to 6 inches from heat 5 minutes. Brush with marinade; turn steak over. Discard remaining marinade. Grill or broil 5 to 7 minutes until internal temperature reaches 140°F on meat thermometer inserted in thickest part of steak.*

4. Transfer steak to cutting board; carve across the grain into thin slices.

Broiling time is for medium-rare doneness. Adjust time for desired doneness.

1 tablespoon soy sauce
2 cloves garlic, minced
¼ teaspoon crushed red pepper
1 boneless beef sirloin, tenderloin or rib eye steak, 1 inch thick (about 1 pound)
2 tablespoons peanut or vegetable oil, divided
1 small red bell pepper, cut into thin strips
1 small yellow or green bell pepper, cut into thin strips
1 small onion, cut into thin strips
¼ cup stir-fry sauce
2 tablespoons rice wine or dry white wine
¼ cup coarsely chopped cilantro
  Hot cooked white rice or Chinese egg noodles (optional)

Pepper Beef

Makes 4 servings

1. Combine soy sauce, garlic and crushed red pepper in medium bowl. Cut beef across the grain into ⅛-inch slices; cut each slice into 1½-inch pieces. Toss beef with soy sauce mixture.

2. Heat wok or large skillet over medium-high heat. Add 1 tablespoon oil; heat until hot. Add half of beef mixture; stir-fry until beef is barely pink in center. Remove and reserve. Repeat with remaining beef mixture; remove and reserve.

3. Heat remaining 1 tablespoon oil in wok; add bell peppers and onion. Reduce heat to medium. Stir-fry 6 to 7 minutes until vegetables are crisp-tender. Add stir-fry sauce and wine; stir-fry 2 minutes or until heated through.

4. Return beef along with any accumulated juices to wok; heat through. Sprinkle with cilantro. Serve over rice, if desired.

BEEFY BEAN & WALNUT STIR-FRY

Makes 4 servings

1 teaspoon vegetable oil
3 cloves garlic, minced
1 pound lean ground beef or ground turkey
1 bag (16 ounces) BIRDS EYE® frozen Cut Green Beans, thawed
1 teaspoon salt
½ cup walnut pieces

■ In large skillet, heat oil and garlic over medium heat about 30 seconds.

■ Add beef and beans; sprinkle with salt. Mix well.

■ Cook 5 minutes or until beef is well browned, stirring occasionally.

■ Stir in walnuts; cook 2 minutes more.

PREP TIME: 5 minutes
COOK TIME: 7 to 10 minutes

Serving Suggestion: Serve over hot cooked egg noodles or rice.

BEEF & NAPA WITH NOODLES

Makes 4 servings

1 small head napa or Chinese cabbage
Boiling water
½ pound boneless tender beef steak (sirloin, rib eye or top loin)
6 tablespoons KIKKOMAN® Stir-Fry Sauce, divided
⅛ to ¼ teaspoon crushed red pepper
2 tablespoons vegetable oil, divided
¼ pound green onions, cut into 2-inch lengths, separating whites from tops
1 large red bell pepper, cut into strips
Hot cooked vermicelli or thin spaghetti

Separate and rinse cabbage; pat dry. Thinly slice enough leaves crosswise to measure 8 cups; place in colander or large strainer. Pour boiling water over cabbage just until leaves wilt. Cool under cold water; drain thoroughly. Cut beef across grain into thin slices, then into strips. Combine 1 tablespoon stir-fry sauce and crushed red pepper in small bowl; stir in beef to coat. Heat 1 tablespoon oil in hot wok or large skillet over high heat. Add beef and stir-fry 1 minute; remove. Heat remaining 1 tablespoon oil in same pan; add white parts of green onions and stir-fry 1 minute. Add bell pepper; stir-fry 2 minutes. Add green onion tops; stir-fry 2 minutes longer. Add beef, cabbage and remaining 5 tablespoons stir-fry sauce; cook and stir until vegetables are coated with sauce. Serve immediately over vermicelli.

BEEFY BEAN & WALNUT STIR-FRY

SENSATIONAL PORK

¾ pound boneless pork
1 teaspoon vegetable oil
1 bag (16 ounces)
    BIRDS EYE® frozen Farm
    Fresh Mixtures Pepper
    Stir Fry vegetables
1 tablespoon water
1 jar (14 ounces) sweet and
    sour sauce
1 can (8 ounces) pineapple
    chunks, drained

SWEET AND SOUR PORK

Makes 4 servings

■ Cut pork into thin strips.

■ In large skillet, heat oil over medium-high heat.

■ Add pork; stir-fry until pork is browned.

■ Add vegetables and water; cover and cook over medium heat 5 to 7 minutes or until vegetables are crisp-tender.

■ Uncover; stir in sweet and sour sauce and pineapple. Cook until heated through.

PREP TIME: 5 minutes
COOK TIME: 15 to 18 minutes

Serving Suggestion: *Serve over hot cooked rice.*

SWEET AND SOUR PORK

BARBECUED RIBS

Makes 4 main-dish or 8 appetizer servings

3 to 4 pounds lean pork baby back ribs or spareribs
⅓ cup hoisin sauce
4 tablespoons soy sauce, divided
3 tablespoons dry sherry
3 cloves garlic, minced
2 tablespoons honey
1 tablespoon dark sesame oil

1. Place ribs in large resealable plastic bag. Combine hoisin sauce, 3 tablespoons soy sauce, sherry and garlic in cup; pour over ribs. Seal bag; turn to coat. Marinate in refrigerator at least 4 hours or up to 24 hours.

2. Preheat oven to 375°F. Drain ribs; reserve marinade. Place ribs on rack in shallow, foil-lined roasting pan. Bake 30 minutes. Turn; brush ribs with half of reserved marinade. Bake 15 minutes. Turn ribs over; brush with remaining marinade. Bake 15 minutes.

3. Combine remaining 1 tablespoon soy sauce, honey and sesame oil in small bowl; brush over ribs. Bake 5 to 10 minutes until ribs are browned and crisp.* Cut into serving-size pieces.

Ribs may be made ahead to this point; cover and refrigerate ribs up to 3 days. To reheat ribs, wrap in foil; cook in preheated 350°F oven 40 minutes or until heated through. Cut into serving-size pieces.

BARBECUED RIBS

1 pound lean boneless pork loin, cut into 1½-inch pieces
1 large red bell pepper, cut into 1-inch pieces
1 large yellow bell pepper, cut into 1-inch pieces
1 large green bell pepper, cut into 1-inch pieces
¼ cup soy sauce
3 cloves garlic, minced
¼ cup sweet and sour sauce
1 tablespoon Chinese hot mustard

GLAZED PORK AND PEPPER KABOBS

Makes 4 servings

1. Place pork and peppers in large resealable plastic bag. Combine soy sauce and garlic in cup; pour over meat and peppers. Seal bag; turn to coat. Marinate in refrigerator at least 30 minutes or up to 2 hours, turning once.

2. Drain meat and peppers; discard marinade. Alternately thread meat and peppers onto metal skewers.

3. Combine sweet and sour sauce and hot mustard in small bowl; reserve half of sauce for dipping. Grill or broil kabobs 5 to 6 inches from heat 14 to 16 minutes until pork is no longer pink, turning occasionally and brushing with remaining sauce mixture during last 5 minutes of cooking. Serve with reserved sauce.

1 large or 2 small pork
   tenderloins (about
   1¼ pounds)
¼ cup soy sauce
2 cloves garlic, minced
3 tablespoons honey
2 tablespoons brown sugar
1 teaspoon minced fresh
   ginger
1 tablespoon toasted
   sesame seeds*

*To toast sesame seeds, spread
seeds in small skillet. Shake skillet
over medium heat 2 minutes or
until seeds begin to pop and turn
golden.*

HONEY-GLAZED PORK

Makes 4 servings

1. Place pork in large resealable plastic bag. Combine soy sauce and garlic in small cup; pour over pork. Seal bag; turn to coat. Marinate in refrigerator up to 2 hours.

2. Preheat oven to 400°F. Drain pork; reserve 1 tablespoon marinade. Combine honey, brown sugar, ginger and reserved marinade in small bowl.

3. Place pork in shallow, foil-lined roasting pan. Brush with half of honey mixture. Roast 10 minutes. Turn pork over; brush with remaining honey mixture and sprinkle with sesame seeds. Roast 10 minutes for small or 15 minutes for large tenderloin or until meat thermometer inserted in thickest part of pork reaches 155°F.

4. Let pork stand, tented with foil, on cutting board 5 minutes. (Temperature will rise to 160°F.). Cut pork across the grain into ½-inch slices. Serve with pan juices, if desired.

MEATBALLS
1 pound lean ground pork
4 ounces shrimp, shelled, deveined and finely chopped
¼ cup sliced water chestnuts, finely chopped
1 egg, lightly beaten
1 green onion with top, finely chopped
1 tablespoon cornstarch
1 tablespoon soy sauce
1 tablespoon dry sherry
1 teaspoon minced fresh ginger
½ teaspoon salt
½ teaspoon sugar
2 tablespoons vegetable oil

SAUCE
1½ cups chicken broth
2 tablespoons soy sauce
½ teaspoon sugar
1 head napa cabbage (1½ to 2 pounds)
3 tablespoons cold water
2 tablespoons cornstarch
1 teaspoon dark sesame oil
Green onion curls and fresh dill sprigs for garnish

BRAISED LION'S HEAD

Makes 4 to 6 servings

1. For meatballs, combine all meatball ingredients except oil in large bowl; mix well. Divide mixture into eight portions; shape each portion into ball.

2. Heat vegetable oil in wok or large nonstick skillet over medium-high heat. Add meatballs; cook 6 to 8 minutes until browned, stirring occasionally.

3. Transfer meatballs to 5-quart saucepan; discard drippings. Add chicken broth, soy sauce and sugar. Bring to a boil. Reduce heat to low; cover. Simmer 30 minutes.

4. While meatballs are cooking, core cabbage. Cut base of leaves into 2-inch squares. Cut leafy tops in half. Place over meatballs; cover. Simmer an additional 10 minutes.

5. Using slotted spoon, transfer cabbage and meatballs to serving platter. Add water to cornstarch in small cup. Gradually add to pan juices, stirring constantly; cook until slightly thickened. Stir in sesame oil. Serve over meatballs and cabbage. Garnish, if desired.

Note: To make green onion curls, cut green onion tops into short thin lengthwise strips. Place strips in bowl of ice water; refrigerate until onion strips curl, about 1 hour.

BRAISED LION'S HEAD

¾ **pound lean pork, cut into thin 2-inch strips**
2 **tablespoons LA CHOY® Soy Sauce**
1 **teaspoon minced fresh garlic**
4 **tablespoons WESSON® Oil, divided**
1½ **cups diagonally sliced celery**
1 **cup chopped red bell pepper**
1 **(10-ounce) jar LA CHOY® Sweet & Sour Sauce**
1 **(8-ounce) can LA CHOY® Sliced Water Chestnuts, drained**
1 **(6-ounce) package frozen pea pods, thawed and drained**
3 **green onions, diagonally cut into 1-inch pieces**
⅛ **teaspoon cayenne pepper**
1 **(5-ounce) can LA CHOY® Chow Mein Noodles**

IVORY, RUBIES AND JADE

Makes 4 servings

In medium bowl, combine pork, soy sauce and garlic; cover and marinate 30 minutes in refrigerator. Drain. In large nonstick skillet or wok, heat *3 tablespoons* oil. Add pork mixture; stir-fry until pork is no longer pink in center. Remove pork from skillet; set aside. Heat *remaining 1 tablespoon* oil in same skillet. Add celery and bell pepper; stir-fry until crisp-tender. Return pork to skillet with *all remaining* ingredients *except* noodles; heat thoroughly, stirring occasionally. Serve over noodles.

IVORY, RUBIES AND JADE

3 pounds baby back pork ribs, cut into halves
2 tablespoons fresh lemon juice
2 tablespoons orange juice
2 tablespoons soy sauce
2 cloves garlic, minced
1/4 cup orange marmalade
1 tablespoon hoisin sauce

LEMON-ORANGE GLAZED RIBS

Makes 4 servings

1. Place ribs in large resealable plastic bag. Combine lemon and orange juices, soy sauce and garlic in small bowl; pour over ribs. Seal bag; turn to coat. Marinate in refrigerator at least 4 hours or up to 24 hours, turning once.

2. Preheat oven to 350°F. Drain ribs; reserve marinade. Place ribs on rack in shallow, foil-lined roasting pan. Brush half of marinade evenly over ribs; bake 20 minutes. Turn ribs over; brush with remaining marinade. Bake 20 minutes.

3. Remove ribs from oven; pour off drippings. Combine marmalade and hoisin sauce in cup; brush half of mixture over ribs. Return to oven; bake 10 minutes or until glazed. Turn ribs over; brush with remaining marmalade mixture. Bake 10 minutes more or until ribs are browned and glazed.

3 tablespoons hoisin sauce
1 tablespoon dry sherry
1 tablespoon soy sauce
2 cloves garlic, minced
½ teaspoon crushed
    Szechuan peppercorns
    or crushed red pepper
2 whole pork tenderloins
    (1¼ to 1½ pounds total)

ROASTED PORK

Makes 4 to 6 servings

1. Preheat oven to 350°F. Combine hoisin sauce, sherry, soy sauce, garlic and peppercorns in small bowl.

2. Brush ¼ of hoisin sauce mixture evenly over each pork tenderloin. Place pork on rack in shallow, foil-lined roasting pan. Bake 15 minutes; turn and brush with remaining hoisin sauce mixture. Continue to bake until meat thermometer inserted in thickest part of pork reaches 155°F. (Timing will depend on thickness of pork; test after 30 minutes.)

3. Let pork stand, tented with foil, on cutting board 5 minutes. (Temperature of pork will rise to 160°F.) Slice diagonally and serve warm. Or, for use in other recipes, cut into portions and refrigerate up to 3 days or freeze up to 3 months.

Variation: For Chinese Barbecued Pork, add 1 tcaspoon red food coloring to hoisin sauce mixture. Prepare pork as directed in recipe. Pork may be grilled over medium coals until meat thermometer inserted in pork reaches 155°F. (Turn pork after 8 minutes; check temperature after 16 minutes.)

2½ cups water
1⅓ cups long-grain white rice
8 ounces ground pork or pork sausage
1 tablespoon vegetable oil
1 medium onion, thinly sliced
1 tablespoon minced fresh ginger
1 jalapeño pepper,* seeded and minced
3 cloves garlic, minced
½ teaspoon ground turmeric or paprika
2 tablespoons fish sauce
2 cups chopped cooked vegetables, such as broccoli, zucchini, red bell peppers, carrots, bok choy or spinach
3 eggs, lightly beaten
3 green onions, thinly sliced
½ cup cilantro leaves

Jalapeños can sting and irritate the skin; wear rubber gloves when handling peppers and do not touch eyes. Wash hands after handling.

THAI FRIED RICE

Makes 4 servings

1. Bring water and rice to a boil in medium saucepan over high heat. Reduce heat to medium-low; cover and simmer 20 minutes or until water is absorbed.

2. Transfer rice to large bowl and fluff with fork. Let cool to room temperature, 30 to 40 minutes, stirring occasionally. Cover and refrigerate until cold, at least 1 hour or up to 24 hours.

3. When rice is cold, cook pork in wok or medium skillet over medium-high heat until no longer pink. Drain off excess fat; transfer pork to bowl and set aside.

4. Heat wok or large skillet over medium-high heat. Add oil and swirl to coat surface. Add onion, ginger, jalapeño pepper, garlic and turmeric; stir-fry 4 to 6 minutes or until onion is very tender.

5. Stir in fish sauce; mix well. Stir in cold rice, vegetables and pork; cook and stir 3 to 4 minutes or until heated through.

6. Push rice mixture to side of wok and pour eggs into center. Cook eggs 2 to 3 minutes or just until set, lifting and stirring to scramble. Stir rice mixture into eggs.

7. Stir in green onions. Transfer to serving bowl; sprinkle with cilantro. Garnish as desired.

THAI FRIED RICE

1 pound pork tenderloin
2 tablespoons cornstarch
4 green onions with tops
1 piece fresh ginger (1 inch long), peeled
3 tablespoons vegetable oil, divided
2 cloves garlic, minced
¼ cup dry sherry
1 tablespoon soy sauce
1 to 2 tablespoons water
2 teaspoons brown sugar
¼ teaspoon crushed red pepper
¼ cup unsalted roasted cashews, chopped
Hot cooked rice
Fresh herb sprigs and bell pepper triangles for garnish

ASIAN GINGER GLAZED PORK

Makes 4 servings

1. Cut pork crosswise into ¼-inch-thick slices. Coat both sides of pork with cornstarch, reserving remaining cornstarch. Set aside.

2. Cut onions into 1-inch pieces. Thinly slice ginger. Stack ginger, a few slices at a time, and cut into fine strips.

3. Heat wok over high heat about 1 minute or until hot. Drizzle 1 tablespoon oil into wok and heat 30 seconds. Add half the pork; stir-fry until well browned on both sides. Remove pork to plate. Repeat with 1 tablespoon oil and remaining pork. Reduce heat to medium.

4. Add remaining 1 tablespoon oil to wok and heat 30 seconds. Add ginger, garlic and onions to wok; stir-fry 1 minute. Combine sherry, soy sauce, 1 tablespoon water, reserved cornstarch, brown sugar and crushed red pepper; add to wok. Cook and stir until sauce comes to a boil and thickens. Stir in additional water if needed.

5. Spoon sauce over pork until coated and glazed. Sprinkle with cashews. Serve with rice. Garnish, if desired.

ASIAN GINGER GLAZED PORK

Sweet and Sour Cooking
Sauce (recipe follows)
2 tablespoons vegetable oil,
divided
1 clove garlic, crushed or
finely chopped
½ pound lean, boneless
pork, cut into thin strips
2 cups broccoli florets
1 sweet red or green bell
pepper, seeded and
sliced into thin strips
1 Golden Delicious apple,
cored and cut into
16 slices
4 cups sliced napa cabbage
Hot cooked rice or
noodles (optional)

GOLDEN PORK STIR-FRY

Makes 4 servings

1. Prepare Sweet and Sour Cooking Sauce; set aside. In large skillet or wok, heat 1 tablespoon oil over medium-high heat. Add garlic and stir-fry until lightly browned. Remove and discard garlic. Add pork to seasoned oil in skillet and stir-fry until browned; remove pork to bowl and reserve.

2. Add remaining tablespoon oil to skillet. Add broccoli and bell pepper; stir-fry about 1 minute. Add apple, cabbage, and reserved pork; stir-fry 2 minutes longer. Add Sweet and Sour Cooking Sauce and cook, stirring, until sauce thickens and coats all ingredients. Serve over rice or noodles, if desired.

SWEET AND SOUR COOKING SAUCE

In small bowl, combine 2 tablespoons chicken broth or water, 1 tablespoon reduced-sodium soy sauce, 1 teaspoon cornstarch, 1 teaspoon sugar, 1 teaspoon grated gingerroot, 1 teaspoon rice wine or cider vinegar, and ⅛ teaspoon crushed red pepper; stir until well-blended.

Favorite recipe from **WASHINGTON APPLE COMMISSION**

1 tablespoon soy sauce
2 cloves garlic, minced
1 boneless lean pork loin or tenderloin* (about 1 pound)
1 can (8 ounces) pineapple chunks in juice, undrained
2 tablespoons peanut or vegetable oil, divided
2 medium carrots, diagonally cut into thin slices
1 large green bell pepper, cut into 1-inch pieces
⅓ cup stir-fry sauce
1 tablespoon white wine or white vinegar
Hot cooked rice (optional)

*Or, substitute 1 pound boneless skinless chicken breasts or thighs.

SWEET & SOUR PORK

Makes 4 servings

1. Combine soy sauce and garlic in medium bowl. Cut pork across the grain into 1-inch pieces; toss with soy sauce mixture.

2. Drain pineapple; reserve 2 tablespoons juice.

3. Heat wok or large skillet over medium-high heat. Add 1 tablespoon oil; heat until hot. Add pork mixture; stir-fry 4 to 5 minutes until pork is no longer pink. Remove and reserve.

4. Heat remaining 1 tablespoon oil in wok. Add carrots and bell pepper; stir-fry 4 to 5 minutes until vegetables are crisp-tender. Add pineapple; heat through.

5. Add stir-fry sauce, reserved pineapple juice and vinegar; stir-fry 30 seconds or until sauce boils.

6. Return pork along with any accumulated juices to wok; heat through. Serve over rice, if desired.

½ teaspoon Szechuan peppercorns*
1 teaspoon cornstarch
4 teaspoons soy sauce, divided
4 teaspoons dry sherry, divided
7½ teaspoons vegetable oil, divided
8 ounces boneless lean pork
2 teaspoons red wine vinegar
½ teaspoon sugar
2 cloves garlic, minced
½ small yellow onion, cut into ¼-inch slices
8 green onions with tops, cut into 2-inch pieces
½ teaspoon sesame oil

*Szechuan peppercorns are deceptively potent. Wear rubber or plastic gloves when crushing them and do not touch your eyes or lips when handling.

TWO-ONION PORK SHREDS

Makes 2 to 3 servings

1. For marinade, place peppercorns in small skillet. Cook over medium-low heat, shaking skillet frequently, until fragrant, about 2 minutes. Let cool. Crush peppercorns with mortar and pestle (or place between paper towels and crush with hammer).

2. Transfer peppercorns to medium bowl. Add cornstarch, 2 teaspoons soy sauce, 2 teaspoons sherry and 1½ teaspoons vegetable oil; mix well.

3. Slice meat ⅛-inch thick; cut into 2×½-inch pieces. Add to marinade; stir to coat well. Let stand 30 minutes.

4. Combine remaining 2 teaspoons soy sauce, 2 teaspoons sherry, vinegar and sugar in small bowl; mix well.

5. Heat remaining 6 teaspoons vegetable oil in wok or large skillet over high heat. Stir in garlic. Add meat; stir-fry until no longer pink in center, about 2 minutes. Add yellow onion; stir-fry 1 minute. Add green onions; stir-fry 30 seconds. Add soy-vinegar mixture; cook and stir 30 seconds. Stir in sesame oil.

TWO-ONION PORK SHREDS

1 pound boneless pork, cut into strips

¼ cup GREY POUPON® Dijon Mustard, divided

3 teaspoons soy sauce, divided

1 (3-ounce) package chicken-flavored ramen noodles

1 (8-ounce) can pineapple chunks, drained, reserving juice

½ cup water

2 tablespoons firmly packed light brown sugar

1 tablespoon cornstarch

½ teaspoon grated fresh ginger

2 cups broccoli flowerettes

½ cup chopped red or green cabbage

½ cup chopped red bell pepper

½ cup coarsely chopped onion

2 tablespoons vegetable oil

SWEET & SOUR MUSTARD PORK

Makes 4 servings

In medium bowl, combine pork strips, 2 tablespoons mustard and 1 teaspoon soy sauce. Cover and refrigerate for 1 hour.

In small bowl, combine remaining mustard and soy sauce, chicken flavor packet from noodles, reserved pineapple juice, water, brown sugar, cornstarch and ginger; set aside. Cook ramen noodles according to package directions; drain and set aside.

In large skillet, over medium-high heat, stir-fry vegetables in oil until tender-crisp; remove from skillet. Add pork mixture; stir-fry for 3 to 4 minutes or until no longer pink. Return vegetables to skillet with pineapple chunks and cornstarch mixture; heat until mixture thickens and begins to boil. Add cooked noodles, tossing to coat well. Garnish as desired. Serve immediately.

SWEET & SOUR MUSTARD PORK

1 pound boneless lean pork
  loin or tenderloin roast
2 cloves garlic, minced
2 teaspoons minced fresh
  ginger
2 tablespoons peanut or
  vegetable oil, divided
1 jar (7 ounces) baby corn,
  rinsed and drained
6 ounces (2 cups) fresh
  snow peas or 1 package
  (6 ounces) thawed
  frozen snow peas, cut
  into halves, if large
½ cup stir-fry sauce
  Hot cooked rice or
  Chinese egg noodles
  (optional)

STIR-FRIED PORK AND VEGETABLES

Makes 4 servings

1. Cut pork across the grain into ¼-inch slices; cut each slice into 1¼×¼-inch strips. Toss pork with garlic and ginger in small bowl.

2. Heat wok or large skillet over medium-high heat. Add 1 tablespoon oil; heat until hot. Add pork mixture; stir-fry 3 minutes or until pork is no longer pink. Remove and reserve.

3. Heat remaining 1 tablespoon oil in wok. Add corn and snow peas; stir-fry 3 minutes for fresh or 2 minutes for frozen snow peas or until crisp-tender and corn is hot. Add stir-fry sauce; stir-fry 30 seconds or until sauce boils.

4. Return pork along with any accumulated juices to wok; heat through. Serve over rice, if desired.

4 boneless pork chops, cut
   into ¾-inch cubes
2 teaspoons ground cumin
1 teaspoon ground
   cardamom
1 teaspoon ground
   cinnamon
1 teaspoon ground
   coriander
1 teaspoon ground mace
½ teaspoon pepper
¼ teaspoon salt
1 tablespoon vegetable oil
2 large onions, chopped
3 cloves garlic, minced
¾ cup beef broth
3 tablespoons honey
2 tablespoons lemon juice
1 container (8 ounces)
   nonfat plain yogurt
2 tablespoons flour
¼ cup chopped parsley
2 cups hot cooked rice
   Sliced almonds, toasted
    (optional)
   Mandarin orange sections
    (optional)

INDIAN PORK WITH HONEY

Makes 4 servings

In a plastic or paper bag combine cumin, cardamom, cinnamon, coriander, mace, pepper and salt. Add pork cubes; shake until pork is coated with spice mixture. Set aside. In a large skillet, heat oil over medium-high heat. Cook and stir onions and garlic until tender but not brown. Add pork to skillet. Cook and stir pork for 2 to 3 minutes or until browned. Stir beef broth, honey and lemon juice into skillet. Bring to boiling; reduce heat. Cover and simmer about 10 minutes or until pork is tender, stirring occasionally. In a small bowl combine yogurt and flour; add to skillet. Stir in parsley. Cook over medium heat, stirring constantly, until mixture thickens. Spoon pork mixture over rice. If desired, sprinkle with almonds and garnish with mandarin orange segments.

Favorite recipe from **NATIONAL PORK PRODUCERS COUNCIL**

6 dried Asian mushrooms
1 slice (4 ounces) smoked or baked ham, cut into 2×¼×¼-inch strips
3 green onions with tops, cut diagonally into thin slices
1 pound ground pork
¼ cup chopped water chestnuts
1 tablespoon cornstarch
1 tablespoon dark sesame oil
1 tablespoon soy sauce
1 teaspoon minced fresh ginger
½ teaspoon sugar
Red pearl onion slices and chives for garnish

STEAMED PORK AND HAM

Makes 4 servings

1. Place mushrooms in small bowl; cover with hot water. Let stand 30 minutes; drain.

2. Squeeze excess water from mushrooms. Cut stems from mushrooms and discard. Cut caps into thin strips; place in medium bowl. Set aside.

3. Reserve 2 tablespoons ham strips. Finely chop remaining ham; add to mushrooms. Reserve 1 tablespoon green onion slices and stir remaining slices into mushroom mixture.

4. Add pork, water chestnuts, cornstarch, oil, soy sauce, ginger and sugar to mushroom-ham mixture; mix lightly. Spread mixture into greased 9-inch shallow ovenproof serving dish or pie plate.

5. To steam pork mixture, place wire rack in wok. Add water to 1 inch below rack. (Water should not touch rack.) Cover wok; bring water to a boil over high heat. Carefully place dish with pork on rack. Cover and reduce heat to medium. Steam pork mixture about 25 to 30 minutes until firm. Carefully remove dish from wok.

6. Sprinkle dish with reserved ham and onion slices. Garnish, if desired. Serve immediately.

STEAMED PORK AND HAM

1½ pounds lean pork
    shoulder or pork loin
    roast, cut into 1-inch
    pieces
1 teaspoon ground ginger
¼ teaspoon ground
    cinnamon
¼ teaspoon ground red
    pepper
1 tablespoon peanut or
    vegetable oil
1 large onion, coarsely
    chopped
3 cloves garlic, minced
1 can (about 14 ounces)
    chicken broth
¼ cup dry sherry
1 package (about
    10 ounces) frozen baby
    carrots, thawed
1 large green bell pepper,
    cut into 1-inch pieces
3 tablespoons soy sauce
1½ tablespoons cornstarch
    Fresh cilantro for garnish

CANTON PORK STEW

Makes 6 servings

1. Sprinkle pork with ginger, cinnamon and red pepper; toss well. Heat large saucepan or Dutch oven over medium-high heat. Add oil; heat until hot.

2. Add pork to saucepan; brown on all sides. Add onion and garlic; cook 2 minutes, stirring frequently. Add broth and sherry. Bring to a boil over high heat. Reduce heat to medium-low. Cover and simmer 40 minutes.

3. Stir in carrots and bell pepper; cover and simmer 10 minutes or until pork is fork tender. Blend soy sauce into cornstarch in cup until smooth. Stir into stew. Cook and stir 1 minute or until stew boils and thickens. Ladle into soup bowls. Garnish with cilantro.

CANTON PORK STEW

1 cup water
6 tablespoons lemon juice
6 tablespoons soy sauce
4 cloves garlic, finely chopped
1 ½ teaspoons cornstarch
½ teaspoon white pepper
¼ teaspoon salt
Pinch cayenne pepper
4 pork chops, about 1 inch thick
1 tablespoon vegetable oil
⅔ cup plum jam
¼ cup BLUE DIAMOND® Sliced Natural Almonds, lightly toasted
¼ cup sliced green onion tops

PORK CHOPS WITH ALMOND PLUM SAUCE

Makes 4 servings

Combine first 8 ingredients ending with cayenne pepper. Marinate pork chops in mixture 1 hour or overnight. Remove pork chops, reserving marinade. Sauté pork chops in oil in large skillet over high heat 2 to 3 minutes on each side or until golden brown. Remove from skillet and set aside. Add reserved marinade and plum jam to skillet. Cook over medium heat until mixture thickens and coats the back of a spoon, about 5 minutes. Return pork chops to skillet in single layer. Simmer, covered, for 5 to 7 minutes. Remove cover and continue cooking 3 to 4 minutes or until pork chops are just cooked through and tender. To serve, remove pork chops to serving plate; sprinkle 1 tablespoon almonds over each pork chop. Pour sauce over pork chops and garnish with green onions.

PEANUT PORK TENDERLOIN

Makes 4 to 6 servings

⅓ cup chunky unsweetened peanut butter
⅓ cup regular or light canned coconut milk
¼ cup lemon juice or dry white wine
3 tablespoons soy sauce
3 cloves garlic, minced
2 tablespoons sugar
1 piece (1-inch cube) fresh ginger, minced
½ teaspoon salt
¼ to ½ teaspoon cayenne pepper
¼ teaspoon ground cinnamon
1½ pounds pork tenderloin

Combine peanut butter, coconut milk, lemon juice, soy sauce, garlic, sugar, ginger, salt, cayenne pepper and cinnamon in 2-quart glass dish until blended. Add pork; turn to coat. Cover and refrigerate at least 30 minutes or overnight. Remove pork from marinade; discard marinade. Grill pork on covered grill over medium KINGSFORD® briquets about 20 minutes until just barely pink in center, turning 4 times. Cut crosswise into ½-inch slices. Serve immediately.

THAI PORK BURRITOS

Makes 4 servings

1 pound lean ground pork
1 small onion, thinly sliced
2 tablespoons grated fresh gingerroot
1 clove garlic, peeled and crushed
2 cups cole slaw mix with carrots
3 tablespoons soy sauce
2 tablespoons lime juice
1 tablespoon honey
2 teaspoons ground coriander
1 teaspoon sesame oil
½ teaspoon crushed red pepper
4 large (10-inch) flour tortillas, warmed
Fresh cilantro, chopped for garnish

Heat large nonstick skillet over high heat. Add pork; cook and stir until pork is no longer pink, about 3 to 4 minutes. Add onion, ginger, garlic and cole slaw mix; stir-fry with pork for 2 minutes, until vegetables are wilted. Combine all remaining ingredients except tortillas and cilantro in small bowl and add to skillet. Stir constantly to blend all ingredients well, about 1 minute. Spoon equal portions of mixture onto warm tortillas; garnish with cilantro. Roll up to encase filling and serve.

PREPARATION TIME: 15 minutes

Favorite recipe from **NATIONAL PORK PRODUCERS COUNCIL**

1 pound pork steak or loin or boneless chicken breast
¾ cup orange juice
⅓ cup honey
3 tablespoons soy sauce
1 tablespoon cornstarch
¼ teaspoon ground ginger
2 tablespoons vegetable oil, divided
2 large carrots, sliced diagonally
2 stalks celery, sliced diagonally
½ cup cashews or peanuts
Hot cooked rice

HONEY NUT STIR-FRY

Makes 4 to 6 servings

Cut pork into thin strips; set aside. Combine orange juice, honey, soy sauce, cornstarch and ginger in small bowl; mix well. Heat 1 tablespoon oil in large skillet over medium-high heat. Add carrots and celery; stir-fry about 3 minutes. Remove vegetables; set aside. Pour remaining 1 tablespoon oil into skillet. Add meat; stir-fry about 3 minutes. Return vegetables to skillet; add sauce mixture and nuts. Cook and stir over medium-high heat until sauce comes to a boil and thickens. Serve over rice.

Favorite recipe from **NATIONAL HONEY BOARD**

⅓ cup KIKKOMAN® Teriyaki Baste & Glaze
1 tablespoon dry sherry
½ teaspoon ginger juice*
¼ teaspoon grated orange peel
2 pork tenderloins (¾ pound each)

Press enough fresh gingerroot pieces through garlic press to measure ½ teaspoon juice.

ORIENTAL GLAZED TENDERLOINS

Makes 4 to 6 servings

Combine teriyaki baste & glaze, sherry, ginger juice and orange peel; set aside. Place tenderloins on grill 4 to 5 inches from hot coals. Cook 25 minutes, turning over occasionally. Brush both sides of tenderloins with baste & glaze mixture. Cook 10 minutes longer, or until meat thermometer inserted into thickest part of meat registers 160°F, turning over and brushing frequently with remaining baste & glaze mixture. Let stand 10 minutes. To serve, cut meat across grain into thin slices.

HONEY NUT STIR-FRY

Nutty Rice (recipe follows)
8 ounces lean pork, cut into
2×½-inch strips
½ cup sliced onion
1 clove garlic, minced
4 fresh California plums,
halved, pitted and cut
into thick wedges
1 cup plain low-fat yogurt
1 tablespoon all-purpose
flour
1½ teaspoons grated fresh
ginger
½ teaspoon ground turmeric
⅛ teaspoon black pepper
Additional plum wedges,
orange sections and
sliced green onions

TANDOORI PORK SAUTÉ

Makes 4 servings

Prepare Nutty Rice. Cook pork in nonstick skillet 2 minutes or until browned, turning occasionally. Transfer to platter. Add onion and garlic to skillet; cook 1 minute. Add plums; cook and stir 1 minute. Remove from heat and return pork to pan. Combine yogurt and flour; add to skillet. Stir in ginger, turmeric and pepper. Bring to a boil; reduce heat and simmer 10 minutes, stirring occasionally. Serve over Nutty Rice and surround with plum wedges, orange sections and green onions.

NUTTY RICE

Bring 2 cups water to a boil in medium saucepan. Add ¾ cup brown rice and ¼ cup wheat berries. (Or, omit wheat berries and use 1 cup brown rice.) Return to a boil. Reduce heat to low; cover and simmer 40 to 45 minutes or until rice is tender and liquid is absorbed.

Makes about 3 cups

Favorite recipe from **CALIFORNIA TREE FRUIT AGREEMENT**

TANDOORI PORK SAUTÉ

1/3 cup water
1/3 cup soy sauce
1/4 cup thinly sliced green
  onions
3 tablespoons honey
3 tablespoons dark sesame
  oil
2 tablespoons minced garlic
2 tablespoons sesame seeds
1 tablespoon grated fresh
  ginger
1 teaspoon black pepper
3 1/2 pounds pork back ribs

August Moon Korean Ribs

Makes 8 servings

To prepare marinade, combine all ingredients except ribs in small bowl. Place ribs in large resealable plastic food storage bag. Pour marinade over ribs, turning to coat. Seal bag. Marinate in refrigerator overnight. Arrange medium KINGSFORD® briquets on each side of rectangular metal or foil drip pan. Grill ribs in center of grid on covered grill 35 to 45 minutes or until ribs are browned and cooked through, turning once.

1 block tofu
1/2 pound ground pork
1 tablespoon dry sherry
1 teaspoon minced fresh
  gingerroot
1 clove garlic, minced
1/2 cup chicken broth
1 tablespoon cornstarch
3 tablespoons KIKKOMAN®
  Soy Sauce
1 tablespoon vinegar
1/2 teaspoon crushed red
  pepper
1 tablespoon vegetable oil
1 onion, cut into 3/4-inch
  pieces
1 green bell pepper, cut into
  3/4-inch pieces
  Hot cooked rice

Hunan Stir-Fry with Tofu

Makes 4 servings

Cut tofu into 1/2-inch cubes; drain well on several layers of paper towels. Meanwhile, combine pork, sherry, ginger and garlic in small bowl; let stand 10 minutes. Blend broth, cornstarch, soy sauce, vinegar and red pepper; set aside. Heat wok or large skillet over medium-high heat; add pork. Cook, stirring to separate pork, about 3 minutes, or until lightly browned; remove. Heat oil in same pan. Add onion and bell pepper; stir-fry 4 minutes. Add pork and soy sauce mixture. Cook and stir until mixture boils and thickens. Gently fold in tofu; heat through. Serve immediately over rice.

¼ cup GRANDMA'S®
    Molasses
2 tablespoons HOLLAND
    HOUSE® Sherry Cooking
    Wine
2 tablespoons soy sauce
1 tablespoon hoisin sauce
1 pound boneless pork, cut
    into thin strips
2 tablespoons oil, divided
1 cup diagonally cut fresh
    asparagus or pea pods
1 cup (2 medium) diagonally
    sliced carrots
¾ cup beef broth or water
2 tablespoons cornstarch
    Toasted sesame seed,
    (optional)
    Cooked vermicelli or
    oriental noodles

STIR-FRIED PORK AND VEGGIES

Makes 4 servings

In medium bowl, combine molasses, wine, soy sauce and hoisin sauce; blend well. Add pork; stir to coat. Cover; refrigerate 1 to 2 hours or overnight.

In large skillet, heat 1 tablespoon oil. Stir-fry asparagus and carrots 3 to 5 minutes or until tender-crisp. Remove vegetables from pan. Add remaining 1 tablespoon oil and pork mixture to pan. Stir-fry 5 minutes or until brown. In small bowl, combine broth and cornstarch; blend well. Stir into pork mixture; cook until mixture thickens, stirring constantly. Return vegetables to pan; heat thoroughly. Sprinkle with sesame seed, if desired. Serve with vermicelli or oriental noodles.

2 pounds pork spareribs,
   cut in half lengthwise*
¼ cup plus 1 tablespoon soy
   sauce, divided
3 tablespoons hoisin sauce
3 tablespoons dry sherry,
   divided
1 tablespoon sugar
1 teaspoon minced fresh
   ginger
2 cloves garlic, minced
¼ teaspoon Chinese 5-spice
   powder
2 tablespoons honey
1 tablespoon cider vinegar

*Ask your butcher to cut the
spareribs in half.*

HONEY-GLAZED SPARERIBS

Makes about 4 servings

1. Cut spareribs between bones to make 6-inch pieces. Trim excess fat. Place ribs in large heavy resealable plastic bag.

2. To prepare marinade, combine ¼ cup soy sauce, hoisin sauce, 2 tablespoons sherry, sugar, ginger, garlic and 5-spice powder in small bowl; mix well. Pour over ribs. Seal bag tightly; place in large bowl. Refrigerate 8 hours or overnight, turning bag occasionally.

3. Preheat oven to 350°F. Line large baking pan with foil. Place ribs on rack in pan, reserving marinade. Bake 30 minutes; turn ribs over. Brush with marinade; continue baking 40 minutes or until ribs are tender when pierced with fork.

4. For glaze, combine honey, vinegar, remaining 1 tablespoon soy sauce and 1 tablespoon sherry in small bowl; mix well. Brush ½ of mixture over ribs. Place under broiler 4 to 6 inches from heat source; broil until ribs are glazed, 2 to 3 minutes. Turn ribs over. Brush with remaining honey mixture. Broil until glazed. Cut into serving-size pieces. Garnish, if desired.

HONEY-GLAZED SPARERIBS

SAUCE

¼ cup water
1 ½ tablespoons LA CHOY® Soy Sauce
1 tablespoon cornstarch
1 tablespoon dry sherry
1 teaspoon Oriental sesame oil
¼ teaspoon black pepper

PORK AND VEGETABLES

1 tablespoon LA CHOY® Soy Sauce
1 tablespoon cornstarch
½ pound lean boneless pork, cut into thin 2-inch strips
2 tablespoons WESSON® Oil, divided
4 eggs, well beaten
1 teaspoon minced fresh garlic
1 teaspoon minced gingerroot
1 (1-ounce) package dried Oriental mushrooms, soaked in water for 20 minutes, stems removed and sliced into thin strips
2 cups shredded cabbage
1 (14-ounce) can LA CHOY® Chop Suey Vegetables, drained
10 (8- to 10-inch) flour tortillas, warmed
1 (10-ounce) jar LA CHOY® Sweet & Sour Sauce

MU SHU PORK

Makes 5 servings

In small bowl, combine sauce ingredients; set aside. In medium bowl, combine soy sauce and cornstarch. Add pork; toss gently. Set aside. In large nonstick skillet, heat *1 tablespoon* Wesson Oil over low heat. Add eggs; cook like a pancake. Remove eggs from skillet; slice into thin 2-inch strips. Set aside. Heat *remaining 1 tablespoon* oil in same skillet. Add pork mixture, garlic and ginger; stir-fry until pork is no longer pink. Remove pork from skillet; drain. Add mushrooms to skillet; stir-fry 1 minute. Stir reserved sauce; add to skillet. Cook, stirring constantly, until sauce is thick and bubbly. Return pork and eggs to skillet with cabbage and vegetables; heat thoroughly, stirring occasionally. Spread *each* tortilla with desired amount of sweet & sour sauce; top with *½ cup* pork mixture. Roll up. Serve with remaining sweet & sour sauce.

MU SHU PORK

1 pound boneless pork loin, cut into ½-inch cubes
1 cup plain lowfat yogurt
2 tablespoons orange juice
1 tablespoon ground coriander
½ teaspoon turmeric
½ teaspoon ground cumin
½ teaspoon salt
¼ teaspoon ground ginger
4 barbecue skewers (if using bamboo skewers, soak in cold water for an hour before using)

CURRIED PORK KABOBS

Makes 4 servings

For marinade, in medium bowl stir together yogurt, orange juice and seasonings. Blend well. Add pork cubes to bowl, stir to coat with marinade. Cover and refrigerate 4 to 24 hours. Remove pork from marinade, discarding marinade; with paper towels lightly pat pork dry. Skewer pork evenly on skewers. Grill over medium-hot coals, turning frequently, for about 10 minutes, until nicely browned.

PREPARATION TIME: 10 minutes
COOKING TIME: 10 minutes

Favorite recipe from **NATIONAL PORK PRODUCERS COUNCIL**

---

1 whole pork tenderloin
½ cup reduced-sodium soy sauce
¼ cup dry sherry
2 tablespoons sliced green onion
1 tablespoon brown sugar
1 tablespoon grated fresh ginger *or* ½ teaspoon dried ground ginger
1 clove garlic, minced

TERIYAKI PORK TENDERLOIN

Makes 4 servings

Combine all ingredients in self-sealing bag; seal bag and mix well. Let rest at room temperature for 20 to 30 minutes (or overnight in the refrigerator). Remove tenderloin from marinade, discarding leftover marinade. Roast tenderloin in shallow pan in 450° F. oven for 20 to 25 minutes, until meat thermometer inserted in thickest part reads 155° to 160°F. Remove from oven and let tenderloin rest for 5 to 10 minutes before slicing.

Favorite recipe from **NATIONAL PORK PRODUCERS COUNCIL**

1 pound pork tenderloin
½ cup soy sauce
2 cloves garlic, minced
1 tablespoon grated fresh
    ginger *or* 1 teaspoon
    dried ground ginger
1 tablespoon sesame oil
¼ cup honey
2 tablespoons brown sugar
4 tablespoons sesame seed

Honey Sesame Tenderloin

Makes 4 servings

Combine soy sauce, garlic, ginger and sesame oil. Place tenderloin in a heavy plastic bag, pour soy mixture over to coat. Let marinate 2 hours at room temperature, or overnight in refrigerator. Remove pork from marinade, discarding marinade; pat pork dry. Mix together honey and brown sugar on shallow plate. Place sesame seed on a separate shallow plate. Roll pork in honey mixture, coating well; then roll in sesame seed. Roast in shallow pan at 400°F. for 20 to 30 minutes, until meat thermometer inserted in pork registers 160°F. Remove to serving platter, slice thinly to serve.

Preparation Time: 10 minutes
Cooking Time: 30 minutes

Favorite recipe from **National Pork Producers Council**

PERFECT POULTRY

LEMON CASHEW CHICKEN STIR-FRY

Makes 6 servings

1 tablespoon peanut oil
1 pound chicken tenders, cut into 1½-inch pieces
½ cup sliced mushrooms
¼ cup sliced green onions
2 cloves garlic, minced
1 cup carrot strips
½ cup reduced-sodium chicken broth
1 to 2 tablespoons dry sherry
2 teaspoons sugar
½ teaspoon grated lemon peel
3 tablespoons lemon juice
1 tablespoon cornstarch
⅛ teaspoon white pepper
1 package (6 ounces) frozen snow peas, thawed
⅓ cup chopped cashews

HEAT oil in large skillet over medium-high heat until hot. Add chicken; cook and stir 7 to 8 minutes or until chicken is no longer pink in center.

ADD mushrooms, green onions and garlic; cook and stir 1 minute or until vegetables are tender. Add carrots, chicken broth, sherry, sugar and lemon peel; cook and stir 1 to 2 minutes more.

COMBINE lemon juice, cornstarch and pepper in small bowl; stir until smooth. Pour over chicken mixture; cook and stir 1 to 2 minutes or until slightly thickened.

ADD snow peas; cook and stir 1 minute or until heated through. Serve over hot cooked rice, if desired; sprinkle with cashews.

LEMON CASHEW CHICKEN STIR-FRY

½ cup plus 1 tablespoon
   cornstarch, divided
1 cup water
3 tablespoons dry sherry
3 tablespoons cider vinegar
3 tablespoons hoisin sauce
4 teaspoons soy sauce
2 teaspoons chicken
   bouillon granules
1 broiler-fryer chicken
   (3 to 4 pounds), cut into
   pieces*
   Vegetable oil for frying
2 teaspoons minced fresh
   ginger
2 medium yellow onions,
   chopped
8 ounces fresh broccoli, cut
   into 1-inch pieces
1 red or green bell pepper,
   chopped
2 cans (4 ounces each)
   whole button
   mushrooms, drained
8 ounces Chinese rice
   vermicelli, softened in
   boiling water (optional)
   Red bell pepper strips for
   garnish

*Cut each drumstick, thigh and
breast half into three pieces. Cut
each wing into two pieces.

HOISIN CHICKEN

Makes 6 servings

1. Combine 1 tablespoon cornstarch, water, sherry, vinegar, hoisin sauce, soy sauce and bouillon granules in small bowl; mix well. Set aside.

2. Place remaining ½ cup cornstarch in large bowl. Add chicken pieces; stir to coat well.

3. Pour oil into large skillet or wok to 1-inch depth. Heat over high heat to 375°F. Add ⅓ of the chicken pieces, one at a time; cook until no longer pink in center, about 5 minutes. Drain chicken pieces on paper towels. Repeat with remaining chicken.

4. Remove all but 2 tablespoons oil from skillet. Add ginger to skillet; stir-fry 1 minute. Add onions; stir-fry 1 minute. Add broccoli, chopped bell pepper and mushrooms; stir-fry 2 minutes.

5. Stir cornstarch mixture; add to skillet. Cook and stir until sauce boils and turns translucent. Return chicken to skillet. Cook and stir until chicken is thoroughly heated, about 2 minutes. Serve over hot vermicelli and garnish, if desired.

HOISIN CHICKEN

½ cup orange juice
2 tablespoons sesame oil, divided
2 tablespoons soy sauce
1 tablespoon dry sherry
2 teaspoons grated fresh ginger
1 teaspoon grated orange peel
1 clove garlic, minced
1½ pounds boneless, skinless chicken breast, cut into strips
3 cups mixed fresh vegetables, such as green bell pepper, red bell pepper, snow peas, carrots, green onions, mushrooms and/or onions
1 tablespoon cornstarch
½ cup unsalted cashew bits or halves
3 cups hot cooked rice

ORANGE CHICKEN STIR-FRY

Makes 6 servings

Combine orange juice, 1 tablespoon oil, soy sauce, sherry, ginger, orange peel and garlic in large glass bowl. Add chicken; cover and marinate in refrigerator 1 hour. Drain chicken, reserving marinade. Heat remaining 1 tablespoon oil in large skillet or wok over medium-high heat. Add chicken; stir-fry 3 minutes or until chicken is light brown. Add vegetables; stir-fry 3 to 5 minutes or until vegetables are crisp-tender. Combine cornstarch and reserved marinade; add to skillet and stir until sauce boils and thickens. Stir in cashews; cook 1 minute more. Serve with rice.

Favorite recipe from **NATIONAL BROILER COUNCIL**

½ cup honey
2 tablespoons lime juice
2 tablespoons chopped fresh cilantro
1 tablespoon soy sauce
2 teaspoons seeded, minced jalapeño pepper
1½ teaspoons minced garlic
6 bone-in chicken breast halves (about 3 pounds)

HONEY-LIME GLAZED CHICKEN

Makes 6 servings

Combine all ingredients except chicken in small bowl until well blended. Place chicken in shallow baking dish; pour half of marinade over chicken. Cover and refrigerate 2 hours or overnight. Reserve remaining marinade. Grill chicken over medium-hot coals about 15 minutes or until chicken is no longer pink in center, turning and basting with reserved marinade halfway through cooking.

Favorite recipe from **NATIONAL HONEY BOARD**

ORANGE CHICKEN STIR-FRY

½ cup soy sauce
¼ cup prepared mustard
2 tablespoons honey
2 tablespoons lemon juice
½ teaspoon ground ginger
4 chicken quarters
Hot cooked rice pilaf
(optional)

ORIENTAL GRILLED CHICKEN

Makes 4 servings

Combine soy sauce, mustard, honey, lemon juice and ginger in large glass bowl. Add chicken, turning to coat. Cover; marinate in refrigerator 1 hour. Remove chicken. Place marinade in small saucepan. Bring to a boil over medium-high heat; keep warm. Place chicken on prepared grill, skin sides up, about 8 inches from heat. Grill, turning occasionally, 45 minutes. Grill, basting occasionally with marinade, 15 minutes more or until fork can be inserted into chicken with ease and juices run clear, not pink. Serve with rice pilaf, if desired.

Favorite recipe from **NATIONAL BROILER COUNCIL**

½ cup soy sauce
Juice of 2 to 3 lemons
¼ cup white wine
2 teaspoon sugar
2 teaspoon CHRISTOPHER
RANCH Chopped Ginger
or 1 teaspoon fresh
grated ginger
3 cloves CHRISTOPHER
RANCH Whole Peeled
Garlic, crushed
14 chicken drummettes

JEN'S GINGER-GARLIC CHICKEN DRUMMETTES

Makes 4 servings

To prepare marinade, combine soy sauce, lemon juice, wine, sugar, ginger and garlic in small bowl. Place drummettes in resealable plastic food storage bag. Pour marinade over drummettes. Press air out of bag and seal tightly. Turn bag over to completely coat drummettes with marinade. Refrigerate 6 hours or overnight, turning bag once or twice. Place drummettes with marinade in a large glass baking dish sprayed with nonstick cooking spray. Bake at 350°F for 1 hour or until juices run clear. Marinade should form a glaze on drummettes.

ASIAN SESAME RICE (PAGE 323) AND ORIENTAL GRILLED CHICKEN

Chicken Thai Stir-Fry

Makes 4 servings

4 broiler-fryer chicken
  breast halves, boned,
  skinned, cut in ½-inch
  strips
2 tablespoons vegetable oil
2 teaspoons grated fresh
  ginger
2 cloves garlic, minced
2 cups broccoli florets
1 medium yellow squash,
  cut into ¼-inch slices
1 medium red bell pepper,
  cut into 2-inch strips
⅓ cup creamy peanut butter
¼ cup reduced-sodium soy
  sauce
2 tablespoons white vinegar
2 teaspoons sugar
½ teaspoon crushed red
  pepper
⅓ cup fat-free reduced-
  sodium chicken broth
8 ounces linguine, cooked
  according to package
  directions
2 green onions, white and
  green parts, thinly sliced

In large skillet, place oil and heat over medium-high heat. Add chicken, ginger, and garlic; cook, stirring, about 5 minutes or until chicken is lightly browned and no longer pink. Remove chicken mixture to bowl; set aside. To drippings in same skillet, add broccoli, squash, and bell pepper strips. Cook, stirring, about 5 minutes or until vegetables are crisp-tender. Remove vegetables to bowl with chicken; set aside. To same skillet, add peanut butter, soy sauce, vinegar, sugar, and crushed red pepper; stir in chicken broth. Return chicken and vegetables to skillet; heat through. Serve over linguine. Sprinkle with green onions.

Favorite recipe from **Delmarva Poultry Industry, Inc.**

1 package (1 ounce) dried black Chinese mushrooms
¼ cup reduced-sodium soy sauce
2 tablespoons rice vinegar
3 cloves garlic, minced
1 pound boneless skinless chicken breasts
½ cup chicken broth
1 tablespoon cornstarch
2 tablespoons peanut or vegetable oil, divided
1 jar (7 ounces) straw mushrooms, drained
3 green onions, cut into 1-inch pieces
Hot cooked white rice or Chinese egg noodles (optional)

Moo Goo Gai Pan

Makes 4 servings

1. Place dried mushrooms in small bowl; cover with warm water. Soak 20 minutes to soften. Drain; squeeze out excess water. Discard stems; slice caps.

2. Combine soy sauce, vinegar and garlic in medium bowl. Cut chicken crosswise into ½-inch strips. Toss chicken with soy sauce mixture. Marinate at room temperature 20 minutes.

3. Blend broth into cornstarch in cup until smooth.

4. Heat wok or large skillet over medium-high heat. Add 1 tablespoon oil; heat until hot. Drain chicken; reserve marinade. Add chicken to wok; stir-fry chicken 3 minutes or until no longer pink. Remove and set aside.

5. Heat remaining 1 tablespoon oil in wok; add dried and straw mushrooms and green onions. Stir-fry 1 minute.

6. Stir broth mixture and add to wok along with reserved marinade. Stir-fry 1 minute or until sauce boils and thickens.

7. Return chicken along with any accumulated juices to wok; heat through. Serve over rice, if desired.

ALMOND CHICKEN

Makes 4 servings

⅓ cup blanched whole almonds
1 pound boneless skinless chicken breasts or thighs
2 cloves garlic, minced
1 teaspoon minced fresh ginger
¼ teaspoon crushed red pepper
¾ cup chicken broth
¼ cup soy sauce
4 teaspoons cornstarch
4 large ribs bok choy (about ¾ pound)
2 tablespoons peanut or vegetable oil, divided
2 medium carrots, thinly sliced
Chow mein noodles or hot cooked rice

1. Preheat oven to 350°F. Spread almonds on baking sheet. Toast 6 to 7 minutes until golden brown, stirring once. Set aside.

2. Cut chicken into 1-inch pieces. Toss chicken with garlic, ginger and crushed red pepper in medium bowl. Marinate chicken at room temperature 15 minutes.

3. Blend chicken broth and soy sauce into cornstarch in small bowl until smooth.

4. Cut bok choy stems into ½-inch pieces. Cut leaves crosswise into halves.

5. Heat wok or large skillet over medium-high heat. Add 1 tablespoon oil; heat until hot. Add chicken mixture; stir-fry 3 minutes or until chicken is no longer pink. Remove and set aside.

6. Heat remaining 1 tablespoon oil in wok; add bok choy stems and carrots. Stir-fry 5 minutes or until vegetables are crisp-tender. Stir broth mixture and add to wok along with bok choy leaves. Stir-fry 1 minute or until sauce boils and thickens.

7. Return chicken along with any accumulated juices to wok; heat through. Stir in almonds. Serve over chow mein noodles.

ALMOND CHICKEN

1 lemon
1 teaspoon dried thyme
  leaves
½ teaspoon salt
¼ teaspoon ground white
  pepper
1 pound turkey cutlets, cut
  into 2½×1-inch strips
1 pound fresh broccoli
1 cup chicken broth
1 tablespoon cornstarch
3 tablespoons vegetable oil,
  divided
1 tablespoon butter
¼ pound fresh button
  mushrooms, cleaned
  and sliced
1 medium red onion,
  peeled, sliced and
  separated into rings
1 can (14 ounces) pre-cut
  baby corn, rinsed and
  drained*
  Hot cooked rice
  Lemon slices for garnish

*Or, substitute 15-ounce can whole
baby corn, cut into 1-inch lengths.

STIR-FRIED TURKEY WITH BROCCOLI

Makes 4 to 6 servings

1. Finely grate peel of lemon. Extract juice from lemon to measure 2 tablespoons. Combine lemon juice, lemon peel, thyme, salt and pepper.

2. Add turkey to lemon mixture; coat well. Marinate 30 minutes.

3. Cut broccoli tops into florets. Peel stems, then slice diagonally into 2-inch pieces; set aside.

4. Combine broth and cornstarch in cup; set aside.

5. Place 4 cups water in wok; bring to a boil over medium-high heat. Add broccoli stems; cook 1 minute. Add florets; cook 2 minutes more or until crisp-tender. Drain and rinse with cold water; set aside.

6. Heat wok over medium-high heat until hot. Add 1 tablespoon oil and butter; heat until hot. Add mushrooms; stir-fry 2 minutes or until mushrooms are wilted. Add onion; stir-fry 2 minutes. Remove to large bowl.

7. Heat 1 tablespoon oil in wok. Stir-fry half of turkey strips in single layer 1½ minutes or until well browned on all sides. Transfer to bowl with mushrooms. Repeat with remaining 1 tablespoon oil and turkey.

8. Add corn to wok and heat 1 minute. Stir cornstarch mixture; add to wok and cook until bubbly. Add turkey, broccoli, mushrooms and onions to wok; cook and stir until heated through. Serve over rice. Garnish, if desired.

STIR-FRIED TURKEY WITH BROCCOLI

2 teaspoons paprika
½ teaspoon ground cumin
½ teaspoon ground
    coriander
¼ teaspoon ground ginger
⅛ teaspoon ground red
    pepper
8 boneless, skinless chicken
    thighs (about
    1¼ pounds)
2 tablespoons plus
    1 teaspoon lemon juice,
    divided
2 tablespoons reduced-
    calorie margarine,
    melted
1 cup plain dry bread
    crumbs
  Vegetable cooking spray
8 ounces plain nonfat
    yogurt, at room
    temperature
½ cup fresh cilantro leaves
¼ cup fresh mint leaves
¼ teaspoon salt
  Lemon slices for garnish
  Hot cooked rice (optional)

BAKED CHICKEN BOMBAY

Makes 4 servings

Combine paprika, cumin, coriander, ginger and red pepper in small bowl. Place chicken between plastic wrap; pound with meat mallet or rolling pin to ½-inch thickness. Sprinkle paprika mixture on both sides of chicken. Combine 2 tablespoons lemon juice and margarine in shallow bowl. Dip chicken in margarine mixture. Roll in bread crumbs to coat. Place on baking sheet coated with cooking spray. Bake at 425°F 17 to 20 minutes or until no longer pink in center. Combine yogurt, cilantro, mint, remaining 1 teaspoon lemon juice and salt in blender or food processor; process until smooth. To serve, pour sauce over chicken. Garnish with lemon slices. Serve with rice, if desired.

Favorite recipe from **NATIONAL BROILER COUNCIL**

BAKED CHICKEN BOMBAY AND BROWN RICE AND SHIITAKE PILAF (PAGE 319)

1 teaspoon ground cumin
½ teaspoon salt
¼ teaspoon cayenne pepper
¼ teaspoon ground
   cinnamon
¼ teaspoon ground cloves
   Raita (recipe follows)
2 small cloves garlic,
   minced
1 small jalapeño pepper,
   seeded and minced
   (optional)
1 tablespoon minced or
   grated fresh ginger
1 turkey breast tenderloin
   (1 to 1¼ pounds), cut
   into ¾-inch cubes
1 to 2 tablespoons
   vegetable oil
4 pita breads, halved
   (optional)

TANDOORI TURKEY KABOBS

Makes 4 servings

Combine cumin, salt, cayenne pepper, cinnamon and cloves in small bowl; reserve ½ teaspoon cumin mixture for Raita. Prepare Raita. Add garlic, jalapeño pepper and ginger to remaining cumin mixture in bowl. Place turkey in large bowl; drizzle with oil and toss to coat. Sprinkle cumin mixture over turkey; toss to coat. Thread turkey onto metal or wooden skewers. (Soak wooden skewers in hot water 30 minutes to prevent burning.) Lightly oil hot grid to prevent sticking. Grill turkey on covered grill over medium-hot KINGSFORD® briquets 7 to 12 minutes or until turkey is no longer pink, turning once. Serve in pita breads, if desired, with Raita.

RAITA

1 cup plain low-fat yogurt
¾ cup finely diced seeded peeled cucumber
1½ tablespoons minced fresh mint
2 to 3 teaspoons honey
½ teaspoon cumin mixture reserved from recipe
   above

Combine all ingredients in small bowl. Cover and refrigerate until ready to serve.   *Makes 1½ cups*

TERIYAKI STIR-FRY CHICKEN DINNER

Makes 4 to 6 servings

1 package (about
    1¾ pounds) PERDUE®
    OVEN STUFFER® or
    Chicken Wingettes
Salt to taste
Ground black pepper to
    taste
2 tablespoons vegetable oil
1 cup broccoli florets
1 can (8 ounces) sliced
    water chestnuts, drained
4 carrots, sliced
4 scallions, thinly sliced
½ cup water
¼ cup brown sugar
¼ cup soy sauce
3 tablespoons dry sherry or
    white vinegar
2 cloves garlic, finely
    chopped
2 teaspoons grated
    gingerroot
2 cups hot cooked rice
    Additional sliced scallion
    for garnish (optional)

Sprinkle wingettes with salt and pepper.

In large nonstick wok or skillet over medium-high heat, heat oil. Stir-fry broccoli 1 minute. Add water chestnuts and carrots; stir-fry 1 minute longer. Add scallions; stir-fry a few seconds. Remove vegetables and reserve.

Add wingettes to wok and cook until lightly browned on all sides, about 5 minutes. Reduce heat to low; cover and cook 10 minutes, turning occasionally until no longer pink. Remove wingettes to paper towel and pour off drippings. Return wingettes and vegetables to pan. Add all remaining ingredients except rice and garnish; stir until well mixed. Cook, turning frequently until wingettes and vegetables are glazed and sauce is thickened, about 3 to 5 minutes. Serve hot over rice, sprinkling with additional sliced scallion, if desired.

BRAISED CORNISH HENS

Makes 2 to 4 servings

2 Cornish hens, thawed if
    frozen (1½ to
    1¾ pounds each)
¼ cup soy sauce
2 tablespoons dry sherry
1 teaspoon sugar
⅔ cup plus 1 tablespoon
    cornstarch, divided
¼ cup vegetable oil
1 piece fresh ginger (about
    1-inch square) peeled
    and cut into 4 slices
2 cloves garlic, crushed
1 cup chicken broth
1 large yellow onion,
    coarsely chopped
12 ounces snow peas
    Yellow squash, zucchini,
    carrot and red bell
    pepper crescents for
    garnish

1. Remove neck and giblets from hens; wrap and freeze for another use or discard. Rinse hens and cavities under cold running water; pat dry with paper towels. Cut each hen into quarters, removing backbone and breast bone.

2. To prepare marinade, combine soy sauce, sherry and sugar in large bowl; mix well. Add hen quarters; stir to coat well. Cover and refrigerate 1 hour to marinate, stirring occasionally.

3. Drain hens and reserve marinade. Place ⅔ cup cornstarch in shallow dish or pie plate. Coat hens with cornstarch. Combine remaining 1 tablespoon cornstarch with marinade; mix well.

4. Heat wok over medium-high heat about 1 minute or until hot. Drizzle oil into wok and heat 30 seconds. Add ginger and garlic; cook and stir about 1 minute or until oil is fragrant. Remove and discard ginger and garlic with slotted spoon. Add hens to oil and fry about 10 to 15 minutes until well browned on all sides.

5. Add broth and onion to wok; bring to a boil. Cover and reduce heat to low; simmer hens about 20 minutes or until fork-tender and juices run clear, turning occasionally. Move hens up side of wok and add snow peas to bottom of wok.

6. Cover and cook 3 to 5 minutes until peas are crisp-tender. Stir cornstarch mixture and add to wok. Cook and stir until sauce thickens and boils. Transfer to serving platter. Garnish, if desired. Serve immediately.

BRAISED CORNISH HENS

1 can (8 ounces) pineapple chunks in unsweetened juice
2 teaspoons cornstarch
2 tablespoons peanut oil
3 boneless skinless chicken breast halves (about 1 pound), cut into ¾-inch pieces
2 to 4 red serrano peppers,* seeded and cut into thin strips (optional)
2 cloves garlic, minced
2 green onions, cut into 1-inch pieces
¾ cup roasted, unsalted cashews
¼ cup chopped fresh basil (do not use dried)
1 tablespoon fish sauce
1 tablespoon soy sauce
Hot cooked rice (optional)
Kumquat flower for garnish

*Serrano peppers can sting and irritate the skin; wear rubber gloves when handling peppers and do not touch eyes. Wash hands after handling.

PINEAPPLE BASIL CHICKEN SUPREME

Makes 4 servings

1. Drain pineapple, reserving juice. Combine reserved juice and cornstarch in small bowl; set aside.

2. Heat wok over high heat 1 minute or until hot. Drizzle oil into wok and heat 30 seconds. Add chicken, peppers, if desired, and garlic; stir-fry 3 minutes or until chicken is no longer pink. Add green onions; stir-fry 1 minute.

3. Stir cornstarch mixture; add to wok. Cook 1 minute or until thickened.

4. Add pineapple, cashews, basil, fish sauce and soy sauce; stir-fry 1 minute or until heated through. Serve over rice and garnish, if desired.

PINEAPPLE BASIL CHICKEN SUPREME

1 teaspoon Garam Masala,
   divided (recipe follows)
½ cup unsalted butter
4 boneless skinless chicken
   breast halves or thighs
   (1 pound)
1 egg, beaten
3 cloves garlic, minced and
   divided
2 teaspoons minced ginger,
   divided
½ teaspoon salt, divided
½ teaspoon turmeric,
   divided
½ cup chopped onion
2 tablespoons shredded
   unsweetened coconut*
¾ cup plain yogurt
¼ cup whipping cream
¼ cup whole cashews for
   garnish

*Sweetened coconut that has been rinsed with boiling water may be substituted.

MOGUL-STYLE FRIED CHICKEN

Makes 4 servings

1. Prepare Garam Masala. Set aside.

2. To prepare clarified butter or ghee, melt butter in small skillet over low heat. Remove from heat. Skim off and discard white foam that forms on top. Skim off clear clarified butter and reserve. Discard white milk solids.

3. Place chicken between two pieces of plastic wrap. Pound with flat side of meat mallet to ¼-inch thickness.

4. Blend egg, ½ teaspoon garlic, 1½ teaspoons ginger, ½ teaspoon Garam Masala, ¼ teaspoon salt and ¼ teaspoon turmeric in shallow bowl. Dip chicken in mixture; turn to coat.

5. Heat clarified butter in large skillet over medium-high heat. Add chicken. Cook 4 to 5 minutes per side or until golden brown and no longer pink in center. Remove chicken from skillet; drain on paper towels.

6. To prepare sauce, pour off all but 2 tablespoons clarified butter from skillet. Reduce heat to medium. Add onion. Cook and stir 3 to 5 minutes or until soft and golden.

7. Add coconut, remaining garlic, remaining ½ teaspoon ginger, ½ teaspoon Garam Masala, ¼ teaspoon salt and ¼ teaspoon turmeric. Cook and stir 30 seconds.

8. Remove skillet from heat. Place yogurt in small bowl. Stir in several spoonfuls hot sauce mixture. Stir yogurt mixture into skillet. Add chicken; turn to coat. Heat over low heat until hot. Remove chicken to serving dish.

9. Stir cream into sauce. *Do not boil.* Spoon sauce over chicken. Garnish with cashews.

GARAM MASALA

2 teaspoons cumin seeds
2 teaspoons whole black peppercorns
1 ½ teaspoons coriander seeds
1 teaspoon fennel seeds
¾ teaspoon whole cloves
½ teaspoon whole cardamom seeds (pods removed)
1 cinnamon stick, broken

Preheat oven to 250°F. Combine spices on pizza pan or baking sheet; bake 30 minutes, stirring occasionally. Grind warm spices in clean coffee or spice grinder (or use mortar and pestle). Store in tightly covered glass jar.

Makes about 2½ tablespoons

CHINESE CHICKEN & WALNUT STIR-FRY

Makes 4 servings

¼ cup chicken broth or bouillon
2 tablespoons soy sauce
2 teaspoons cornstarch
2 teaspoons vegetable oil
¾ pound boneless skinless chicken breasts, cut into ¼-inch-thick strips
2 to 3 tablespoons slivered fresh ginger
1 clove garlic, minced
4 cups fresh vegetables (snow peas, bean sprouts, very thinly sliced carrots and celery)
1 cup toasted walnut pieces
Hot cooked rice

Combine chicken broth, soy sauce and cornstarch; reserve. In wok or heavy skillet, heat oil until very hot but not smoking. Add chicken, ginger and garlic. Stir-fry over high heat 2 minutes; remove and reserve. Add vegetables to wok; toss until crisp-tender, 3 to 4 minutes. Return chicken to wok. Add cornstarch mixture; stir-fry 1 minute to thicken and coat. Add walnuts; toss. Serve immediately with rice.

Favorite recipe from **WALNUT MARKETING BOARD**

4 whole boneless skinless
  chicken breasts
½ cup cornstarch
½ teaspoon salt
⅛ teaspoon black pepper
4 egg yolks, lightly beaten
¼ cup water
  Vegetable oil for frying
4 green onions with tops,
  sliced

LEMON SAUCE

3 tablespoons cornstarch
1½ cups water
½ cup lemon juice
3½ tablespoons brown sugar
3 tablespoons honey
2 teaspoons instant chicken
  bouillon granules
1 teaspoon minced fresh
  ginger
  Lemon peel and lemon
  balm for garnish

LEMON CHICKEN

Makes 4 to 6 servings

1. Cut chicken breasts in half; place between two sheets of plastic wrap. Pound with meat mallet or rolling pin to flatten slightly.

2. Combine cornstarch, salt and pepper in small bowl. Gradually blend in egg yolks and water.

3. Pour oil into large skillet or wok to 1-inch depth. Heat over high heat to 375°F. Meanwhile, dip chicken breasts, one at a time, into cornstarch mixture.

4. Add chicken breasts, two at a time to hot oil; cook until golden brown, about 5 minutes or until chicken is no longer pink in center. Drain chicken on paper towels. Keep warm while cooking remaining chicken.

5. Cut each breast into four pieces. Arrange chicken pieces on serving plate. Sprinkle with green onions.

6. Combine cornstarch, water, lemon juice, brown sugar, honey, bouillon granules and ginger in medium saucepan; mix well. Cook over medium heat, stirring constantly, until sauce boils and thickens, about 5 minutes. Pour over chicken. Garnish, if desired.

LEMON CHICKEN

THAI CHICKEN SATAYS

1 cup plain yogurt
½ cup coconut milk
1 tablespoon curry powder
1 teaspoon grated fresh
    ginger
1 clove garlic, crushed
1 teaspoon lemon juice
½ teaspoon salt
½ teaspoon black pepper
1 pound chicken tenders
6 (6-inch) pita bread
    rounds, cut in half
Chopped fresh cilantro
Additional plain yogurt

Makes 6 servings

COMBINE 1 cup yogurt, coconut milk, curry powder, ginger, garlic, lemon juice, salt and pepper in medium bowl; reserve ⅓ cup marinade. Add chicken to remaining marinade; cover and refrigerate at least 8 hours.

SOAK 12 (10-inch) wooden skewers in water 20 minutes; set aside.

REMOVE chicken from marinade; discard marinade. Thread chicken onto skewers. Place skewers on broiler rack coated with nonstick cooking spray; place rack on broiler pan. Broil 4 to 5 inches from heat source 4 to 5 minutes. Turn skewers; brush with reserved marinade. Broil 4 minutes more or until chicken is no longer pink in center.

REMOVE chicken from skewers. Fill pitas with chicken and top with cilantro and dollop of yogurt.

Serving Suggestion: *Serve with a fruit salad of pineapple, mandarin oranges and bananas.*

TERIYAKI PLUM CHICKEN

½ cup LA CHOY® Teriyaki
    Sauce
½ cup plum jam
2 tablespoons WESSON®
    Vegetable Oil
2 plums, finely chopped
1½ to 2 pounds chicken
    pieces
Fresh plum slices
    (optional)

Makes 4 servings

In a large bowl, combine *all* ingredients *except* chicken and plum slices; mix well. Add chicken, cover and marinate in refrigerator at least 2 hours. Place chicken on grill over medium-hot coals. Grill, basting occasionally with marinade and turning often, for 20 minutes or until meat is no longer pink. Garnish with fresh plum slices, if desired.

THAI CHICKEN SATAYS

5 teaspoons dry sherry,
    divided
5 teaspoons soy sauce,
    divided
3½ teaspoons cornstarch,
    divided
¼ teaspoon salt
3 boneless skinless chicken
    breast halves, cut into
    bite-size pieces
2 tablespoons chicken broth
    or water
1 tablespoon red wine
    vinegar
1½ teaspoons sugar
3 tablespoons vegetable oil,
    divided
⅓ cup salted peanuts
6 to 8 small dried hot chili
    peppers
1½ teaspoons minced fresh
    ginger
2 green onions with tops,
    cut into 1½-inch pieces
Additional green onion
    and dried hot chili
    pepper for garnish

KUNG PAO CHICKEN

Makes 3 servings

1. For marinade, combine 2 teaspoons sherry, 2 teaspoons soy sauce, 2 teaspoons cornstarch and salt in large bowl; mix until smooth. Add chicken; stir to coat well. Let stand 30 minutes.

2. Combine remaining 3 teaspoons sherry, 3 teaspoons soy sauce, 1½ teaspoons cornstarch, chicken broth, vinegar and sugar in small bowl; mix well. Set aside.

3. Heat 1 tablespoon oil in wok or large skillet over medium heat. Add peanuts; cook and stir until lightly toasted. Remove peanuts from wok; set aside.

4. Heat remaining 2 tablespoons oil in wok over medium heat. Add chili peppers; stir-fry until peppers just begin to char, about 1 minute.

5. Increase heat to high. Add chicken mixture; stir-fry 2 minutes. Add ginger; stir-fry until chicken is no longer pink in center, about 1 minute.

6. Add peanuts and green onions. Stir cornstarch mixture; add to wok. Cook and stir until sauce boils and thickens. Garnish, if desired.

5 teaspoons cornstarch, divided
4 teaspoons soy sauce, divided
1 tablespoon dry sherry
1 teaspoon sesame oil
3 boneless skinless chicken breast halves, cut into bite-size pieces
1 tablespoon fermented, salted black beans
1 teaspoon minced fresh ginger
1 clove garlic, minced
½ cup chicken broth
1 tablespoon oyster sauce
1 medium yellow onion
3 tablespoons vegetable oil, divided
1 pound fresh asparagus spears, trimmed and diagonally cut into 1-inch pieces
2 tablespoons water
Fresh cilantro leaves for garnish

Asparagus Chicken with Black Bean Sauce

Makes 3 to 4 servings

1. For marinade, combine 2 teaspoons cornstarch, 2 teaspoons soy sauce, sherry and sesame oil in large bowl; mix well. Add chicken; stir to coat well. Cover and refrigerate 30 minutes.

2. Place black beans in sieve; rinse under cold running water. Finely chop beans. Combine with ginger and garlic; set aside.

3. Combine chicken broth, oyster sauce, remaining 3 teaspoons cornstarch and 2 teaspoons soy sauce in small bowl; mix well. Set aside.

4. Cut onion into eight wedges. Separate wedges; set aside.

5. Heat 2 tablespoons vegetable oil in wok or large skillet over high heat. Add chicken; stir-fry until no longer pink in center, about 3 minutes. Remove from wok; set aside.

6. Heat remaining 1 tablespoon vegetable oil in wok. Add onion and asparagus; stir-fry 30 seconds.

7. Add water; cover. Cook, stirring occasionally, until asparagus is crisp-tender, about 2 minutes. Return chicken to wok.

8. Stir chicken broth mixture; add to wok with bean mixture. Cook until sauce boils and thickens, stirring constantly. Garnish, if desired.

1 cup coarsely chopped
   fresh cilantro
8 cloves garlic, peeled and
   coarsely chopped
2 tablespoons fish sauce
2 jalapeño peppers,* seeded
   and coarsely chopped
1 tablespoon packed brown
   sugar
1 teaspoon curry powder
   Grated peel of 1 lemon
1 cut-up frying chicken
   (about 3 pounds)

*Jalapeños can sting and irritate the
skin; wear rubber gloves when
handling peppers and do not touch
eyes. Wash hands after handling.

THAI BARBECUED CHICKEN

Makes 4 servings

Place cilantro, garlic, fish sauce, jalapeño peppers,
brown sugar, curry powder and lemon peel in blender
or food processor; blend to form coarse paste.

Rinse chicken pieces; pat dry with paper towels. Work
fingers between skin and meat on breast and thigh
pieces. Rub about 1 teaspoon seasoning paste under
skin on each piece. Rub chicken pieces on all sides with
remaining paste. Place chicken in large resealable
plastic food storage bag or covered container; marinate
in refrigerator 3 to 4 hours or overnight.

Prepare coals for grill. Brush grid lightly with oil. Grill
chicken over medium coals, skin side down, about 10
minutes or until well browned. Turn chicken and grill 20
to 30 minutes more or until chicken is no longer pink in
center and juices run clear. (Thighs and legs may
require 10 to 15 minutes more cooking time than
breasts.) If chicken is browned on both sides but still
needs additional cooking, move to edge of grill, away
from direct heat, to finish cooking. Garnish as desired.

Note: *To bake, place chicken skin side up in lightly oiled
baking pan. Bake in preheated 375°F oven 30 to 45
minutes or until no longer pink in center.*

THAI BARBECUED CHICKEN

½ cup uncooked rice
1 small onion
2 boneless skinless chicken
   breast halves
1 tablespoon butter or
   margarine
1 clove garlic, minced
1 teaspoon curry powder
¼ teaspoon ground ginger
3 tablespoons raisins
1 cup coarsely chopped
   apple, divided
1 teaspoon chicken bouillon
   granules
¼ cup plain nonfat yogurt
2 teaspoons all-purpose
   flour
   Green onion slivers
   (optional)

CHICKEN CURRY

Makes 2 servings

1. Cook rice according to package directions.

2. While rice is cooking, cut onion into thin slices. Cut chicken into ¾-inch cubes.

3. Heat butter, garlic, curry powder and ginger in medium skillet over medium heat. Add chicken; cook and stir 2 minutes. Add onion, raisins and ¾ cup apple; cook and stir 3 minutes. Stir in chicken bouillon and ¼ cup water. Reduce heat to low; cover and cook 2 minutes.

4. Combine yogurt and flour in small bowl. Stir several tablespoons liquid from skillet into yogurt mixture. Stir yogurt mixture into skillet. Cook and stir just until mixture starts to boil.

5. Serve chicken curry over rice; garnish with remaining ¼ cup apple and green onion slivers, if desired.

PREP AND COOK TIME: 28 minutes

CHICKEN CURRY

1½ **pounds skinless chicken thighs (4 to 6 thighs)**
2 **stalks lemongrass**
¼ **cup sugar**
3 **tablespoons fish sauce**
2 **cloves garlic, slivered**
¼ **teaspoon black pepper**
1 **tablespoon vegetable oil**
1 **tablespoon lemon juice**

CARAMELIZED LEMONGRASS CHICKEN

Makes 4 servings

1. Rinse chicken and pat dry with paper towels.

2. Remove outer leaves from lemongrass and discard. Trim off and discard upper stalks. Flatten lemongrass with meat mallet or flat side of cleaver.

3. Cut flattened lemongrass into 1-inch pieces.

4. Place chicken in large resealable plastic food storage bag; add sugar, fish sauce, garlic, pepper and lemongrass. Seal bag tightly; turn to coat. Marinate in refrigerator at least 1 hour or up to 4 hours, turning occasionally.

5. Heat oil in large skillet over medium heat. Remove chicken from marinade; reserve marinade. Cook chicken 10 minutes or until browned, turning once.

6. Pour reserved marinade into skillet; bring to a boil. Boil 1 to 2 minutes. Reduce heat to low; cover and simmer 30 minutes or until chicken is tender and no longer pink in center, turning occasionally.

7. Stir lemon juice into skillet. Turn chicken pieces over to coat. Garnish as desired.

CARAMELIZED LEMONGRASS CHICKEN

2 oranges
¼ cup mild-flavored
   molasses
1 tablespoon soy sauce
2 teaspoons cornstarch
¾ cup all-purpose flour
½ teaspoon salt
¼ teaspoon baking powder
¾ cup water
1 pound boneless skinless
   chicken breasts or
   thighs, cut into 1-inch
   pieces
   Vegetable oil for frying
1 teaspoon chili oil
4 whole dried chili peppers
2 cloves garlic, minced
1½ teaspoons finely chopped
   fresh ginger
   Hot cooked rice
   Orange and chili flowers
   for garnish

SPICY ORANGE CHICKEN

Makes 4 servings

1. Remove ½-inch wide strips of peel from 1 orange with vegetable peeler. Slice peel into 1-inch pieces; set aside. (Remove colored portion of skin only; white pith has a bitter taste.) Extract juice from oranges.

2. Combine ½ cup orange juice, molasses, soy sauce and cornstarch in small bowl; set aside.

3. Combine flour, salt and baking powder in medium bowl. Stir in water with wire whisk to form smooth batter. Add chicken; mix well.

4. Heat about 3 cups vegetable oil in wok over medium-high heat until oil registers 375°F on deep-fry thermometer. Shake off excess batter from ⅓ of chicken; carefully add chicken to wok.

5. Cook about 4 minutes or until chicken is golden brown and no longer pink in center, stirring occasionally to break up pieces with spoon. Remove chicken with slotted spoon to tray lined with paper towels; drain. Repeat 2 more times with remaining chicken, reheating oil between batches.

6. Pour off all oil from wok. Reheat wok over medium-high heat until hot. Add chili oil, orange peel, dried chili peppers, garlic and ginger; stir-fry about 30 seconds to 1 minute or until fragrant.

7. Stir cornstarch mixture; add to wok. Cook and stir until sauce boils and thickens. Return chicken to wok; mix well. Serve with rice. Garnish, if desired.

SPICY ORANGE CHICKEN

1 pound boneless skinless chicken breast halves
1/3 cup soy sauce
2 tablespoons fresh lime juice
2 cloves garlic, minced
1 teaspoon grated fresh ginger
3/4 teaspoon crushed red pepper
2 tablespoons water
3/4 cup canned unsweetened coconut milk
1 tablespoon creamy peanut butter
4 green onions with tops, cut into 1-inch pieces

THAI SATAY CHICKEN SKEWERS

Makes 4 servings

1. Slice chicken crosswise into 3/8-inch-wide strips; place in shallow glass dish.

2. Combine soy sauce, lime juice, garlic, ginger and crushed red pepper in small bowl. Reserve 3 tablespoons mixture; cover and refrigerate. Add water to remaining mixture. Pour over chicken; toss to coat well. Cover; marinate in refrigerator at least 30 minutes or up to 2 hours, stirring mixture occasionally.

3. Cover 8 wooden skewers (10 to 12 inches long) with cold water. Soak 20 minutes to prevent burning; drain.

4. Prepare grill for direct cooking.

5. Meanwhile for peanut sauce, combine coconut milk, reserved soy sauce mixture and peanut butter in small saucepan. Bring to a boil over medium-high heat, stirring constantly. Reduce heat to low and simmer, uncovered, 2 to 4 minutes or until sauce thickens. Keep warm.

6. Drain chicken; reserve marinade from dish. Weave 3 to 4 chicken pieces accordion style onto each skewer, alternating with green onion pieces placed crosswise on skewer. Brush reserved marinade from dish over chicken and green onions. Discard remaining marinade.

7. Place skewers on grid. Grill skewers, on uncovered grill, over medium-hot coals 6 to 8 minutes or until chicken is no longer pink, turning halfway through grilling time. Serve with warm peanut sauce for dipping.

THAI SATAY CHICKEN SKEWERS

2 tablespoons soy sauce
1 tablespoon Chinese chili sauce
1 tablespoon dry sherry
2 cloves garlic, minced
¼ teaspoon crushed red pepper
16 chicken tenders (about 1 pound)
1 tablespoon peanut oil
Hot cooked rice

SZECHUAN CHICKEN TENDERS

Makes 4 servings

COMBINE soy sauce, chili sauce, sherry, garlic and crushed red pepper in shallow dish. Add chicken; coat well.

HEAT oil in large nonstick skillet over medium heat until hot. Add chicken; cook 6 minutes, turning once, until chicken is browned and no longer pink in center.

SERVE chicken with rice.

½ pound boneless skinless chicken breasts, finely chopped
1 tablespoon soy sauce
1 clove garlic, minced
¾ teaspoon ginger
¾ teaspoon chili powder
1 tablespoon oil
½ cup chopped celery
¾ cup chopped DIAMOND® Walnuts
¼ cup sliced green onions
2 tablespoons ketchup
1 tablespoon cider vinegar
Iceberg lettuce leaves or warm flour tortillas

CHINESE CHICKEN ROLLS

Makes 2½ cups

Combine chicken, soy sauce, garlic, ginger and chili powder; let stand 15 minutes. Heat oil in skillet; cook chicken mixture until chicken is no longer pink. Add celery; cook 1 minute. Stir in walnuts, onions, ketchup and vinegar; heat through. Serve rolled inside lettuce leaves or tortillas.

CHICKEN FRIED RICE

Makes 6 servings

1 bag SUCCESS® Rice
½ pound boneless skinless chicken, cut into ½-inch pieces
½ teaspoon salt
¼ teaspoon black pepper
2 tablespoons vegetable oil
1 clove garlic, minced
½ teaspoon grated fresh ginger
2 cups diagonally sliced green onions
1 cup sliced fresh mushrooms
2 tablespoons reduced-sodium soy sauce
1 teaspoon sherry
1 teaspoon Asian-style hot chili sesame oil (optional)

Prepare rice according to package directions.

Sprinkle chicken with salt and pepper; set aside. Heat vegetable oil in large skillet over medium-high heat. Add garlic and ginger; cook and stir 1 minute. Add chicken; stir-fry until no longer pink in center. Add green onions and mushrooms; stir-fry until tender. Stir in soy sauce, sherry and sesame oil, if desired. Add rice; heat thoroughly, stirring occasionally.

SZECHUAN WINGS

Makes 3 to 4 servings

1 package (about 1¾ pounds) PERDUE® Fresh OVEN STUFFER® or Chicken Wingettes
6 tablespoons white vinegar
6 tablespoons chili sauce
6 tablespoons soy sauce
2 tablespoons canola oil
2 tablespoons minced fresh gingerroot
1½ tablespoons sugar
1½ tablespoons crushed red pepper
1½ teaspoons salt

Place wingettes in large bowl. In small bowl, combine remaining ingredients; set aside ¼ cup. Pour soy sauce mixture over wingettes; cover and refrigerate 1 hour or longer.

Prepare lightly greased grill for cooking. Remove wingettes to grill and discard marinade. Grill wingettes, uncovered, 5 to 6 inches over medium-hot coals 25 to 30 minutes or until wingettes are no longer pink and juices run clear, turning and basting frequently with reserved soy sauce mixture.

4 to 6 boneless skinless
  chicken thighs
1 cup plain yogurt, divided
2 cloves garlic, minced and
  divided
1 teaspoon salt
3 tablespoons Clarified
  Butter (page 170),
  divided
1 cinnamon stick, broken
1 teaspoon coriander seeds
½ teaspoon cumin seeds
¼ teaspoon cardamom
  seeds
¼ teaspoon whole black
  peppercorns
¼ teaspoon ground turmeric
1 large onion, chopped
2 teaspoons finely chopped
  fresh ginger
½ cup chicken broth
1 Granny Smith or Jonathan
  apple, unpeeled, cut into
  ½-inch pieces
  Hot cooked rice, shredded
  coconut, raisins,
  chopped nuts and
  cilantro (optional)

CHICKEN CURRY

Makes 4 servings

1. Cut chicken into 1-inch cubes; place in medium bowl.

2. Combine ½ cup yogurt, half of garlic and salt in small bowl. Pour over chicken; toss to coat well. Cover and refrigerate at least 30 minutes or up to 2 hours, stirring occasionally.

3. Prepare Clarified Butter.

4. To prepare curry powder, grind cinnamon stick, coriander, cumin, cardamom and peppercorns in clean coffee or spice grinder or use mortar and pestle to pulverize. Stir in turmeric.

5. Heat 2 tablespoons Clarified Butter in large skillet over medium heat. Add curry powder; cook and stir 2 minutes. Add onion, remaining garlic and ginger; cook and stir 5 minutes or until onion is soft.

6. Push mixture to side of skillet. Heat remaining 1 tablespoon Clarified Butter. Add chicken with yogurt marinade; cook and stir about 4 to 5 minutes or until chicken begins to turn opaque.

7. Whisk chicken broth into remaining ½ cup yogurt. Add mixture to skillet; bring to a boil, stirring constantly.

8. Reduce heat to medium-low; cover and cook 20 to 25 minutes. Uncover and cook 5 minutes. Stir in apple; cook 2 minutes more. Serve with rice and condiments, if desired.

continued on page 170

CHICKEN CURRY

Chicken Curry, continued

CLARIFIED BUTTER
1 cup unsalted butter

1. Melt butter in medium saucepan over low heat. Skim off white foam with spoon; discard. Continue skimming until only clear liquid remains.

2. Strain Clarified Butter through cheesecloth into container. Discard milky white residue at bottom of saucepan. Store butter covered in refrigerator up to 2 months. *Makes about ¾ cup*

**1 tablespoon peanut or
    vegetable oil**
½ teaspoon hot chili oil
**8 chicken thighs
    (1½ to 2 pounds)**
2 cloves garlic, minced
¼ cup sweet and sour sauce
1 tablespoon soy sauce
**2 teaspoons minced fresh
    ginger**
**Cilantro and strips of
    orange peel for garnish**

GINGERED CHICKEN THIGHS

Makes 4 servings

1. Heat large nonstick skillet over medium-high heat. Add peanut oil and chili oil; heat until hot. Cook chicken, skin side down, 4 minutes or until golden brown.

2. Reduce heat to low; turn chicken skin side up. Cover and cook 15 to 18 minutes until juices run clear.

3. Spoon off fat. Increase heat to medium. Add garlic and cook 2 minutes. Combine sweet and sour sauce, soy sauce and ginger. Brush half of mixture over chicken; turn chicken over. Brush remaining mixture over chicken. Cook 5 minutes, turning once more, until sauce is thickened and chicken is browned. Transfer chicken to serving platter; pour sauce evenly over chicken. Garnish with cilantro and orange peel.

GINGERED CHICKEN THIGHS

4 tablespoons soy sauce, divided
2 teaspoons dry sherry
1 pound boneless chicken, skinned and cut into matchstick pieces
¼ cup creamy peanut butter
2 tablespoons rice vinegar
1 tablespoon low-fat chicken broth or water
2 teaspoons sugar
1½ teaspoons sesame oil
10 ounces dried rice stick noodles
1 tablespoon vegetable oil
2 teaspoons minced fresh ginger
1 teaspoon minced garlic
½ medium red onion, thinly sliced
½ cucumber, peeled, seeded and cut into matchstick pieces
1 medium carrot, shredded
¼ cup unsalted dry-roasted Texas peanuts, coarsely chopped

Glass Noodles with Peanut Sauce

Makes 4 servings

To prepare marinade, combine 1 tablespoon soy sauce and sherry in small bowl. Add chicken and stir to coat. Cover and refrigerate for 30 minutes.

To prepare peanut sauce, combine peanut butter, remaining 3 tablespoons soy sauce, rice vinegar, chicken broth, sugar and sesame oil in another bowl and set aside.

Bring 4 cups water to a boil in medium saucepan. Add noodles, stirring to separate strands. Cook, stirring, for 30 seconds or until noodles are slightly soft. Drain in colander and rinse under cold running water. Drain well; cut noodles in half and set aside.

Heat wok or large frying pan over high heat. Add vegetable oil, swirling to coat sides. Add ginger and garlic; cook, stirring, until fragrant, about 5 seconds. Add chicken and stir-fry for 1 minute or until opaque. Add onion and stir-fry for 1 minute. Add cucumber, carrot and peanut sauce; cook, stirring, until slightly thickened. Remove from heat. Add noodles and toss until evenly coated. Sprinkle with peanuts.

Favorite recipe from **Texas Peanut Producers Board**

SPICY THAI CHICKEN

Makes 4 servings

¾ cup canned cream of coconut
3 tablespoons lime juice
3 tablespoons soy sauce
8 sprigs cilantro
3 large cloves garlic
3 large green onions, cut up
3 anchovy fillets
1 teaspoon TABASCO® pepper sauce
2 whole boneless skinless chicken breasts, cut in half (about 1½ pounds)

In container of blender or food processor, combine cream of coconut, lime juice, soy sauce, cilantro, garlic, green onions, anchovies and TABASCO® sauce. Cover; process until smooth. Place chicken in large shallow dish or plastic bag; add marinade. Cover; refrigerate at least 2 hours, turning chicken occasionally.

Remove chicken from marinade; reserve marinade. Place chicken on grill about 5 inches from source of heat. Brush generously with marinade. Grill 5 minutes. Turn chicken; brush with marinade. Grill 5 minutes longer or until chicken is cooked. Heat any remaining marinade to a boil. Serve as a dipping sauce for chicken.

SWEET AND SOUR CHICKEN BREASTS

Makes 3 to 4 servings

1 package (about 1½ pounds) PERDUE® FIT 'N EASY® Fresh Skinless & Boneless OVEN STUFFER® Roaster Breast
1 cup diced onions
½ cup soy sauce
¼ cup canola oil
3 tablespoons grated fresh gingerroot
¾ cup brown sugar
2 tablespoons cornstarch

With a meat mallet, flatten breast halves; place in large, shallow bowl. In small bowl, combine onions, soy sauce, oil and gingerroot; set aside 1 cup for basting. Pour remaining marinade over chicken; cover and refrigerate 1 hour or longer, turning occasionally.

Prepare lightly greased grill for cooking. Drain chicken and discard marinade. Grill breasts, uncovered, 5 to 6 inches over medium-hot coals 6 to 10 minutes on each side or until no longer pink in center, turning occasionally. Meanwhile, in small saucepan over medium heat, combine reserved marinade with sugar and cornstarch; bring to a boil. Reduce heat to low; simmer 5 to 6 minutes or until thickened. Reserve half of sauce. Baste chicken with remaining sauce during last 10 minutes of cooking time. To serve, spoon reserved sauce over chicken.

1 tablespoon dried rubbed
  sage
1 teaspoon salt
¼ teaspoon black pepper
1 whole duck, thawed
  (about 5 pounds)
3 cups vegetable oil
1 tablespoon butter or
  margarine
2 large Granny Smith or
  Rome Beauty apples,
  cored and cut into thin
  wedges
½ cup honey
  Fresh sage sprigs and
  crabapples for garnish

CRISPY DUCK

Makes 4 servings

1. Combine sage, salt and pepper in small bowl; set aside.

2. Remove neck and giblets from duck. Cut wing tips and second wing sections off duck. Wrap and freeze for another use. Trim excess fat and excess skin from duck; discard. Rinse duck under cold running water; pat dry with paper towels.

3. Cut duck into quarters, removing backbone and breast bone. Place duck in 13×9-inch baking pan. Rub duck with sage mixture. Cover; refrigerate 1 hour.

4. To steam duck, place wire rack in wok. Add water to 1 inch *below* rack. (Water should not touch rack.) Cover wok; bring water to a boil over high heat. Arrange quarters, skin sides up, on wire rack. Cover; reduce heat to medium-high. Steam 40 minutes or until fork-tender, adding boiling water to wok to keep water at same level.

5. Transfer cooked duck to plate. Carefully remove rack from wok; discard water. Rinse wok and dry.

6. Heat oil in wok over medium-high heat until oil registers 375°F on deep-fry thermometer. Add half of duck, skin sides down, with long-handled tongs. Fry 5 to 10 minutes until crisp and brown, turning once. Drain duck on paper towels. Repeat with remaining duck.

7. Pour off oil. Add butter to wok and melt over medium heat. Add apples; cook and stir with slotted spoon 5 minutes or until soft. Stir in honey and bring to a boil.

8. Transfer apples with slotted spoon to warm serving platter. Arrange duck on apples. Drizzle honey mixture over duck. Garnish, if desired.

CRISPY DUCK

MEATLESS PLEASURES

2 to 3 teaspoons curry powder
1 can (16 ounces) sliced potatoes, drained
1 bag (16 ounces) BIRDS EYE® frozen Farm Fresh Mixtures Broccoli, Cauliflower and Carrots
1 can (15 ounces) chick-peas, drained
1 can (14½ ounces) stewed tomatoes
1 can (13¾ ounces) vegetable or chicken broth
2 tablespoons cornstarch

INDIAN VEGETABLE CURRY

Makes about 6 servings

■ Stir curry powder in large skillet over high heat until fragrant, about 30 seconds.

■ Stir in potatoes, vegetables, chick-peas and tomatoes; bring to a boil. Reduce heat to medium-high; cover and cook 8 minutes.

■ Blend broth with cornstarch; stir into vegetables. Cook until thickened.

PREP TIME: 5 minutes
COOK TIME: 15 minutes

Serving Suggestion: *Add cooked chicken for a heartier main dish. Serve with white or brown rice.*

INDIAN VEGETABLE CURRY

8 ounces firm tofu
1 medium yellow onion,
    peeled
1 medium zucchini
    (½ pound)
1 medium yellow squash
1 cup vegetable oil
8 medium button
    mushrooms, sliced
1 small red bell pepper, cut
    into thin strips
4 ounces fresh snow peas
¼ cup water
1 tablespoon soy sauce
1 tablespoon tomato paste
¼ teaspoon salt
⅛ teaspoon black pepper

STIR-FRIED TOFU AND VEGETABLES

Makes 4 servings

1. Drain tofu on paper towels. Cut crosswise into ¼-inch-thick slices. Set aside.

2. Cut onion into 8 wedges. Cut zucchini and yellow squash crosswise into 1-inch-thick slices. Cut large slices into quartered chunks; set aside.

3. Heat oil in wok over medium-high heat about 4 minutes or until hot. Add tofu and stir-fry about 3 minutes per side or until golden brown, turning once. Remove tofu with slotted spatula to baking sheet or large plate lined with paper towels; drain. Drain oil from wok, reserving 2 tablespoons.

4. Return reserved oil to wok. Heat over medium heat 30 seconds or until hot. Add onion and stir-fry 1 minute. Add zucchini, yellow squash and mushrooms; cook 7 to 8 minutes until zucchini and yellow squash are crisp-tender, stirring occasionally.

5. Add bell pepper, snow peas and water. Stir-fry 2 to 3 minutes until crisp-tender. Stir in soy sauce, tomato paste, salt and black pepper until well mixed. Add fried tofu; stir-fry until heated through and coated with sauce. Transfer to serving platter.

STIR-FRIED TOFU AND VEGETABLES

8 ounces firm tofu, drained
4 tablespoons soy sauce, divided
1 tablespoon dark sesame oil
1 can (about 14 ounces) chicken broth
2 tablespoons dry sherry
1 package (3¾ ounces) bean threads
2 cups frozen mixed vegetable medley, such as broccoli, carrot and red pepper, thawed

BEAN THREADS WITH TOFU AND VEGETABLES

Makes 6 servings

1. Press tofu lightly between paper towels; cut into ¾-inch cubes or triangles. Place on shallow plate; drizzle with 1 tablespoon soy sauce and sesame oil.

2. Combine broth, remaining 3 tablespoons soy sauce and sherry in deep skillet or large saucepan. Bring to a boil; reduce heat. Add bean threads; simmer, uncovered, 7 minutes or until noodles absorb liquid, stirring occasionally to separate noodles.

3. Stir in vegetables; heat through. Stir in tofu mixture; cover and heat through, about 1 minute.

1 cup chicken broth or
   lower sodium chicken
   broth
½ cup GREY POUPON® Dijon
   Mustard
⅓ cup creamy peanut butter
3 tablespoons firmly packed
   light brown sugar
2 tablespoons soy sauce
1 clove garlic, crushed
½ teaspoon minced fresh
   ginger
1 tablespoon cornstarch
4 cups cut-up vegetables
   (red pepper, carrot,
   mushrooms, green
   onions, pea pods)
1 tablespoon vegetable oil
1 pound linguine, cooked
   Chopped peanuts and
   scallion brushes, for
   garnish

THAI PEANUT NOODLE STIR-FRY

Makes 4 to 6 servings

In medium saucepan, combine chicken broth, mustard, peanut butter, sugar, soy sauce, garlic, ginger and cornstarch. Cook over medium heat until mixture thickens and begins to boil; reduce heat and keep warm.

In large skillet, over medium-high heat, sauté vegetables in oil until tender, about 5 minutes. In large serving bowl, combine hot cooked pasta, vegetables and peanut sauce, tossing until well coated. Garnish with chopped peanuts and scallion brushes. Serve immediately.

8 ounces firm tofu, drained
   and cubed
1 cup canned vegetable
   broth, divided
½ cup orange juice
⅓ cup soy sauce
1 to 2 teaspoons hot chili
   oil
½ teaspoon fennel seeds
½ teaspoon black pepper
2 tablespoons cornstarch
3 tablespoons vegetable oil
3 medium carrots,
   diagonally sliced
1 cup sliced green onions
   and tops
3 cloves garlic, minced
2 teaspoons minced ginger
4 ounces button
   mushrooms, sliced
1 medium red bell pepper,
   cut into 1-inch squares
4 ounces fresh snow peas
8 ounces broccoli florets,
   steamed
½ cup peanuts
4 to 6 cups hot cooked rice

SZECHUAN VEGETABLE STIR-FRY

Makes 4 to 6 servings

1. To marinate tofu, place in 8-inch round or square glass baking dish. Combine ½ cup broth, orange juice, soy sauce, chili oil, fennel seeds and black pepper in 2-cup measure; pour over tofu. Let stand 15 to 60 minutes. Drain; reserve marinade.

2. Combine cornstarch and remaining ½ cup broth in medium bowl. Add reserved marinade; set aside.

3. Heat vegetable oil in wok or large skillet over high heat until hot. Add carrots, green onions, garlic and ginger; stir-fry 3 minutes. Add tofu, mushrooms, bell pepper and snow peas; stir-fry 2 to 3 minutes or until vegetables are crisp-tender. Add broccoli; stir-fry 1 minute or until heated through.

4. Stir cornstarch mixture. Add to wok and cook 1 to 2 minutes or until bubbly. Stir in peanuts. Serve over rice.

SZECHUAN VEGETABLE STIR-FRY

1 spaghetti squash
  (3 pounds)
⅓ cup sesame seeds
⅓ cup vegetable broth
2 tablespoons reduced-
  sodium soy sauce
1 tablespoon sugar
2 teaspoons dark sesame
  oil
1 teaspoon cornstarch
1 teaspoon crushed red
  pepper
1 teaspoon Worcestershire
  sauce
1 tablespoon vegetable oil
2 medium carrots, cut into
  matchstick-size strips
1 large red bell pepper,
  seeded and thinly sliced
¼ pound fresh snow peas,
  cut in half diagonally
½ cup coarsely chopped
  unsalted peanuts
⅓ cup minced fresh cilantro

SESAME-PEANUT SPAGHETTI SQUASH

Makes 4 servings

1. Preheat oven to 350°F. Spray 13×9-inch baking dish with nonstick cooking spray. Wash squash; cut in half lengthwise. Remove and discard seeds. Place squash, cut-side down, in prepared dish. Bake 45 minutes to 1 hour or until just tender. Using fork, remove spaghetti-like strands from hot squash and place strands in large bowl. (Use oven mitts to protect hands.) Cover and keep warm.

2. Meanwhile, to toast sesame seeds, heat wok over medium-high heat until hot. Add sesame seeds; cook and stir 45 seconds or until golden brown. Remove to blender. Add vegetable broth, soy sauce, sugar, sesame oil, cornstarch, crushed red pepper and Worcestershire sauce to blender. Process until mixture is coarsely puréed.

3. Heat wok or large skillet over medium-high heat 1 minute or until hot. Drizzle vegetable oil into wok and heat 30 seconds. Add carrots; stir-fry 1 minute. Add bell pepper; stir-fry 2 minutes or until vegetables are crisp-tender. Add snow peas; stir-fry 1 minute. Stir sesame seed mixture and add to wok. Cook and stir 1 minute or until sauce thickens.

4. Pour vegetable mixture over spaghetti squash. Add peanuts and cilantro; toss well.

SESAME-PEANUT SPAGHETTI SQUASH

Peanut Sauce (page 188)
12 flour tortillas (8-inch diameter)
1 tablespoon peanut oil
3 leeks, cut in half lengthwise and thinly sliced
3 carrots, cut into short matchstick-size strips
1 cup thinly sliced fresh shiitake mushrooms
1 small head napa or Savoy cabbage, shredded (4 cups)
2 cups fresh bean sprouts, rinsed and drained
8 ounces firm tofu, drained and cut into 2½×¼-inch strips
3 tablespoons reduced-sodium soy sauce
2 tablespoons dry sherry
1½ tablespoons minced fresh ginger
2 teaspoons cornstarch
1½ teaspoons dark sesame oil
3 cloves garlic, minced
¾ cup finely chopped honey roasted peanuts

Mu Shu Vegetables

Makes 6 servings

1. Prepare Peanut Sauce.

2. To soften and warm tortillas,* preheat oven to 350°F. Stack tortillas and wrap in foil. Heat in oven 10 minutes or until tortillas are warm.

3. Heat wok over medium-high heat 1 minute or until hot. Drizzle peanut oil into wok and heat 30 seconds. Add leeks, carrots and mushrooms; stir-fry 2 minutes. Add cabbage; stir-fry 3 minutes or until just tender. Add bean sprouts and tofu; stir-fry 1 minute or until hot.

4. Combine soy sauce, sherry, ginger, cornstarch, sesame oil and garlic in small bowl until smooth. Add to wok. Cook and stir 1 minute or until thickened.

5. Spread each tortilla with about 1 teaspoon Peanut Sauce. Spoon ½ cup vegetable mixture on bottom half of tortilla; sprinkle with 1 tablespoon peanuts.

6. Fold bottom edge of tortilla over filling; fold in side edges. Roll up to completely enclose filling. Or, spoon ½ cup vegetable mixture on one half of tortilla. Fold bottom edge over filling. Fold in one side edge. Serve with remaining Peanut Sauce.

Tortillas can be softened and warmed in microwave oven just before using. Stack tortillas and wrap in plastic wrap. Microwave at HIGH ½ to 1 minute, turning over and rotating ¼ turn once during heating.

continued on page 188

MU SHU VEGETABLES

Mu Shu Vegetables, continued

PEANUT SAUCE

- **3 tablespoons sugar**
- **3 tablespoons water**
- **3 tablespoons dry sherry**
- **3 tablespoons reduced-sodium soy sauce**
- **2 teaspoons white wine vinegar**
- **⅓ cup creamy peanut butter**

Combine all ingredients except peanut butter in small saucepan. Bring to a boil over medium-high heat, stirring constantly. Boil 1 minute or until sugar melts. Stir in peanut butter until smooth; cool to room temperature.

Makes ⅔ cup

- **2 cups uncooked instant white rice**
- **2 teaspoons vegetable oil**
- **2 cups broccoli florets**
- **1 large carrot, sliced**
- **½ green bell pepper, sliced**
- **¼ cup frozen chopped onion**
- **½ cup orange juice**
- **½ cup teriyaki sauce**
- **1 tablespoon cornstarch**
- **1 teaspoon bottled minced garlic**
- **½ teaspoon ground ginger**
- **¼ to ½ teaspoon hot pepper sauce**
- **1 package (10½ ounces) reduced-fat firm tofu, drained and cubed**

TOFU STIR-FRY

Makes 4 servings

1. Cook rice according to package directions.

2. While rice is cooking, heat oil in large skillet. Add broccoli, carrot, bell pepper and onion; cook and stir 3 minutes.

3. Combine orange juice, teriyaki sauce, cornstarch, garlic, ginger and hot pepper sauce in small bowl; mix well. Pour sauce over vegetables in skillet. Bring to a boil; cook and stir 1 minute.

4. Add tofu to skillet; stir gently to coat with sauce. Serve over rice.

PREP AND COOK TIME: 18 minutes

TOFU STIR-FRY

1 block tofu
2 tablespoons vegetable oil
1 teaspoon minced
    gingerroot
1 medium onion, chunked
⅛ teaspoon salt
6 ounces fresh snow peas,
    trimmed and cut
    diagonally in half
⅓ cup KIKKOMAN® Stir-Fry
    Sauce
2 medium-size fresh
    tomatoes, chunked
¼ cup slivered blanched
    almonds, toasted

VEGETARIAN TOFU STIR-FRY

Makes 4 servings

Cut tofu into ½-inch cubes; drain well on several layers of paper towels. Heat oil in hot wok or large skillet over high heat. Add ginger; stir-fry 30 seconds, or until fragrant. Add onion and salt; stir-fry 2 minutes. Add snow peas; stir-fry 1 minute. Add stir-fry sauce, tomatoes and tofu. Gently stir to coat tofu and vegetables with sauce. Reduce heat and cook only until tomatoes and tofu are heated through. Sprinkle with almonds; serve immediately.

¼ cup soy sauce
1 tablespoon creamy peanut
    butter
1 package (about
    12 ounces) firm tofu,
    drained
1 medium zucchini
1 medium yellow squash
2 teaspoons peanut or
    vegetable oil
½ teaspoon hot chili oil
2 cloves garlic, minced
2 cups (packed) torn fresh
    spinach leaves
¼ cup coarsely chopped
    cashews or peanuts
    (optional)

DRAGON TOFU

Makes 2 servings

Whisk soy sauce into peanut butter in small bowl. Press tofu lightly between paper towels; cut into ¾-inch squares or triangles. Place in single layer in shallow dish. Pour soy sauce mixture over tofu; stir gently to coat all surfaces. Let stand at room temperature 20 minutes. Cut zucchini and yellow squash lengthwise into ¼-inch-thick slices; cut each slice into 2×¼-inch strips. Heat nonstick skillet over medium-high heat. Add peanut and chili oils; heat until hot. Add garlic, zucchini and yellow squash; stir-fry 3 minutes. Add tofu mixture; cook 2 minutes or until tofu is heated through and sauce is slightly thickened, stirring occasionally. Stir in spinach; remove from heat. Sprinkle with cashews, if desired.

¾ pound extra firm tofu
Spicy Peanut Sauce
(recipe follows)
12 ounces vermicelli noodles
2 teaspoons sesame oil
1 tablespoon minced green
onions (green parts
only)
2 cups bean sprouts
1½ cups shredded carrots
½ green bell pepper, cut into
thin strips
½ red bell pepper, cut into
thin strips

ORIENTAL TOFU NOODLE SALAD WITH SPICY PEANUT SAUCE

Makes 6 servings

Wrap tofu in paper towels. Top with a heavy weight to press out excess water; let stand 30 minutes. Cut tofu into 1-inch cubes; place in medium bowl.

Prepare Spicy Peanut Sauce. Add to tofu; toss lightly to coat. Cover with plastic wrap; let stand at room temperature about 30 minutes.

Cook vermicelli according to package directions; rinse and drain.

Heat oil in wok or large skillet. Add green onions; stir-fry 30 seconds. Add bean sprouts, carrots and bell pepper; stir-fry 1 minute. Add vermicelli and tofu mixture; cook until hot, stirring occasionally.

SPICY PEANUT SAUCE

1 tablespoon chopped garlic
1 tablespoon chopped fresh ginger
¼ cup smooth or crunchy reduced-fat peanut
butter
3 tablespoons chicken broth or water
2½ tablespoons reduced-sodium soy sauce
2 tablespoons Worcestershire sauce
1 tablespoon plus 1½ teaspoons sugar
1 tablespoon plus 1½ teaspoons rice wine or sake
1 teaspoon hot chili paste or crushed dried red
chili pepper

Process garlic and ginger in blender until finely chopped. Add remaining ingredients; process until blended. (If sauce is too thick, add 1 tablespoon additional broth or water. If sauce is thin, add additional peanut butter.)

Makes ½ cup

Favorite recipe from **THE SUGAR ASSOCIATION, INC.**

¾ cup sweet (pearl or
   glutinous) rice
1¾ cups water, divided
1 can (about 14 ounces)
   chicken broth
1 tablespoon soy sauce
2 teaspoons sugar
2 teaspoons red wine
   vinegar
2 tablespoons cornstarch
3 tablespoons peanut oil,
   divided
1½ teaspoons finely chopped
   fresh ginger
2 cloves garlic, thinly sliced
1 red bell pepper, cut into
   ¼-inch strips
1 green bell pepper, cut into
   ¼-inch strips
8 ounces button
   mushrooms, quartered
4 ounces fresh shiitake or
   other exotic
   mushrooms, thinly
   sliced
1 teaspoon dark sesame oil
   Vegetable oil for frying

SIZZLING RICE CAKES WITH MUSHROOMS AND BELL PEPPERS

Makes 4 to 6 servings

1. Place rice in colander; rinse under cold running water to remove excess starch. Combine rice and 1½ cups water in medium saucepan.

2. Bring rice and water to a boil over medium-high heat. Reduce heat to low; cover and simmer 15 to 20 minutes until liquid is absorbed. Remove from heat; let cool.

3. Combine chicken broth, soy sauce, sugar and vinegar in medium bowl. Set aside. Combine cornstarch and remaining ¼ cup water in small cup; mix well. Set aside.

4. Heat 1 tablespoon peanut oil in wok over medium-high heat. Add ginger and garlic; stir-fry 10 seconds. Add bell pepper strips; stir-fry 2 to 3 minutes or until crisp-tender. Remove and set aside.

5. Add remaining 2 tablespoons peanut oil to wok. Add mushrooms; stir-fry 2 to 3 minutes or until softened. Remove and set aside.

6. Add chicken broth mixture to wok and bring to a boil. Stir cornstarch mixture; add to wok. Cook until sauce boils and thickens slightly, stirring constantly. Stir in sesame oil. Return vegetables to wok; cover to keep warm.

7. Shape rice into 12 (2-inch) cakes. (Wet hands to make handling rice easier.)

8. Heat 2 to 3 inches vegetable oil in large skillet over medium-high heat until oil registers 375°F on deep-fry thermometer. Add 4 rice cakes; cook 2 to 3 minutes or until puffed and golden, turning occasionally. Remove with slotted spatula to paper towels. Repeat with remaining rice cakes, reheating oil between batches. Serve vegetable mixture over rice cakes.

SIZZLING RICE CAKES WITH MUSHROOMS AND BELL PEPPERS

½ cup reduced-sodium soy sauce

⅓ cup sugar

¼ cup lime juice

2 fresh red Thai chilies *or* 1 large red jalapeño chili,* seeded and finely chopped

8 ounces firm tofu cakes

2 medium sweet potatoes, peeled

1 (about 8 ounces) jicama or 1 can (8 ounces) sliced water chestnuts, drained

2 large leeks

1 cup vegetable oil

8 ounces very thin dried rice vermicelli

¼ cup chopped unsalted dry-roasted peanuts

2 tablespoons chopped mint

2 tablespoons chopped fresh cilantro

Mint leaves for garnish

Chilies can sting and irritate the skin; wear rubber gloves when handling chilies and do not touch eyes. Wash hands after handling.

Vegetarian Rice Noodles

Makes 4 servings

1. Combine soy sauce, sugar, lime juice and chilies in small bowl; mix well. Set aside.

2. Drain tofu on paper towels. Cut into 4 slices; cut each slice diagonally into 2 triangles. Set aside.

3. Cut sweet potatoes into ¼-inch slices. Set aside.

4. Peel jicama and cut into ¼-inch slices. Cut slices into 1-inch squares; set aside. (Omit step if using water chestnuts.)

5. Cut leeks lengthwise in half. Rinse and cut crosswise into ¼-inch slices; set aside.

6. Heat oil in wok over medium-high heat about 4 minutes or until hot. Add tofu and stir-fry about 4 minutes per side or until golden brown. Remove tofu with slotted spatula to baking sheet or large plate lined with paper towels; drain.

7. Reheat oil. Add jicama and stir-fry about 5 minutes or until lightly browned, stirring occasionally. Remove with slotted spoon to baking sheet lined with paper towels; drain. Repeat with sweet potatoes in 2 batches, reheating oil each time.

8. Add leeks. Stir-fry 1 minute. Pour leeks into large strainer over heatproof bowl to drain; set aside. Reserve 1 tablespoon oil.

continued on page 196

VEGETARIAN RICE NOODLES

Vegetarian Rice Noodles, continued

9. Place 4 cups water in wok; bring to a boil over high heat. Add vermicelli and cook 3 minutes or until tender but still firm, stirring frequently. Drain in colander and rinse under cold running water to stop cooking; drain again and place vermicelli in large bowl. Add 1 tablespoon reserved oil; toss lightly to coat.

10. Cut cooked vermicelli several times to shorten strands to 8- or 10-inch lengths.

11. Stir soy sauce mixture and add to wok; heat over medium heat just until sugar dissolves. Add vermicelli and toss until coated. Gently stir in tofu, sweet potatoes, jicama, leeks, peanuts, mint and cilantro. Garnish with mint leaves.

---

1 package (about 12 ounces) firm tofu, drained
2 tablespoons soy sauce
2 teaspoons minced fresh ginger
1 cup chicken broth, divided
1 tablespoon cornstarch
1½ cups broccoli florets
1 teaspoon hot chili oil
2 teaspoons dark sesame oil
¼ cup coarsely chopped cilantro or green onion tops

Ma Po Tofu

Makes 2 main-dish or 4 side-dish servings

1. Press tofu lightly between paper towels; cut into ¾-inch squares or triangles. Place in shallow dish; sprinkle with soy sauce and ginger.

2. Blend ¼ cup broth into cornstarch in cup until smooth. Combine remaining ¾ cup broth, broccoli and chili oil in 10-inch skillet. Bring to a boil over high heat. Reduce heat to medium. Cover and cook 3 minutes or until broccoli is crisp-tender.

3. Stir broth mixture and add to skillet. Cook and stir 1 minute or until sauce boils and thickens. Stir in tofu mixture. Simmer, uncovered, until tofu is hot. Stir in sesame oil. Sprinkle with cilantro.

2 eggs
2 egg whites
½ cup fresh or canned bean
sprouts, rinsed and
drained
½ cup chopped fresh
mushrooms
2 tablespoons thinly sliced
green onion
2 tablespoons soy sauce,
divided
1 tablespoon peanut or
vegetable oil
1 cup chicken broth
1 tablespoon cornstarch
¼ teaspoon sugar
¼ teaspoon black pepper

Egg Foo Yung

Makes 2 main-dish or 4 side-dish servings

1. Beat eggs and egg whites in large bowl. Stir in bean sprouts, mushrooms, green onion and 1 tablespoon soy sauce.

2. Heat large nonstick skillet over medium-high heat. Add oil; heat until hot. To form each pancake, pour ¼ cup egg mixture into skillet (egg mixture will run; do not crowd skillet). Cook 1 to 2 minutes until bottoms of pancakes are set. Turn pancakes over; cook 1 to 2 minutes until pancakes are cooked through. Remove and keep warm. Repeat with remaining egg mixture.

3. Blend broth into cornstarch in small bowl until smooth. Stir into skillet. Stir in sugar and pepper; cook and stir 1 minute or until sauce boils and thickens.

4. Pour sauce over warm pancakes; serve immediately.

Variation: Add ½ cup chopped cooked shrimp or ½ cup diced roasted pork to egg mixture.

1 large head cauliflower
(about 1¼ pounds)
2 tablespoons olive oil
1 cup sliced green onions
3 cloves garlic, minced
2 tablespoons minced fresh
ginger
2 teaspoons curry powder
½ teaspoon ground cumin
½ teaspoon ground turmeric
3 cups water
1 can (about 14 ounces)
stewed tomatoes,
undrained
½ teaspoon salt
1 cup red lentils
1 tablespoon lemon juice
Fragrant Basmati Rice
(recipe follows)

LENTIL RICE CURRY

Makes 6 servings

1. Trim cauliflower and cut into florets. Set aside.

2. Heat oil in large saucepan over medium heat until hot. Add green onions, garlic, ginger, curry, cumin and turmeric; cook and stir 5 minutes. Add water, tomatoes with juice and salt; bring to a boil over high heat.

3. Meanwhile, rinse lentils under cold running water, picking out and discarding any debris or blemished lentils. Add lentils to saucepan. Reduce heat to low. Cover and simmer 35 to 40 minutes or until lentils are tender. Add cauliflower and lemon juice. Cover and simmer 8 to 10 minutes more or until cauliflower is tender.

4. Meanwhile prepare Fragrant Basmati Rice.

5. Spoon lentil mixture over Fragrant Basmati Rice. Garnish, if desired.

FRAGRANT BASMATI RICE

2 cups apple juice
¾ cup water
½ teaspoon salt
1½ cups white basmati or Texmati rice
2 thin slices ginger
1 piece cinnamon stick (2 inches long)

Bring juice, water and salt to a boil in medium saucepan. Add remaining ingredients; reduce heat to low. Cover; simmer 25 to 30 minutes or until liquid is absorbed. Remove ginger and cinnamon stick; discard.

Makes 4 cups

LENTIL RICE CURRY

⅓ cup water
4 teaspoons reduced-
  sodium soy sauce
1 tablespoon rice wine or
  dry white wine
2 teaspoons cornstarch
1½ teaspoons sugar
¼ teaspoon chicken bouillon
  granules
1 package (10½ ounces)
  extra-firm tofu, drained
3 teaspoons vegetable oil,
  divided
3 cups sliced fresh
  mushrooms
1 cup sliced leek
2 cloves garlic, minced
2 teaspoons minced fresh
  ginger
2 cups diagonally sliced
  carrots
3 cups torn stemmed
  spinach
4 cups hot cooked rice

VEGETABLE-TOFU STIR-FRY

Makes 4 servings

Combine water, soy sauce, rice wine, cornstarch, sugar and bouillon granules in small bowl. Press tofu lightly between paper towels; cut into ¾-inch squares or triangles.

Spray wok or large skillet with nonstick cooking spray; heat over medium-high heat. Add 1 teaspoon oil. Add mushrooms, leek, garlic and ginger. Stir-fry 2 to 3 minutes or until vegetables are tender. Remove from wok.

Add remaining 2 teaspoons oil to wok; add carrots. Stir-fry 5 to 6 minutes or until crisp-tender. Add cornstarch mixture; stir-fry about 1 minute or until mixture boils and thickens. Stir in mushroom mixture, tofu and spinach. Cover; cook about 1 minute or until heated through. Serve over rice.

VEGETABLE-TOFU STIR-FRY

1 pound spaghetti
1 cup chunky peanut butter
1 cup orange juice
¼ cup soy sauce
¼ cup sesame oil
¼ cup vegetable oil
2 tablespoons cider vinegar
1 tablespoon TABASCO®
    pepper sauce
1 teaspoon salt
2 large green onions, sliced
1 medium cucumber, sliced

SESAME NOODLES

Makes 6 servings

■ Prepare spaghetti as package directs. Drain.

■ Meanwhile, in large bowl, whisk peanut butter, orange juice, soy sauce, sesame oil, vegetable oil, cider vinegar, TABASCO® sauce and salt until smooth. Add cooked spaghetti and green onions; toss well. Serve warm or cover and refrigerate to serve cold later. Just before serving, toss with additional orange juice, if necessary. Garnish with cucumber slices

2 tablespoons vegetable oil,
    divided
8 ounces firm bean curd
    (tofu), drained and cut
    into ½-inch cubes
½ cup water
2 tablespoons oyster sauce
4 teaspoons dry sherry
4 teaspoons soy sauce
1 tablespoon cornstarch
4 ounces fresh mushrooms,
    sliced
6 green onions, cut into
    1-inch pieces
3 stalks celery, diagonally
    cut into ½-inch pieces
1 red or green bell pepper,
    cut into ½-inch squares

BEAN CURD WITH OYSTER SAUCE

Makes 4 servings

Heat 1 tablespoon oil in wok or large skillet over high heat. Add tofu and stir-fry until light brown, about 3 minutes. Remove and set aside. Combine water, oyster sauce, sherry, soy sauce and cornstarch in small bowl until smooth. Heat remaining 1 tablespoon oil in wok over high heat. Add mushrooms, green onions, celery and bell pepper; stir-fry 1 minute. Return tofu to wok; toss lightly to combine. Stir oyster sauce mixture and add to wok. Cook and stir until liquid comes to a boil; cook 1 minute more.

6 ounces spaghetti, cooked
8 ounces firm tofu, drained
    and cut into 1-inch
    cubes
1 tablespoon reduced-
    sodium soy sauce
1 ½ cups vegetable broth or
    water
2 tablespoons cornstarch
1 tablespoon vegetable oil
2 cups sliced celery
1 cup broccoli florets
¾ cup red bell pepper
    chunks
⅓ cup sliced green onions
8 strips (1 ½ × ½ inch) orange
    peel
1 teaspoon minced fresh
    ginger
  Orange slices for garnish

CRISPY ORANGE VEGETABLES AND TOFU

Makes 4 servings

Cook spaghetti according to package directions; drain and keep warm. Meanwhile, combine tofu and soy sauce in medium bowl; set aside. Combine vegetable broth and cornstarch in cup until smooth. Heat oil in large nonstick skillet or wok. Add celery, broccoli, bell pepper, green onions, orange peel and ginger. Stir-fry until vegetables are crisp-tender, about 4 to 5 minutes. Stir cornstarch mixture and add to vegetable mixture; bring to a boil, stirring constantly until mixture is slightly thickened, about 1 minute. Gently stir in tofu mixture; cook until heated through, about 1 minute. Serve over spaghetti. Garnish with orange slices.

8 ounces uncooked soba (Japanese buckwheat noodles)
1 tablespoon light olive oil
2 cups sliced shiitake mushrooms
1 medium red bell pepper, cut into thin strips
2 whole small dried red chili peppers *or* ¼ teaspoon crushed red pepper
1 clove garlic, minced
2 cups shredded napa cabbage
½ cup reduced-sodium chicken broth
2 tablespoons reduced-sodium tamari or soy sauce
1 tablespoon rice wine or dry sherry
2 teaspoons cornstarch
1 package (14 ounces) firm tofu, drained and cut into 1-inch cubes
2 green onions, thinly sliced

Soba Stir-Fry

Makes 4 (2-cup) servings

1. Cook soba according to package directions, omitting salt. Drain and set aside.

2. Heat oil in large nonstick skillet or wok over medium heat. Add mushrooms, bell pepper, dried peppers and garlic. Cook 3 minutes or until mushrooms are tender.

3. Add cabbage. Cover and cook 2 minutes or until cabbage is wilted.

4. Combine chicken broth, tamari, rice wine and cornstarch in small bowl. Stir sauce into vegetable mixture. Cook 2 minutes or until sauce is bubbly.

5. Stir in tofu and soba; toss gently until heated through. Sprinkle with green onions.

SOBA STIR-FRY

Splendid Seafood

½ cup A.1. THICK &
   HEARTY® Steak Sauce
⅓ cup apricot preserves
2 teaspoons curry powder
2 cloves garlic, minced
1 pound large shrimp,
   peeled, deveined
1 (1-pound) beef top round
   steak, cut into 1-inch
   cubes
1 cup snow peas, cut in half
   Hot cooked couscous

Curried Apricot Glazed Shrimp and Beef

Makes 4 servings

Soak 8 (10-inch) wooden skewers in water at least 30 minutes.

In small bowl, combine steak sauce, preserves, curry and garlic. Place shrimp and steak in nonmetal dish; coat with ½ cup steak sauce mixture. Cover; refrigerate 2 hours, stirring occasionally.

Remove shrimp and steak from marinade; discard marinade. Alternately thread shrimp, beef and snow peas onto wooden or metal skewers. Grill kabobs over medium heat or broil 6 inches from heat source 5 minutes on each side or until steak is desired doneness and shrimp turn opaque, basting with remaining steak sauce mixture. Serve immediately with couscous.

CURRIED APRICOT GLAZED SHRIMP AND BEEF

**Coconut Ginger Rice
(recipe follows)**
1 tablespoon vegetable oil
1 pound raw medium
    shrimp, peeled and
    deveined
3 cloves garlic, minced
1 cup finely chopped fresh
    pineapple *or* 1 can
    (8 ounces) crushed
    pineapple, drained
2 tablespoons packed
    brown sugar
1 tablespoon fish sauce
2 teaspoons curry powder
¼ teaspoon crushed red
    pepper
3 green onions, thinly sliced
    Chives for garnish
¼ cup toasted coconut
¼ cup chopped roasted
    peanuts, salted or
    unsalted
¼ cup chopped cilantro
¼ cup diced red bell pepper

CURRIED SHRIMP WITH COCONUT GINGER RICE

Makes 4 servings

Prepare Coconut Ginger Rice.

Meanwhile, heat wok or large skillet over high heat. Add oil and swirl to coat surface. Add shrimp and garlic; cook and stir 2 to 3 minutes, until all shrimp turn pink and opaque. Transfer to bowl with slotted spoon. Add pineapple, brown sugar, fish sauce, curry powder and crushed red pepper to wok; bring to a boil over high heat, stirring constantly. Reduce heat to medium; cook 2 minutes. Stir in shrimp mixture and green onions; cook 1 minute or until shrimp are heated through.

Mound Coconut Ginger Rice on serving platter. Pour shrimp and sauce over rice; garnish with chives, if desired. Serve toasted coconut, peanuts, cilantro and bell pepper in small bowls to sprinkle on individual servings.

COCONUT GINGER RICE
3 cups water
2 cups long-grain white rice
1 cup unsweetened coconut milk
2 tablespoons sugar
2 teaspoons grated fresh ginger

Bring water, rice, coconut milk, sugar and ginger to a boil in medium saucepan over high heat. Reduce heat to low; cover and simmer 25 minutes or until liquid is absorbed. Fluff rice with fork. *Makes about 6 cups*

CURRIED SHRIMP WITH COCONUT GINGER RICE

8 ounces flat rice noodles
3 tablespoons ketchup
3 tablespoons fish sauce
2 tablespoons packed
    brown sugar
1 tablespoon lime juice
1 jalapeño pepper, seeded
    and finely chopped
1 teaspoon curry powder
2 tablespoons peanut oil,
    divided
1 pound medium shrimp,
    peeled and deveined
3 cloves garlic, minced
3 eggs, lightly beaten
2 cups fresh bean sprouts,
    rinsed, drained and
    divided
⅔ cup roasted skinless
    peanuts (salted or
    unsalted), chopped
3 green onions, thinly sliced
1 small carrot, shredded
¾ cup shredded red or green
    cabbage
½ cup cilantro, coarsely
    chopped
1 lime, cut into wedges

Pad Thai

Makes 4 servings

1. Place noodles in large bowl; cover with hot water. Let stand 10 to 30 minutes or until soft and pliable.

2. To prepare sauce, combine ¼ cup water, ketchup, fish sauce, sugar, lime juice, jalapeño pepper and curry powder in medium bowl; set aside.

3. Heat wok or large skillet over high heat. Add 1 tablespoon oil and swirl to coat surface. Add shrimp; stir-fry 2 minutes or until shrimp turn pink and opaque. Transfer to bowl with slotted spoon.

4. Reduce heat to medium. Add remaining 1 tablespoon oil and heat 15 seconds. Add garlic; cook and stir 20 seconds or until golden. Add eggs; cook 2 minutes or just until set, turning and stirring every 30 seconds to scramble. Stir in sauce.

5. Increase heat to high. Add noodles; stir to coat with sauce. Cook 2 to 4 minutes, stirring often, until noodles are tender. (Add water, 1 tablespoon at a time, if sauce is absorbed and noodles are still dry.)

6. Add cooked shrimp, 1½ cups bean sprouts, peanuts and green onions; cook and stir 1 to 2 minutes or until heated through.

7. Transfer mixture to large serving platter. Pile remaining ½ cup sprouts, carrot, cabbage, cilantro and lime wedges around noodles. Squeeze lime over noodles before eating.

PAD THAI

1 package (1 ounce) dried
   black Chinese
   mushrooms*
1 cup chicken broth
3 tablespoons soy sauce
2 tablespoons dry sherry
4½ teaspoons cornstarch
2 tablespoons peanut or
   vegetable oil, divided
½ pound medium shrimp,
   peeled and deveined
½ pound bay scallops or
   halved sea scallops
2 cloves garlic, minced
6 ounces (2 cups) fresh
   snow peas, cut
   diagonally into halves
Sesame Noodle Cake
   (page 306) or hot
   cooked rice (optional)
¼ cup thinly sliced green
   onions (optional)

*Or, substitute 1½ cups sliced fresh
mushrooms. Omit step 1.

EASY SEAFOOD STIR-FRY

Makes 4 servings

1. Place mushrooms in small bowl; cover with warm water. Soak 20 minutes to soften. Drain; squeeze out excess water. Discard stems; slice caps.

2. Blend broth, soy sauce and sherry into cornstarch in another small bowl until smooth.

3. Heat wok or large skillet over medium-high heat. Add 1 tablespoon oil; heat until hot. Add shrimp, scallops and garlic; stir-fry 3 minutes or until seafood is opaque. Remove and reserve.

4. Add remaining 1 tablespoon oil to wok. Add mushrooms and snow peas; stir-fry 3 minutes or until snow peas are crisp-tender.

5. Stir broth mixture and add to wok. Stir-fry 2 minutes or until sauce boils and thickens.

6. Return seafood along with any accumulated juices to wok; heat through. Serve over Sesame Noodle Cake, if desired. Garnish with green onions.

3 to 5 tablespoons
    vegetable oil, divided
8 mushrooms, finely
    chopped
4 teaspoons cornstarch
1 cup water
2 teaspoons instant chicken
    bouillon granules
2 teaspoons soy sauce
1 teaspoon sugar
8 eggs
½ teaspoon salt
⅛ teaspoon black pepper
8 ounces bean sprouts,
    rinsed and drained
8 ounces shrimp, peeled,
    deveined and finely
    chopped
4 green onions with tops,
    finely chopped
1 stalk celery, finely
    chopped
  Cooked whole shrimp and
    slivered green onions
    for garnish

Shrimp Omelets

Makes 4 servings

1. Heat 1 tablespoon oil in small skillet. Add mushrooms; cook 1 minute. Remove from skillet; set aside.

2. Combine cornstarch, water, bouillon granules, soy sauce and sugar in small saucepan until smooth. Cook and stir over medium heat until mixture boils and thickens, about 5 minutes. Keep warm.

3. Combine eggs, salt and pepper in large bowl. Beat until frothy. Add sprouts, shrimp, green onions, celery and mushrooms; mix well.

4. For each omelet, heat ½ tablespoon oil in 7-inch omelet pan or skillet. Pour ½ cup egg mixture into pan. Cook until lightly browned, 2 to 3 minutes on each side, gently pushing cooked portion to center and tilting skillet to allow uncooked portion to flow underneath.

5. Stack omelets on serving plate. Pour warm soy sauce mixture over omelets. Garnish, if desired.

SAUCE

2 tablespoons vegetable oil
1 small yellow onion, finely chopped
1 teaspoon curry powder
1½ tablespoons dry sherry
1 tablespoon satay sauce
2 teaspoons soy sauce
1 teaspoon sugar
¼ cup cream or milk

SHRIMP

2 egg whites, lightly beaten
4 teaspoons cornstarch
1 tablespoon dry sherry
1 tablespoon soy sauce
2 cans (6½ ounces each) crabmeat, drained and flaked
8 green onions with tops, finely chopped
2 stalks celery, finely chopped
1½ pounds large shrimp, peeled and deveined
½ cup all-purpose flour
3 eggs
3 tablespoons milk
2 to 3 cups soft bread crumbs (from 8 to 10 bread slices)
Vegetable oil for frying

CRAB-STUFFED SHRIMP

Makes 4 servings

For sauce, heat 2 tablespoons oil in small saucepan over medium heat. Add yellow onion; cook and stir until tender, about 3 minutes. Add curry powder; cook and stir 1 minute. Add 1½ tablespoons sherry, satay sauce, 2 teaspoons soy sauce and sugar; cook and stir 2 minutes. Stir in cream; bring to a boil. Simmer 2 minutes, stirring occasionally. Keep warm.

For shrimp, blend egg whites, cornstarch, 1 tablespoon sherry and 1 tablespoon soy sauce in medium bowl until smooth. Add crabmeat, green onions and celery; mix well.

Cut deep slit into but not through back of each shrimp. Flatten shrimp slightly by pounding gently with mallet or rolling pin. Spoon crab mixture onto each shrimp, pressing into slit with back of spoon or small spatula. Coat each shrimp lightly with flour.

Beat eggs and milk with fork in shallow bowl until blended. Place each shrimp, stuffed side up, in egg mixture, spooning egg mixture over shrimp to cover completely. Coat each shrimp with bread crumbs, pressing crumbs lightly onto shrimp. Place shrimp in single layer on baking sheets or plates. Refrigerate 30 minutes.

Pour oil into large skillet or wok to 1-inch depth. Heat over high heat to 375°F. Add four or five shrimp at a time; cook until golden brown, about 3 minutes. Drain on paper towels. Serve with sauce.

CRAB-STUFFED SHRIMP

2 medium zucchini
2 medium yellow squash
¼ cup sake
¼ cup soy sauce
2 tablespoons sugar
1½ pounds red salmon fillet
with skin (1¼ inches
thick)
2 tablespoons vegetable oil,
divided
1 tablespoon butter
¼ teaspoon salt
¼ teaspoon black pepper
1 tablespoon sesame seeds,
toasted*
Lemon slices (optional)

*To toast sesame seeds, cook and stir in wok over medium-high heat about 45 seconds or until seeds begin to pop and turn golden. Remove from wok to small bowl.

SEARED SALMON TERIYAKI

Makes 4 servings

1. Cut zucchini and yellow squash into matchstick-size strips. Combine sake, soy sauce and sugar in cup; stir until sugar dissolves. Set aside.

2. Rinse and dry salmon. Run fingers over cut surface of salmon; remove any bones that remain. Cut crosswise into 4 pieces.

3. Heat wok over high heat until hot. Add 1 tablespoon oil; heat 30 seconds. Add zucchini, yellow squash and butter. Cook and stir 4 to 5 minutes until lightly browned and tender. Sprinkle squash mixture with salt and pepper. Transfer to serving platter. Sprinkle with sesame seeds; cover and keep warm.

4. Add remaining 1 tablespoon oil to wok and heat over high heat until sizzling hot. Carefully place fish in wok, skin sides up. Cook 4 minutes or until browned. Reduce heat to medium-high. Turn fish. Cook, skin sides down, 8 to 10 minutes or until fish flakes easily when tested with fork, loosening fish on bottom occasionally. Place fish over squash mixture on platter. Cover and keep warm.

5. Pour off fat from wok. Stir soy mixture and pour into wok. Boil until mixture is reduced by half and slightly thickened. Spoon sauce over fish. Serve with lemon slices, if desired.

SEARED SALMON TERIYAKI

SEASONING
- 1 tablespoon LEE KUM KEE® Black Bean Garlic Sauce
- 1 teaspoon water
- ½ teaspoon sugar

- 1 pound fish fillet
- 1 tablespoon cornstarch
- 1½ teaspoons LEE KUM KEE® Oyster Flavored Sauce
- 2 tablespoons vegetable oil
- 2 green onions, cut into pieces
- 2 stalks celery, cut into strips
- 1 medium carrot, cut into strips

BLACK BEAN GARLIC FISH

Makes 4 servings

1. In bowl, combine seasoning ingredients. Set aside.

2. Rinse fish and pat dry with paper towel. Cut fish into 1-inch pieces; place in medium bowl.

3. Combine cornstarch and oyster flavored sauce. Add to fish; stirring until coated. Marinate 10 minutes.

4. Heat oil in wok or skillet over medium-high heat. Add green onions; stir-fry until fragrant.

5. Add fish and stir-fry until half cooked, about 1 minute.

6. Add celery, carrot and seasoning mixture. Stir-fry until all ingredients are cooked.

- 3 teaspoons dark sesame oil, divided
- 3 tablespoons Chinese rice wine or sherry
- 2 tablespoons soy sauce
- 2 teaspoons minced fresh ginger
- 2 teaspoons sugar
- ¼ teaspoon black pepper
- 1½ pounds swordfish, halibut or salmon fillets, ¾ inch thick
- 1 tablespoon vegetable oil
- 1 pound fresh mushrooms, sliced
- 2 green onions, sliced
- ¼ cup cilantro leaves
  Dash salt

ASIAN SWORDFISH

Makes 4 to 6 servings

Combine 2 teaspoons sesame oil, wine, soy sauce, ginger, sugar and pepper in 2-quart dish. Add swordfish; turn to coat. Cover and refrigerate at least 2 hours. Heat vegetable oil in medium skillet over high heat. Add mushrooms; cook and stir until well browned. Remove from heat; stir in green onions, cilantro, salt and remaining 1 teaspoon sesame oil; keep warm. Remove swordfish from marinade; discard marinade. Lightly oil grid to prevent sticking. Grill swordfish over medium-hot KINGSFORD® briquets about 4 minutes per side or until swordfish flakes easily when tested with a fork. Spoon mushroom mixture over swordfish.

1 cup SMUCKER'S® Orange
  Marmalade
3 tablespoons soy sauce
2 tablespoons white vinegar
2 teaspoons hot pepper
  sauce
4½ teaspoons cornstarch
2 tablespoons vegetable oil
1 tablespoon fresh ginger,
  chopped
1 tablespoon garlic,
  chopped
24 fresh jumbo shrimp,
  peeled and deveined
1 red bell pepper, chopped
1 yellow or green bell
  pepper, chopped
3 cups broccoli florets
  (about 1 bunch)
½ cup water
1 cup chopped scallions

SMUCKER'S® MANDARIN SHRIMP AND VEGETABLE STIR-FRY

Makes 4 to 6 servings

Combine Smucker's® Orange Marmalade, soy sauce, vinegar, hot pepper sauce and cornstarch in small bowl. Stir to dissolve cornstarch and set aside.

Place large skillet or wok over high heat. Heat pan for 1 minute, then add vegetable oil. Heat oil for 30 seconds, then add ginger, garlic and shrimp. Stir-fry for 2 to 3 minutes until shrimp begin to turn rosy pink in color. Remove shrimp from skillet and set aside.

Add bell peppers and broccoli florets to skillet and cook on high heat for 1 minute. Add water; cover and reduce heat to medium. Cook 4 to 5 minutes or until vegetables are tender.

Uncover skillet and increase heat to high. Add shrimp and Smucker's® Orange Marmalade mixture. Cook shrimp for another 2 minutes until sauce is thickened and shrimp are completely cooked. Season with salt and freshly ground black pepper to taste.

Stir in scallions and serve with boiled rice.

1 tablespoon sesame seeds
1 pound sea scallops
8 ounces whole wheat
    spaghetti
3 tablespoons sesame oil,
    divided
¼ cup chicken broth or clam
    juice
3 tablespoons lemon juice
2 tablespoons oyster sauce
1 tablespoon cornstarch
1 tablespoon soy sauce
½ teaspoon grated lemon
    peel
1 tablespoon vegetable oil
2 carrots, cut into
    matchstick-size strips
1 yellow bell pepper, cut
    into thin strips
4 slices peeled fresh ginger
1 clove garlic, minced
6 ounces fresh snow peas,
    trimmed or 1 (6-ounce)
    package frozen snow
    peas, thawed
2 green onions, thinly sliced

LEMON SESAME SCALLOPS

Makes 4 servings

1. To toast sesame seeds, heat small skillet over medium heat. Add sesame seeds; cook and stir about 5 minutes or until golden. Set aside.

2. Rinse scallops and pat dry with paper towels.

3. Cook spaghetti according to package directions. Drain in colander. Place spaghetti in large bowl; toss with 2 tablespoons sesame oil. Cover to keep warm.

4. Combine broth, lemon juice, oyster sauce, cornstarch, soy sauce and lemon peel until smooth; set aside.

5. Heat remaining 1 tablespoon sesame oil and vegetable oil in large skillet or wok over medium heat. Add carrots and bell pepper; stir-fry 4 to 5 minutes or until crisp-tender. Transfer to large bowl; set aside.

6. Add ginger and garlic to skillet. Stir-fry 1 minute over medium high-heat. Add scallops; stir-fry 1 minute. Add snow peas and green onions; stir-fry 2 to 3 minutes or until snow peas turn bright green and scallops turn opaque. Remove slices of ginger; discard. Transfer scallop mixture to bowl with vegetable mixture, leaving any liquid in skillet.

7. Stir broth mixture; add to liquid in skillet. Cook and stir 5 minutes or until thickened. Return scallop mixture to skillet; cook 1 minute. Serve immediately over warm spaghetti; sprinkle with toasted sesame seeds.

LEMON SESAME SCALLOPS

SHRIMP JAVA

Makes 4 servings

¼ cup reduced-sodium soy sauce
2 tablespoons lime juice
1 tablespoon brown sugar
1 teaspoon ground cumin
2 cloves garlic, minced
½ teaspoon chili powder
1 pound large shrimp, peeled and deveined
3 tablespoons vegetable oil
½ small bunch fresh cilantro, coarsely chopped and divided
Hot cooked rice

■ Combine soy sauce, lime juice, brown sugar, cumin, garlic and chili powder in large bowl; stir until well mixed. Add shrimp and toss to coat. Marinate 15 minutes.

■ Heat wok over high heat about 1 minute or until hot. Drizzle oil into wok and heat 30 seconds. Add shrimp mixture; stir-fry about 4 minutes or until shrimp turn pink and opaque. Add half the cilantro; toss to combine. Transfer to serving dish. Garnish with remaining cilantro. Serve with rice.

THAI SHRIMP CURRY

Makes 4 servings

½ cup vegetable oil
2 large shallots, thinly sliced
1 can (14 ounces) unsweetened coconut milk, divided
1 teaspoon red Thai curry paste
⅓ cup water
1 tablespoon brown sugar
1 tablespoon fish sauce
Peel of 1 lime, finely chopped
1 pound large shrimp, peeled, deveined and tails removed
½ cup fresh basil leaves, cut into thin strips
Hot cooked jasmine rice
2 cups fresh pineapple wedges for garnish
½ cup peanuts for garnish
Fresh basil leaves for garnish

Heat oil in wok over high heat until oil registers 375°F on deep-fry thermometer. Add shallots; fry until crisp and golden brown. Remove shallots from wok with slotted spoon; drain on paper towels. Reserve for garnish.

Pour half of the coconut milk into large skillet. Bring to a boil over medium heat, stirring occasionally. Cook 5 to 6 minutes until oil rises to surface. Stir in curry paste. Cook and stir 2 minutes. Stir together remaining coconut milk and water. Add to skillet with sugar, fish sauce and lime peel. Cook over medium-low heat 10 to 15 minutes or until sauce reduces and thickens. Add shrimp and basil strips; reduce heat to low. Cook 3 to 5 minutes or until shrimp turn pink and opaque.

Serve over jasmine rice; garnish with pineapple, peanuts, basil and reserved shallots, if desired.

SHRIMP JAVA

BAKED FISH WITH THAI PESTO

Makes 4 to 6 servings

1 to 2 jalapeño peppers,*
   coarsely chopped
1 lemon
1 ½ cups lightly packed fresh
   basil leaves
1 cup lightly packed fresh
   cilantro leaves
¼ cup lightly packed fresh
   mint leaves
¼ cup roasted peanuts
   (salted or unsalted)
4 green onions, thinly sliced
2 tablespoons sweetened
   shredded coconut
2 tablespoons chopped
   ginger
3 cloves garlic, minced
½ teaspoon sugar
½ cup peanut oil
2 pounds boneless fish
   fillets (such as salmon,
   halibut, cod or orange
   roughy)
   Lemon and cucumber
   slices for garnish

Jalapeños can sting and irritate the skin; wear rubber gloves when handling peppers and do not touch eyes. Wash hands after handling.

1. Place jalapeño peppers in blender or food processor. Grate peel of lemon; add peel to blender.

2. Extract juice from lemon to measure 2 tablespoons juice. Add to blender.

3. Add basil, cilantro, mint, peanuts, green onions, coconut, ginger, garlic and sugar to blender; blend until finely chopped. With blender running, slowly pour oil into blender; blend just until mixed.

4. Preheat oven to 375°F. Rinse fish and pat dry with paper towels.

5. Lay fillets on lightly oiled baking sheet. Spread thin layer of pesto over each fillet.

6. Bake 10 minutes or until fish flakes easily when tested with fork and is just opaque in center. Transfer fish to serving platter with wide spatula. Garnish, if desired.

BAKED FISH WITH THAI PESTO

ORIENTAL SHRIMP & STEAK KABOBS

Makes about 8 servings

1 envelope LIPTON® Recipe Secrets® Savory Herb with Garlic or Onion Soup Mix
¼ cup soy sauce
¼ cup lemon juice
¼ cup olive or vegetable oil
¼ cup honey
½ pound uncooked medium shrimp, peeled and deveined
½ pound boneless sirloin steak, cut into 1-inch cubes
16 cherry tomatoes
2 cups mushroom caps
1 medium green bell pepper, cut into chunks

In 15×9-inch glass baking dish, blend savory herb with garlic soup mix, soy sauce, lemon juice, oil and honey; set aside.

On metal skewers, alternately thread shrimp, steak, tomatoes, mushrooms and green pepper. Add prepared skewers to baking dish; turn to coat. Cover and marinate in refrigerator at least 2 hours, turning skewers occasionally. Remove prepared skewers, reserving marinade.

Grill or broil, turning and basting frequently with reserved marinade, until shrimp turn pink and steak is done. (Do not brush with marinade during last 5 minutes of cooking.)

Serving Suggestion: *Serve with corn-on-the-cob, a mixed green salad and grilled garlic bread.*

LEMON TERIYAKI HALIBUT

Makes 4 servings

3 tablespoons KIKKOMAN® Lite Teriyaki Marinade & Sauce
2 tablespoons minced fresh parsley
1 teaspoon lemon juice
2 halibut steaks, ¾ inch thick, cut crosswise in half
4 lemon slices, cut in half

Combine lite teriyaki sauce, parsley and lemon juice; pour over halibut in large plastic food storage bag. Press air out of bag; close top securely. Turn bag over several times to coat all pieces well. Refrigerate 1 hour, turning bag over occasionally. Meanwhile, prepare coals for grilling. Reserving marinade, remove fish; place on grill 4 to 5 inches from hot coals. Cook 4 minutes; turn fish over. Brush with reserved marinade and top with lemon slices. Cook 4 minutes longer, or until fish flakes easily with fork. (Or, place fish on rack of broiler pan. Broil 4 to 5 inches from heat 5 minutes. Turn fish over; brush with reserved marinade and top with lemon slices. Broil 4 to 5 minutes longer, or until fish flakes easily with fork.)

ORIENTAL SHRIMP & STEAK KABOBS

2 cups water
1 cup long-grain rice
2 tablespoons soy sauce
½ teaspoon crushed red
   pepper
¼ cup olive oil
½ cup chopped green onions
½ cup chopped celery
½ cup chopped green or red
   bell pepper
½ cup chopped mushrooms
1 cup chopped broccoli
2 cups loosely packed
   spinach leaves or red
   cabbage
1 cup fresh bean sprouts,
   rinsed and drained
2 cloves garlic, crushed
1 cup tomato wedges *or*
   1 medium tomato
12 ounces crab- or lobster-
   flavored surimi seafood,
   flaked or chunked
½ cup cucumber slices
¼ cup chopped hard cooked
   egg
¼ cup dry roasted peanuts

SEAFOOD STIR-FRY WITH INDONESIAN RICE

Makes 6 servings

Combine water, rice, soy sauce and crushed red pepper in 2-qt. saucepan. Cover and bring to a boil. Reduce heat to low and cook 15 minutes or until rice is tender and water is absorbed.

Meanwhile, heat oil in wok or 12-inch skillet over medium heat. Add green onions, celery, bell pepper and mushrooms; cook 3 minutes, stirring often. Add broccoli, cook and stir 2 minutes. Stir in spinach, bean sprouts and garlic, then stir in cooked rice. Reduce heat to low; top with tomato wedges and surimi. Cover and heat until hot, about 3 minutes. Garnish with cucumber, egg and peanuts. Serve hot or at room temperature.

Favorite recipe from **SURIMI SEAFOOD EDUCATION CENTER**

SAUCE

⅓ cup GRANDMA'S®
    Molasses
¼ cup cider vinegar
2 tablespoons cornstarch
2 tablespoons pineapple
    juice, reserved from
    chunks
2 tablespoons catsup
2 tablespoons soy sauce

1 pound swordfish or red
    snapper, cut into 1-inch
    cubes
¼ cup cornstarch
3 tablespoons vegetable oil,
    divided
1 green, red or yellow bell
    pepper, cut into strips
2 green onions, chopped
1 (8-ounce) can pineapple
    chunks in its own juice,
    drained and
    2 tablespoons juice
    reserved for sauce
Cherry tomatoes, halved
Hot cooked rice or
    noodles

SWEET AND SOUR FISH

Makes 4 servings

In medium bowl, combine all sauce ingredients; blend well. Set aside. Coat swordfish with ¼ cup cornstarch. In large skillet, heat 2 tablespoons oil. Stir-fry swordfish 5 minutes or until fish flakes easily with a fork. Remove from pan. Heat remaining 1 tablespoon oil. Stir-fry bell pepper and green onions 2 minutes or until tender-crisp. Add sauce. Cook until thickened. Add fish, pineapple and tomatoes; cook until thoroughly heated. Serve with rice or noodles.

4 orange roughy or tilefish fillets (4 to 6 ounces each)

¼ cup mirin* or white wine

3 tablespoons soy sauce

1 tablespoon dark sesame oil

1½ teaspoons grated fresh ginger

¼ teaspoon crushed red pepper

1 package (10 ounces) fresh spinach leaves

1 tablespoon peanut or vegetable oil

1 clove garlic, minced

*Mirin is a Japanese sweet wine available in Japanese markets and the gourmet section of large supermarkets.

SHANGHAI FISH PACKETS

Makes 4 servings

1. Prepare grill for direct cooking.

2. Place orange roughy in single layer in large shallow dish. Combine mirin, soy sauce, sesame oil, ginger and crushed red pepper in small bowl; pour over orange roughy. Cover; marinate in refrigerator while preparing spinach.

3. Meanwhile, wash spinach; pat dry with paper towels. Remove and discard stems.

4. Heat peanut oil in large skillet over medium heat. Add garlic; cook and stir 1 minute. Add spinach; cook and stir until wilted, about 3 minutes, tossing with 2 wooden spoons.

5. Place spinach mixture in center of four 12×12-inch squares of heavy-duty foil. Remove orange roughy from marinade; reserve marinade. Place 1 orange roughy fillet over each mound of spinach. Drizzle reserved marinade evenly over orange roughy. Wrap in foil.

6. Place packets on grid. Grill packets, on covered grill, over medium coals 15 to 18 minutes or until orange roughy flakes easily when tested with fork.

SHANGHAI FISH PACKET

MALABAR SHRIMP

Makes 4 servings

4 green onions with tops
1 tablespoon vegetable oil
2 tablespoons butter or
    margarine
1 pound medium shrimp,
    peeled and deveined
1 tablespoon curry powder
2 cloves garlic, minced
½ teaspoon salt
½ teaspoon sugar
½ teaspoon grated lemon
    peel
½ cup heavy cream
¼ cup diced mild green
    chilies
    Cooked bulgur
3 tablespoons coarsely
    chopped unsalted dry-
    roasted peanuts
    Toasted coconut or
    bottled chutney
    (optional)
    Enoki mushrooms and red
    bell pepper strips for
    garnish

■ Cut green onions diagonally into 1-inch pieces.

■ Heat wok over high heat about 1 minute or until hot. Drizzle oil into wok and heat 30 seconds. Add green onions; stir-fry about 1 minute or until crisp-tender. Remove to small bowl.

■ Add butter to wok; swirl to coat bottom and heat 30 seconds. Add shrimp, curry powder, garlic, salt, sugar and lemon peel; stir-fry about 3 minutes or until shrimp turn pink and opaque. Add cream and chilies; cook and stir until heated through. Stir in green onions.

■ Serve shrimp over bulgur. Sprinkle with peanuts and coconut, if desired. Garnish, if desired.

Note: To toast coconut, preheat oven to 300°F. Spread coconut on baking sheet and bake 4 to 6 minutes or until light golden brown, stirring frequently.

CHILI GARLIC PRAWNS

Makes 4 servings

2 tablespoons vegetable oil
1 pound prawns, peeled and
    deveined
3 tablespoons LEE KUM
    KEE® Chili Garlic Sauce
1 green onion, cut into
    slices

1. Heat oil in wok or skillet.

2. Add prawns and stir-fry until just pink.

3. Add chili garlic sauce and stir-fry until prawns are completely cooked.

4. Sprinkle with green onion and serve.

MALABAR SHRIMP

3 tablespoons soy sauce
2 tablespoons dry sherry
2 cloves garlic, minced
1 pound salmon steaks or
   fillets
2 tablespoons finely
   chopped fresh cilantro

GRILLED CHINESE SALMON

Makes 4 servings

1. Combine soy sauce, sherry and garlic in shallow dish. Add salmon; turn to coat. Cover and refrigerate at least 30 minutes or up to 2 hours.

2. Drain salmon; reserve marinade. Arrange steaks (arrange fillets skin side down) on oiled rack of broiler pan or oiled grid over hot coals. Broil or grill 5 to 6 inches from heat 10 minutes. Baste with reserved marinade after 5 minutes of broiling; discard any remaining marinade. Sprinkle with cilantro.

1 pound Florida shrimp,
   peeled and deveined
½ cup chicken broth
¼ cup soy sauce
3 tablespoons dry sherry or
   white wine
2 tablespoons cornstarch
2 teaspoons minced fresh
   ginger
¼ cup oil
1 (6-ounce) package frozen
   snow peas, thawed and
   patted dry *or* ½ pound
   fresh snow peas
3 green onions, cut into
   1-inch pieces
½ (8-ounce) can water
   chestnuts, sliced
   Hot cooked rice (optional)

SHRIMP WITH SNOW PEAS

Makes 4 servings

Combine chicken broth, soy sauce, sherry, cornstarch and ginger and set aside. Heat oil in skillet or wok. Stir-fry shrimp over high heat until pink; remove from skillet. Stir-fry snow peas, green onions and water chestnuts separately over high heat for 3 to 4 minutes until tender. Remove from skillet. Return all ingredients to skillet. Stir soy sauce mixture and add to skillet. Cook until sauce thickens slightly, about 2 to 3 minutes. Serve over rice, if desired.

Favorite recipe from **FLORIDA DEPARTMENT OF AGRICULTURE & CONSUMER SERVICES, BUREAU OF SEAFOOD AND AQUACULTURE**

GRILLED CHINESE SALMON

8 ounces firm tofu, drained
1 tablespoon soy sauce
¼ cup chicken broth
3 tablespoons oyster sauce
2 teaspoons cornstarch
1 tablespoon peanut or
    vegetable oil
6 ounces (2 cups) fresh
    snow peas, cut into
    halves
8 ounces thawed frozen
    cooked crabmeat or
    imitation crabmeat,
    broken into ½-inch
    pieces (about 2 cups)
Sesame Noodle Cake
    (page 306, optional)
2 tablespoons chopped
    cilantro or thinly sliced
    green onions

STIR-FRIED CRAB

Makes 4 servings

1. Press tofu lightly between paper towels; cut into ½-inch squares or triangles. Place in shallow dish. Drizzle soy sauce over tofu.

2. Blend broth and oyster sauce into cornstarch in cup until smooth.

3. Heat wok or large skillet over medium-high heat. Add oil; heat until hot. Add snow peas; stir-fry 3 minutes. Add crabmeat; stir-fry 1 minute. Stir broth mixture and add to wok. Stir-fry 30 seconds or until sauce boils and thickens.

4. Stir in tofu mixture; heat through. Serve over Sesame Noodle Cake, if desired. Sprinkle with cilantro.

---

1 teaspoon cornstarch
½ cup chicken broth
1 teaspoon oyster sauce
½ teaspoon minced fresh
    ginger
¼ teaspoon sugar
⅛ teaspoon black pepper
1 tablespoon vegetable oil
1 pound large shrimp,
    peeled and deveined
8 ounces fresh broccoli,
    coarsely chopped
2 cans (4 ounces each)
    whole mushrooms,
    drained
1 can (8 ounces) sliced
    bamboo shoots, drained

BRAISED SHRIMP WITH VEGETABLES

Makes 4 servings

Combine cornstarch, broth, oyster sauce, ginger, sugar and pepper in small bowl; mix until smooth. Set aside.

Heat oil in wok or large skillet over high heat. Add shrimp; stir-fry until shrimp turn pink, about 3 minutes. Add broccoli to wok; stir-fry 1 minute. Add mushrooms and bamboo shoots; stir-fry 1 minute.

Stir cornstarch mixture; add to wok. Cook and stir until sauce boils and thickens, about 2 minutes.

1 ½ **pounds fresh tuna fillets,***
   ¾ inch thick
   ¼ **cup soy sauce**
   2 **tablespoons sake**
   1 **tablespoon sugar**
   ½ **teaspoon minced fresh**
      ginger
   ¼ **teaspoon minced garlic**
1 ½ **tablespoons vegetable oil**
   2 **small limes, cut into**
      halves
   4 **sticks pickled ginger***
      (optional)

Substitute salmon, halibut, swordfish or other firm-fleshed fish if desired.

**Pickled ginger has been preserved in sweet vinegar. It is available in Asian markets.*

TUNA TERIYAKI

Makes 4 servings

1. Cut tuna into 4 equal pieces; place in single layer in shallow bowl.

2. Combine soy sauce, sake, sugar, minced ginger and garlic in small bowl; stir until sugar is dissolved.

3. Pour soy marinade over tuna. Marinate in refrigerator, turning frequently, 40 minutes.

4. Drain tuna, reserving marinade. Heat oil in large skillet over medium heat until hot. Add tuna; cook until light brown, 2 to 3 minutes. Turn tuna over; cook just until opaque, 2 to 3 minutes.

5. Reduce heat to medium-low; pour reserved marinade over tuna. Add limes to skillet, cut side down. Cook, carefully turning tuna once, until coated and sauce is bubbly, 1 to 1 ½ minutes.

6. Serve immediately with limes and pickled ginger, if desired.

4 to 5 tablespoons
vegetable oil, divided
2 eggs, lightly beaten
⅔ cup peeled medium
shrimp chopped into
¾-inch pieces
3 cloves garlic, minced
1 to 2 tablespoons minced
fresh serrano chilies
4 to 6 cups cooked rice,
chilled overnight
1 tablespoon sugar
1 tablespoon nam pla
(fish sauce, optional)
1 tablespoon soy sauce
1 can (6 ounces) STARKIST®
Solid White or Chunk
Light Tuna, drained and
chunked
½ cup chopped dry-roasted
peanuts
¼ cup chopped fresh basil
2 tablespoons chopped
fresh cilantro
Lime wedges for garnish

THAI-STYLE TUNA FRIED RICE

Makes 4 to 6 servings

In wok, heat 1 tablespoon oil over medium-high heat; add eggs and cook, stirring, until partially cooked but still runny. Return eggs to bowl. Wipe out wok with paper towels. Add 2 tablespoons oil to wok; heat.

Add shrimp, garlic and chilies. Stir-fry until shrimp turn pink, about 3 minutes. Remove shrimp mixture; set aside. Add remaining 1 or 2 tablespoons oil to wok; stir-fry rice, sugar, nam pla, if desired, and soy sauce until rice is heated through. Add tuna and peanuts; heat.

Return shrimp mixture and eggs to pan, chopping eggs into pieces with stir-fry spatula. Add basil and cilantro; toss gently to mix. Serve with lime wedges for garnish; squeeze lime juice on fried rice, if desired.

PREP TIME: 15 minutes

THAI-STYLE TUNA FRIED RICE

HOT AND SOUR SHRIMP

Makes 4 servings

½ package (½ ounce) dried shiitake mushrooms*
½ small unpeeled cucumber
1 tablespoon brown sugar
2 teaspoons cornstarch
3 tablespoons rice vinegar
2 tablespoons reduced-sodium soy sauce
1 tablespoon vegetable oil
1 pound medium shrimp, peeled and deveined
2 cloves garlic, minced
¼ teaspoon crushed red pepper
1 large red bell pepper, cut into short, thin strips
Hot cooked Chinese egg noodles (optional)

Or substitute ¾ cup sliced fresh mushrooms. Omit procedure for soaking mushrooms.

Place mushrooms in small bowl; cover with warm water. Soak 20 minutes to soften. Drain; squeeze out excess water. Discard stems; slice caps. Cut cucumber in half lengthwise; scrape out seeds. Slice crosswise. Combine brown sugar and cornstarch in small bowl. Blend in vinegar and soy sauce until smooth.

Heat oil in wok or large nonstick skillet over medium heat. Add shrimp, garlic and crushed red pepper; stir-fry 1 minute. Add mushrooms and bell pepper; stir-fry 2 minutes or until shrimp are opaque. Stir vinegar mixture; add to wok. Cook and stir 30 seconds or until sauce boils and thickens. Add cucumber; stir-fry until heated through. Serve over noodles, if desired.

SPICY HONEY GARLIC SHRIMP

Makes 4 servings

3 tablespoons vegetable oil
1 pound shrimp, peeled and deveined
⅔ teaspoon salt
5 tablespoons LEE KUM KEE® Honey Garlic Sauce
2 green onions, sliced
2 tablespoons LEE KUM KEE® Chili Garlic Sauce

1. Heat oil in wok or skillet over medium heat.

2. Add shrimp and stir-fry until just pink. Sprinkle with salt while cooking.

3. Add honey garlic sauce, green onions and chili garlic sauce.

4. Stir-fry until green onions are tender and sauce is hot.

HOT AND SOUR SHRIMP

4 swordfish or halibut
  steaks (about
  1½ pounds total)
¼ cup chopped green onions
2 tablespoons Sesame Salt
  (recipe follows)
2 tablespoons hot bean
  paste*
2 tablespoons soy sauce
4 teaspoons sugar
1 tablespoon dark sesame
  oil
4 cloves garlic, minced
⅛ teaspoon black pepper

*Available in specialty stores or Asian markets

GRILLED SWORDFISH WITH HOT RED SAUCE

Makes 4 servings

Spray grid of grill or broiler rack with nonstick cooking spray. Prepare coals for grill or preheat broiler.

Rinse swordfish and pat dry with paper towels. Place in shallow glass dish. Combine green onions, Sesame Salt, hot bean paste, soy sauce, sugar, sesame oil, garlic and pepper in small bowl; mix well. Spread half of marinade over fish; turn fish over and spread with remaining marinade. Cover with plastic wrap and refrigerate 30 minutes.

Remove fish from marinade; discard remaining marinade. Place fish on prepared grid. Grill fish over medium-hot coals or broil 4 to 5 minutes per side or until fish is opaque and flakes easily with fork. Garnish as desired.

SESAME SALT
½ cup sesame seeds
¼ teaspoon salt

To toast sesame seeds, heat seeds in large skillet over medium-low heat, stirring or shaking skillet frequently until seeds begin to pop and turn golden, about 4 to 6 minutes. Set aside to cool.

Crush toasted sesame seeds and salt with mortar and pestle or process in clean coffee or spice grinder. Refrigerate in covered jar for use in additional Korean recipes.   *Makes ½ cup*

GRILLED SWORDFISH WITH HOT RED SAUCE

SATISFYING SALADS

8 ounces uncooked angel
   hair pasta
½ cup chunky peanut butter
¼ cup soy sauce
¼ to ½ teaspoon crushed
   red pepper
2 green onions, thinly sliced
1 carrot, shredded

THAI-STYLE WARM NOODLE SALAD

Makes 4 servings

1. Cook pasta according to package directions.

2. While pasta is cooking, blend peanut butter, soy sauce and crushed red pepper in medium bowl until smooth.

3. Drain pasta, reserving 5 tablespoons water. Mix hot pasta water with peanut butter mixture until smooth; toss pasta with sauce. Stir in green onions and carrot. Serve warm or at room temperature.

PREP AND COOK TIME: 12 minutes

THAI-STYLE WARM NOODLE SALAD

¾ **pound sirloin steak**
⅓ **cup vegetable oil, divided**
⅓ **cup rice vinegar***
¼ **cup reduced-sodium soy sauce**
1 **fresh jalapeño or serrano pepper, finely chopped, divided**
2 **cloves garlic, minced**
1 **tablespoon minced fresh gingerroot**
½ **teaspoon red pepper flakes**
1 **(9-ounce) package frozen French-style green beans, thawed and drained**
2 **carrots, halved and thinly sliced**
1 **cucumber, peeled, seeded and sliced**
4 **cups cooked brown rice Chopped fresh mint leaves (optional)**

White wine vinegar may be substituted.

HOT TO GO THAI SALAD

Makes 6 servings

Partially freeze steak; slice across grain into ¼-inch strips. Place in large bowl. Combine all but 1 tablespoon oil, vinegar, soy sauce, ½ of the jalapeño, garlic, gingerroot and red pepper flakes in small bowl. Pour mixture over beef; marinate 1 hour. Drain beef; discard marinade. Heat remaining 1 tablespoon oil in large skillet over medium-high heat until hot. Add beef and remaining jalapeño; cook 3 to 5 minutes or until no longer pink. Combine beef, liquid from skillet, beans, carrots, cucumber and rice in large bowl. Toss to coat. Sprinkle with mint, if desired.

Favorite recipe from **USA RICE FEDERATION**

HOT TO GO THAI SALAD

DRESSING

- 1 cup packed fresh mint or basil leaves, coarsely chopped
- 1 cup prepared olive oil vinaigrette salad dressing
- ⅓ cup FRANK'S® Original REDHOT® Cayenne Pepper Sauce
- 3 tablespoons chopped peeled fresh ginger
- 3 tablespoons sugar
- 3 cloves garlic, chopped
- 2 teaspoons FRENCH'S® Worcestershire Sauce

SALAD

- 1 flank steak (about 1½ pounds)
- 6 cups washed and torn mixed salad greens
- 1 cup sliced peeled cucumber
- ⅓ cup chopped peanuts

THAI BEEF SALAD

Makes 6 servings

Place Dressing ingredients in blender or food processor. Cover and process until smooth. Reserve 1 cup Dressing. Place steak in large resealable plastic food storage bag. Pour remaining Dressing over steak. Seal bag and marinate in refrigerator 30 minutes.

Place steak on grid, reserving marinade. Grill over hot coals about 15 minutes for medium-rare, basting frequently with marinade. Let steak stand 5 minutes. To serve, slice steak diagonally and arrange on top of salad greens and cucumber. Sprinkle with nuts and drizzle with reserved Dressing. Serve warm. Garnish as desired.

PREP TIME: 20 minutes
MARINATE TIME: 30 minutes
COOK TIME: 15 minutes

½ pound boneless tender
    beef steak (sirloin, rib
    eye or top loin)
⅓ cup KIKKOMAN® Stir-Fry
    Sauce
1 teaspoon distilled white
    vinegar
¼ to ½ teaspoon crushed
    red pepper
1 clove garlic, pressed
    Lettuce leaves (optional)
3 cups finely shredded
    iceberg lettuce
3 tablespoons vegetable oil,
    divided
1 medium eggplant, cut into
    julienne strips
1 medium carrot, cut into
    julienne strips
6 green onions, cut into
    1½-inch lengths,
    separating whites from
    tops

Stir-Fried Beef & Eggplant Salad

Makes 2 to 3 servings

Cut beef across grain into thin slices, then into strips. Combine stir-fry sauce, vinegar, red pepper and garlic. Coat beef with 1 tablespoon of the stir-fry sauce mixture; set aside remaining mixture. Line edge of large shallow bowl or large platter with lettuce leaves; arrange shredded lettuce in center. Heat 1 tablespoon oil in hot wok or large skillet over high heat. Add beef and stir-fry 1 minute; remove. Heat remaining 2 tablespoons oil in same pan; add eggplant and stir-fry 6 minutes. Add carrot and white parts of green onions; stir-fry 3 minutes. Add green onion tops; stir-fry 2 minutes longer. Add remaining stir-fry sauce mixture and beef. Cook and stir just until beef and vegetables are coated with sauce. Spoon mixture over shredded lettuce; toss well to combine before serving. Serve immediately.

1 pound medium shrimp, cooked or 2 cups chicken, cooked and shredded
Romaine lettuce leaves
2 fresh California Nectarines, halved, pitted and thinly sliced
2 cups sliced cucumber
2 celery stalks, cut into 3-inch-matchstick pieces
⅓ cup shredded red radishes
Sesame Dressing (recipe follows) or low calorie dressing
2 teaspoons sesame seeds (optional)

JAPANESE PETAL SALAD

Makes 4 servings

Center shrimp on 4 lettuce-lined salad plates. Fan nectarines to right side of shrimp; overlap cucumber slices to left side. Place celery at top of plate; mound radishes at bottom of plate. Prepare dressing; pour 3 tablespoons over each salad. Sprinkle with sesame seeds, if desired.

SESAME DRESSING

In small bowl, combine ½ cup rice wine vinegar (*not* seasoned type), 2 tablespoons reduced-sodium soy sauce, 2 teaspoons sugar and 2 teaspoons dark sesame oil. Stir to dissolve sugar.   *Makes about ⅔ cup*

Favorite recipe from **CALIFORNIA TREE FRUIT AGREEMENT**

¾ pound JONES® Ham, cut into ½-inch cubes
4 tablespoons vegetable oil, divided
4 cups shredded cabbage
1 red bell pepper, cut in thin strips
6 ounces pea pods, cut in half
2 cloves garlic, crushed
½ teaspoon ginger
3 tablespoons dry sherry
3 tablespoons soy sauce
1 tablespoon cider vinegar
½ teaspoon hot pepper sauce
6 ounces macaroni, cooked and drained

JONES® HAM STIR-FRY PASTA SALAD

Makes 6 servings

Heat 2 tablespoons oil in large skillet over medium heat. Add cabbage, bell pepper and pea pods. Stir-fry 3 minutes and remove from pan. Add remaining 2 tablespoons oil. Add garlic and ginger; stir-fry 30 seconds. Add ham and stir-fry 3 minutes.

Add sherry, soy sauce, vinegar and hot pepper sauce. Bring to a boil, stirring constantly. Reduce heat and simmer 1 minute. Remove from heat; add macaroni and vegetables, tossing to coat. Serve chilled.

JAPANESE PETAL SALAD

1 package (1 pound) PERDUE® FIT 'N EASY® Fresh Skinless & Boneless Turkey Tenderloins

6 tablespoons peanut oil, divided

1 small bunch scallions, cut diagonally into 1-inch pieces

1 red bell pepper, julienned

1 medium zucchini, julienned

1 can (8 ounces) sliced water chestnuts, drained

1 clove garlic, minced

1 tablespoon reduced-sodium soy sauce

4 cups cooked oriental noodles or other pasta (8 ounces uncooked)

2 cups shredded Chinese or napa cabbage

⅓ cup Light Teriyaki Sauce (recipe follows)

Fresh cilantro sprigs (optional)

TENDER-NESS TURKEY STIR-FRY SALAD

Makes 6 servings

Slice tenderloins lengthwise in half along natural crease. Cut turkey into 1-inch chunks. In wok or large nonstick skillet over medium-high heat, heat 2 tablespoons oil. Add turkey and stir-fry 2 to 3 minutes. Add scallions and bell pepper; stir-fry 1 minute. Add zucchini, water chestnuts and garlic; stir-fry 1 minute longer or until vegetables are tender-crisp and turkey is cooked through. Stir in soy sauce and set aside.

In large bowl, combine noodles and cabbage. In small bowl, whisk together remaining 4 tablespoons oil and Light Teriyaki Sauce. Add turkey mixture to bowl; toss with teriyaki mixture. Garnish with cilantro. Serve with oriental-style corn or rice chips and iced tea, if desired.

PREPARATION TIME: 10 minutes
COOKING TIME: 6 minutes

LIGHT TERIYAKI SAUCE

- ⅓ **cup fresh lemon juice**
- 1 **piece (1-inch) fresh ginger, peeled and diced**
- 1 **clove garlic**
- 1 **tablespoon reduced-sodium soy sauce**
- 2 **teaspoons dark sesame oil**
- 1 **teaspoon oriental chili paste (optional)**
- **Pinch sugar**

Place lemon juice in small bowl. Using garlic press, squeeze ginger over bowl to collect extract. Discard pulp. Press garlic clove into bowl and add remaining ingredients. Stir well. Cover and store in refrigerator up to 1 week. Use as marinade, dipping sauce or salad dressing. Once used as marinade, discard sauce; do not reuse as dipping sauce or salad dressing.

Makes about ½ cup

PREPARATION TIME: 5 minutes

8 ounces firm tofu, drained
8 small red potatoes
    (1¼ pounds), scrubbed
2 large carrots, peeled
4 ounces fresh green beans,
    stemmed
1 tablespoon soy sauce
2 teaspoons sugar
½ pound green cabbage
4 ounces fresh bean
    sprouts, rinsed and
    drained
1 small cucumber, peeled
    and sliced
    Tangy Peanut Sauce
    (page 256)
⅓ cup vegetable oil
4 hard-cooked eggs, peeled
    and chilled

GADO-GADO (INDONESIAN VEGETABLE SALAD)

Makes 4 servings

1. Cut tofu into 4 thin slices. Wrap in paper towels. Place on plate; top with a heavy weight, such as unopened can of food, to press out excess liquid. Let stand 30 minutes.

2. Meanwhile, to steam vegetables, place 12-inch bamboo steamer in wok. Add water to ½ inch *below* steamer. (Water should not touch steamer.) Remove steamer. Cover wok; bring water to a boil over high heat. Place potatoes in steamer. Place steamer in wok over boiling water. Cover and steam potatoes 10 minutes. Add carrots; cover and steam 5 minutes.

3. Add beans to steamer; cover and steam 5 to 10 minutes more until vegetables are fork-tender. Carefully remove steamer from wok; set aside.

4. Remove paper towels from tofu. Combine soy sauce and sugar in cup; mix well. Drizzle soy mixture over tofu and let stand 30 minutes to marinate, turning tofu occasionally.

5. Place 4 cups water in wok; bring to a boil over high heat. Cut cabbage into ½-inch-thick slices. Add cabbage to wok; cook about 1 minute or *just* until wilted. Remove with slotted spoon to bowl of cold water. Add sprouts to boiling water in wok. Cook 10 seconds and drain in colander. Rinse sprouts under cold water and place in small bowl. Drain cabbage in colander. Refrigerate cabbage, bean sprouts and cucumber in separate bowls. Dry wok with paper towels.

6. Prepare Tangy Peanut Sauce; pour into serving bowl and set aside.

continued on page 256

GADO-GADO (INDONESIAN VEGETABLE SALAD)

Gado-Gado (Indonesian Vegetable Salad), continued

7. Heat wok over high heat about 1 minute or until hot. Add oil and heat 15 seconds. Add marinated tofu and cook about 4 minutes per side or until well browned. Drain on paper towels. Cut tofu into ¾-inch squares.

8. Cut cooked beans into 2-inch lengths. Cut carrots into julienne strips. Cut potatoes into ½-inch-thick slices. Cut eggs lengthwise into quarters.

9. Divide cabbage, carrots and beans among 4 dinner plates. Arrange potatoes, eggs and cucumber on top. Sprinkle with tofu squares and sprouts. Serve with Tangy Peanut Sauce.

TANGY PEANUT SAUCE
- 1 tablespoon vegetable oil
- 3 medium shallots *or* ½ small yellow onion, peeled and finely chopped
- 2 cloves garlic, minced
- 1 tablespoon light brown sugar
- ½ teaspoon salt
- ¼ to ½ teaspoon ground red pepper
- ½ cup creamy peanut butter
- ½ to ⅔ cup water, divided
- 2 to 3 tablespoons lime or lemon juice
- Jalapeño pepper slivers for garnish

Heat oil in small saucepan over medium heat until hot. Add shallots and garlic; cook and stir 1 minute. Stir in brown sugar, salt and red pepper to taste until well mixed. Remove from heat. Stir in peanut butter and ½ cup water until smooth. Stir in lime juice to taste. If sauce is thick, stir in more water, 1 tablespoon at a time, until desired consistency. Garnish, if desired.

Makes about 1⅛ cups

1 quart plus 3 tablespoons
water, divided
3 chicken thighs (about
14 ounces)
2 medium cucumbers, cut in
half lengthwise, seeded
and thinly sliced
1 large carrot, cut into
matchstick-size strips
1 teaspoon salt
2 tablespoons fish sauce
1½ tablespoons sugar
1½ tablespoons fresh lime
juice
1 clove garlic, finely
chopped
½ cup roasted unsalted
peanuts
4 shelled, deveined jumbo
shrimp, cooked
1 tablespoon chopped fresh
cilantro
1 tablespoon chopped fresh
mint leaves
1 tablespoon chopped fresh
basil
1 tablespoon chopped green
onion tops

Chicken and Cucumber Salad (Goi Ga Tom)

Makes 4 servings

1. Heat 1 quart water in medium saucepan over high heat to boiling. Add chicken. Reduce heat to low; simmer, covered, until tender, about 25 minutes. Drain chicken; let stand until cool enough to handle. Skin and debone chicken; cut into ¼-inch cubes.

2. Meanwhile, combine cucumbers and carrot in large bowl; sprinkle with salt. Toss to mix well; let stand 15 minutes.

3. For dressing, combine remaining 3 tablespoons water, fish sauce, sugar, lime juice and garlic in small bowl; stir until sugar is dissolved.

4. Chop peanuts; then crush slightly in mortar with pestle or on board with rolling pin.

5. Squeeze cucumber mixture to extract liquid; discard liquid.

6. Combine cucumber mixture, chicken and peanuts in medium bowl; drizzle with dressing. Toss to mix well; refrigerate, covered, 30 minutes to 2 hours.

7. Cut shrimp in half lengthwise, leaving tails attached. Mix cilantro, mint, basil and green onion in small bowl.

8. Transfer salad mixture to serving dish. Garnish with shrimp; top with mixed herbs.

1 pound beef flank steak
3 tablespoons Thai
    seasoning, divided
1 stalk lemongrass
2 red Thai chili peppers *or* 1
    red jalapeño pepper,*
    seeded and cut into
    slivers
1 clove garlic, minced
2 tablespoons chopped
    fresh cilantro
2 tablespoons chopped
    fresh basil
1 tablespoon minced red
    onion
1 tablespoon fish sauce
    Juice of 1 lime
1 large carrot, grated
1 cucumber, chopped
4 cups assorted salad
    greens
    Fresh chili pepper for
    garnish

Chilies can sting and irritate the skin; wear rubber gloves when handling chilies and do not touch eyes. Wash hands after handling.

THAI GRILLED BEEF SALAD

Makes 4 servings

1. Prepare grill for direct grilling.

2. Place beef on plate. Sprinkle 1 tablespoon Thai seasoning over beef. Cover and marinate 15 minutes.

3. To mince lemongrass, trim roots and any dry outer leaves. Finely chop base to measure 1 tablespoon.

4. Grill or broil beef 5 to 6 minutes per side or until desired doneness is reached. Cool 10 minutes on cutting board.

5. Meanwhile, combine remaining 2 tablespoons Thai seasoning, lemongrass, peppers, garlic, cilantro, basil, onion, fish sauce and lime juice in medium bowl; mix well.

6. Thinly slice beef across grain. Add beef, carrot and cucumber to dressing; toss to coat. Arrange on bed of greens. Garnish, if desired.

THAI GRILLED BEEF SALAD

1 cup BLUE DIAMOND® Blanched Slivered Almonds
1 tablespoon butter
2 whole chicken breasts, skinned, boned and cubed
¼ cup plus 1 tablespoon olive oil, divided
1½ tablespoons soy sauce
1 clove garlic, finely chopped
1 tablespoon white wine vinegar
1½ teaspoons sugar
¾ teaspoon grated fresh ginger *or* ¼ teaspoon ground ginger
½ teaspoon salt
½ teaspoon lemon juice
¼ teaspoon white pepper
2 cups sliced celery
6 green onions, thinly sliced (including part of green tops)
1 large green bell pepper, diced
2 tablespoons chopped fresh cilantro
Lettuce

ALMOND CHICKEN SALAD SHANGHAI

Makes 4 to 6 servings

Sauté almonds in butter until golden; reserve. Sauté chicken in 1 tablespoon oil in large skillet over high heat for 2 to 3 minutes or until chicken is cooked through and moisture has evaporated. Add soy sauce and garlic. Cook 1 to 2 minutes. Cool. Combine vinegar, sugar, ginger, salt, lemon juice and white pepper. Beat in remaining ¼ cup oil. Toss dressing with chicken, celery, green onions, bell pepper and cilantro. Chill. Just before serving, fold in reserved almonds. Divide among individual lettuce-lined plates.

ORIENTAL BEEF SALAD

4 servings

1 pound boneless beef
    sirloin or top round
    steak, ¾ inch thick
¼ cup dry sherry
¼ cup reduced-sodium soy
    sauce
1 tablespoon cornstarch
3 tablespoons vegetable oil,
    divided
8 ounces mushrooms, sliced
1 package (6 ounces) frozen
    pea pods, thawed
4 cups thinly sliced lettuce
    Crisp chow mein noodles
    and red bell pepper
    slices (optional)

Cut beef steak into ⅛-inch-thick strips. Combine sherry, soy sauce and cornstarch; pour over strips, stirring to coat. Heat 2 tablespoons oil in large nonstick skillet over medium-high heat. Add mushrooms and pea pods; stir-fry 3 to 4 minutes. Remove vegetables; reserve. Drain marinade from beef and reserve. Add remaining 1 tablespoon oil to skillet. Stir-fry beef strips (½ at a time), 1 to 2 minutes. Return vegetables, beef and marinade to skillet; cook and stir until sauce thickens. Serve beef mixture over lettuce. Garnish, if desired.

PREP AND COOK TIME: 30 minutes

Favorite recipe from **NORTH DAKOTA BEEF COMMISSION**

1 head napa cabbage or
  romaine lettuce,
  shredded (about 6 cups)
1 medium cucumber,
  peeled, halved
  lengthwise, seeded and
  sliced (about 1¼ cups)
2 medium carrots, coarsely
  grated (about 1 cup)
2 small oranges, peeled and
  cut into segments
½ cup fresh cilantro leaves
  (optional)
2 Honey-Lime Glazed
  Chicken breasts,
  shredded (page 130)
  Honey-Lime Dressing
  (recipe follows)
¼ cup dry-roasted peanuts,
  chopped

Thai-Style Salad with Shredded Glazed Chicken

Makes 4 servings

Combine all ingredients except Honey-Lime Dressing and peanuts in large bowl; toss until well blended. Pour Honey-Lime Dressing over salad; toss until well blended. Sprinkle each serving with peanuts just before serving.

HONEY-LIME DRESSING

Whisk together 6 tablespoons honey, 3 tablespoons peanut butter, 3 tablespoons lime juice, 2 tablespoons chopped fresh mint, 1 tablespoon seeded minced jalapeño pepper, 1½ teaspoons soy sauce, 1 teaspoon minced garlic and ¾ teaspoon grated lime peel in small bowl until well blended.

Favorite recipe from **National Honey Board**

THAI-STYLE SALAD WITH SHREDDED GLAZED CHICKEN

3 tablespoons peanut or
vegetable oil
3 tablespoons rice vinegar
2 tablespoons soy sauce
1 tablespoon honey
1 teaspoon minced fresh
ginger
1 teaspoon dark sesame oil
1 clove garlic, minced
¼ teaspoon crushed red
pepper (optional)
4 cups chopped cooked
chicken or turkey
4 cups packed shredded
napa cabbage or
romaine lettuce
1 cup shredded carrots
½ cup thinly sliced green
onions
1 can (5 ounces) chow mein
noodles (optional)
¼ cup chopped cashews or
peanuts (optional)
Carrot curls and green
onions for garnish

CHINESE CHICKEN SALAD

Makes 4 to 6 servings

1. For dressing, combine peanut oil, vinegar, soy sauce, honey, ginger, sesame oil, garlic and crushed red pepper in small jar with tight-fitting lid; shake well.

2. Place chicken in large bowl. Pour dressing over chicken; toss to coat.*

3. Add cabbage, shredded carrots and sliced green onions to bowl; toss well to coat. Serve over chow mein noodles. Sprinkle cashews over salad. Garnish with carrot curls and green onions.

Salad may be made ahead to this point; cover and refrigerate chicken mixture until ready to serve.

CHINESE CHICKEN SALAD

3 boneless pork chops, cut
  into stir-fry strips
1 medium onion, finely
  chopped
¼ cup lime juice
2 tablespoons soy sauce
1 teaspoon ground
  coriander
½ teaspoon ground cumin
½ teaspoon ground ginger
¼ teaspoon ground turmeric
⅛ teaspoon cayenne pepper
¼ cup peanut butter
1 tablespoon brown sugar
½ cup plain nonfat yogurt
1 teaspoon soy sauce
⅛ teaspoon hot pepper
  sauce
1 tablespoon vegetable oil
4 cups coarsely chopped
  Chinese cabbage or
  shredded cabbage
¼ cup thinly sliced green
  onions
2 cups chow mein noodles

Hot 'n Crunchy Thai Pork Salad with Spicy Peanut Dressing

Makes 4 servings

For marinade, in small bowl combine onion, lime juice, 2 tablespoons soy sauce, coriander, cumin, ginger, turmeric and cayenne. Place pork strips in 1-gallon self-sealing plastic bag; pour marinade over pork strips, seal bag. Marinate in refrigerator for 1 to 2 hours. Drain pork strips, discarding marinade. For dressing, in small saucepan combine peanut butter and brown sugar. Cook over low heat, stirring constantly, until well blended. Remove from heat and stir in yogurt, 1 teaspoon soy sauce and hot pepper sauce. Return to heat. Cook and stir over low heat until just heated through. Keep warm. In large skillet heat vegetable oil over medium-high heat. Cook and stir pork strips for 2 to 3 minutes or until cooked through. Remove from heat; add cabbage and green onions. Toss to combine. Divide cabbage mixture among individual plates. Place chow mein noodles on top of cabbage mixture. Drizzle with dressing.

PREPARATION TIME: 30 minutes

Favorite recipe from **National Pork Producers Council**

1/3 cup GREY POUPON® Dijon Mustard*
1/4 cup orange juice
1/4 cup chopped green onions
2 tablespoons vegetable oil
2 tablespoons honey*
1 tablespoon soy sauce
1/2 teaspoon grated fresh ginger
4 cups mixed salad greens
1 1/2 cups blanched pea pods
1 (11-ounce) can mandarin orange segments, drained
1 (5-ounce) can sliced water chestnuts, drained
8 ounces deli smoked turkey breast, cut into julienne strips
1 cup crispy Chinese noodles

*1/3 cup Grey Poupon Honey Mustard may be substituted for Dijon mustard; omit honey.

CHINATOWN TURKEY SALAD

Makes 6 servings

In small saucepan, over medium heat, heat mustard, orange juice, green onions, oil, honey, soy sauce and ginger for 2 to 3 minutes or until heated through; keep warm.

On large serving platter, layer salad greens, pea pods, orange segments, water chestnuts, turkey strips and noodles. Serve salad drizzled with warm mustard dressing.

COMFORTING SOUPS

4 ounces dried Chinese egg
   noodles
3 cans (14 ounces each)
   reduced-sodium chicken
   broth
2 slices fresh ginger
2 cloves garlic, peeled and
   cut into halves
½ cup fresh snow peas, cut
   into 1-inch pieces
3 tablespoons chopped
   green onions
1 tablespoon chopped fresh
   cilantro
1½ teaspoons hot chili oil
½ teaspoon dark sesame oil

ASIAN NOODLE SOUP

Makes 4 servings

1. Cook noodles according to package directions, omitting salt. Drain and set aside.

2. Combine chicken broth, ginger and garlic in large saucepan; bring to a boil over high heat. Reduce heat to low; simmer about 15 minutes. Remove ginger and garlic with slotted spoon and discard.

3. Add snow peas, green onions, cilantro, chili oil and sesame oil to broth; simmer 3 to 5 minutes. Stir in noodles; serve immediately. Garnish with red chili pepper strips, if desired.

ASIAN NOODLE SOUP

1 package (3 ounces) ramen noodles
¾ pound chicken tenders
2 cans (about 14 ounces each) chicken broth
¼ cup shredded carrot
¼ cup frozen snow peas
2 tablespoons thinly sliced green onion tops
½ teaspoon bottled minced garlic
¼ teaspoon ground ginger
3 tablespoons chopped cilantro
½ lime, cut into 4 wedges

THAI NOODLE SOUP

Makes 4 servings

1. Break noodles into pieces. Cook noodles according to package directions, discarding flavor packet. Drain and set aside.

2. Cut chicken tenders into ½-inch pieces. Combine chicken broth and chicken tenders in large saucepan or Dutch oven; bring to a boil over medium heat. Cook 2 minutes.

3. Add carrot, snow peas, green onion, garlic and ginger. Reduce heat to low; simmer 3 minutes. Add cooked noodles and cilantro; heat through. Serve soup with lime wedges.

PREP AND COOK TIME: 15 minutes

For a special touch, garnish soup with green onion curls.

¼ of small head of cabbage
1½ tablespoons vegetable oil
8 ounces boneless lean pork, cut into thin strips
6 cups chicken broth
2 tablespoons soy sauce
½ teaspoon minced fresh ginger
4 ounces Chinese-style thin egg noodles
8 green onions with tops, diagonally cut into ½-inch slices

LONG SOUP

Makes 4 servings

1. Remove core from cabbage; discard. Shred cabbage.

2. Heat oil in wok or large skillet over medium-high heat. Add pork and cabbage; stir-fry until pork is no longer pink in center, about 5 minutes. Add chicken broth, soy sauce and ginger. Bring to a boil. Reduce heat to low; simmer 10 minutes, stirring occasionally.

3. Add noodles. Stir in green onions. Cook just until noodles are tender, 1 to 4 minutes. Ladle into soup bowls.

THAI NOODLE SOUP

2 tablespoons WESSON® Oil
1 cup chopped onion
1½ teaspoons minced fresh
garlic
1 teaspoon minced
gingerroot
4 (14½-ounce) cans chicken
broth
1 tablespoon plus
1½ teaspoons LA CHOY®
Soy Sauce
¼ teaspoon pepper
¼ teaspoon Oriental sesame
oil
1 cup thinly sliced carrots
½ pound lean pork, cut into
thin strips
1 (8-ounce) can LA CHOY®
Bamboo Shoots, drained
1 (8-ounce) can LA CHOY®
Sliced Water Chestnuts,
drained
1 (6-ounce) package frozen
pea pods
2 eggs, well beaten

HEARTY EGG DROP SOUP

Makes 10 servings

In large saucepan or Dutch oven, heat Wesson Oil over medium heat. Add onion, garlic and ginger; cook and stir until tender. Stir in broth, soy sauce, pepper and sesame oil; bring to a boil. Add carrots; simmer 5 minutes. Stir in pork; simmer 2 minutes. Add *all remaining* ingredients *except* eggs; bring to a boil. Reduce heat to low. Stir in eggs with fork to separate into strands.

1 package (1 ounce) dried black Chinese mushrooms*
1 tablespoon peanut or vegetable oil
1 large yellow onion, coarsely chopped
2 cloves garlic, minced
2 cups sliced mushrooms
2 cans (about 14 ounces each) chicken broth
2 ounces cooked ham, cut into thin slivers (½ cup)
½ cup thinly sliced green onions
1 tablespoon dry sherry
1 tablespoon soy sauce
1 tablespoon cornstarch

*Or, substitute 4 ounces fresh shiitake mushrooms; discard stems and slice caps. Omit step 1.

Shantung Twin Mushroom Soup

Makes 6 appetizer servings

1. Place dried mushrooms in small bowl; cover with warm water. Soak 20 minutes to soften. Drain; squeeze out excess water. Discard stems; slice caps.

2. Heat large saucepan over medium heat. Add oil; heat until hot. Add yellow onion and garlic; cook 1 minute. Add both mushrooms; cook 4 minutes, stirring occasionally.

3. Add broth; bring to a boil over high heat. Reduce heat to medium-low. Cover and simmer 15 minutes.

4. Stir in ham and green onions; heat through. Blend sherry and soy sauce into cornstarch in cup until smooth. Stir into soup. Cook 2 minutes or until soup thickens, stirring occasionally. Ladle into soup bowls.

10 to 12 dried shiitake
   mushrooms (about
   1 ounce)
3 eggs
1 tablespoon chopped fresh
   chives or minced green
   onion tops
2 teaspoons vegetable oil
3 cans (about 14 ounces
   each) reduced-sodium
   chicken broth
2 tablespoons oyster sauce
12 ounces medium shrimp,
   peeled and deveined
3 cups lightly packed fresh
   spinach leaves, washed
   and stemmed
1 tablespoon lime juice
   Crushed red pepper
   Cilantro sprigs and lime
   peel for garnish

SHRIMP, MUSHROOM AND OMELET SOUP

Makes 6 servings

Place mushrooms in bowl; cover with hot water. Let stand 30 minutes or until caps are soft.

Meanwhile, beat eggs and chives in small bowl with wire whisk until blended. Heat large nonstick skillet over medium-high heat until very hot. Add oil and swirl to coat surface. Pour egg mixture into pan. Reduce heat to medium; cover and cook, without stirring, 2 minutes or until set on bottom. Slide spatula under omelet; lift omelet and tilt pan to allow uncooked egg to flow under. Repeat at several places around omelet. Slide omelet onto flat plate. Hold another plate over omelet and turn omelet over. Slide back into pan to cook other side about 20 seconds. Slide back onto plate.

When cool enough to handle, roll up omelet. Slice into ¼-inch-wide strips.

Drain mushrooms; squeeze out excess water. Remove and discard stems. Slice caps into thin strips.

Combine mushrooms, chicken broth and oyster sauce in large saucepan. Cover and bring to a boil over high heat. Reduce heat to low; cook 5 minutes. Increase heat to medium-high; add shrimp and cook 2 minutes or until shrimp turn pink and opaque. Add omelet strips and spinach; remove from heat. Cover and let stand 1 to 2 minutes or until spinach wilts slightly. Stir in lime juice. Ladle soup into bowls. Sprinkle with crushed red pepper; garnish, if desired.

SHRIMP, MUSHROOM AND OMELET SOUP

1 tablespoon plus
  1 ½ teaspoons LA CHOY®
  Soy Sauce, divided
1 tablespoon cornstarch
2 boneless skinless chicken
  breasts, cut into ½-inch
  pieces
1 tablespoon WESSON® Oil
1 cup chopped onion
2 teaspoons minced fresh
  garlic
½ teaspoon minced
  gingerroot
¼ teaspoon pepper
¼ teaspoon Oriental sesame
  oil
4 (14½-ounce) cans chicken
  broth
2 ounces vermicelli or very
  thin spaghetti noodles,
  broken in half
½ cup julienne-cut carrots
½ cup julienne-cut celery
1 (8-ounce) can LA CHOY®
  Sliced Water Chestnuts,
  drained
1 (6-ounce) package frozen
  pea pods
1 tablespoon minced
  cilantro

CHINESE CHICKEN NOODLE SOUP

Makes 9 servings

In small bowl, combine *1 tablespoon* soy sauce and cornstarch; mix well. Add chicken; toss gently to coat. Cover and let stand 30 minutes. In large saucepan or Dutch oven, heat Wesson Oil over medium-high heat. Add chicken, onion, garlic, ginger, pepper and sesame oil; cook and stir until chicken is no longer pink in center. Add *remaining 1½ teaspoons* soy sauce, broth, vermicelli, carrots and celery. Bring to a boil. Reduce heat to low; simmer 5 minutes or until vermicelli is tender. Stir in water chestnuts and pea pods; heat thoroughly, stirring occasionally. Sprinkle with cilantro just before serving.

CHINESE CHICKEN NOODLE SOUP

1 pound boneless beef
   steak, such as sirloin or
   round steak
2 teaspoons dark sesame
   oil, divided
3 cans (about 14 ounces
   each) reduced-sodium
   beef broth
1 package (16 ounces)
   frozen stir-fry
   vegetables
3 green onions, thinly sliced
¼ cup stir-fry sauce

STIR-FRY BEEF & VEGETABLE SOUP

Makes 6 servings

1. Slice beef across grain into ⅛-inch-thick strips; cut strips into bite-size pieces.

2. Heat Dutch oven over high heat. Add 1 teaspoon oil and tilt pan to coat bottom. Add half the beef in single layer; cook 1 minute, without stirring, until slightly browned on bottom. Turn and brown other side about 1 minute. Remove beef from pan with slotted spoon; set aside. Repeat with remaining 1 teaspoon oil and beef; set aside.

3. Add broth to Dutch oven; cover and bring to a boil over high heat. Add vegetables; reduce heat to medium-high and simmer 3 to 5 minutes or until heated through. Add beef, green onions and stir-fry sauce; simmer 1 minute more.

PREP AND COOK TIME: 22 minutes

Serving Suggestion: *To make a quick sesame bread, brush refrigerated dinner roll dough with water and dip in sesame seeds before baking.*

STIR-FRY BEEF & VEGETABLE SOUP

1 package (1 ounce) dried
   black Chinese
   mushrooms
4 ounces firm tofu, drained
4 cups chicken broth
3 tablespoons white vinegar
2 tablespoons soy sauce
½ to 1 teaspoon hot chili oil
¼ teaspoon ground white
   pepper
1 cup shredded cooked
   pork, chicken or turkey
½ cup drained canned
   bamboo shoots, cut into
   thin strips
3 tablespoons water
2 tablespoons cornstarch
1 egg white, slightly beaten
¼ cup thinly sliced green
   onions or chopped
   cilantro
1 teaspoon dark sesame oil

Hot and Sour Soup

Makes 4 to 6 appetizer servings

1. Place mushrooms in small bowl; cover with warm water. Soak 20 minutes to soften. Drain; squeeze out excess water. Discard stems; slice caps. Press tofu lightly between paper towels; cut into ½-inch squares or triangles.

2. Combine broth, vinegar, soy sauce, chili oil and pepper in medium saucepan. Bring to a boil over high heat. Reduce heat to medium. Simmer 2 minutes.

3. Stir in mushrooms, tofu, pork and bamboo shoots; heat through.

4. Blend water into cornstarch until smooth. Stir into soup. Cook and stir 4 minutes or until soup boils and thickens.

5. Remove from heat. Stirring constantly in one direction, slowly pour egg white in thin stream into soup. Stir in green onions and sesame oil. Ladle into soup bowls.

2 tablespoons soy sauce
1 teaspoon minced fresh
  ginger
¼ teaspoon crushed red
  pepper
1 boneless beef top sirloin
  steak, 1 inch thick
  (about ¾ pound)
1 tablespoon peanut or
  vegetable oil
2 cups sliced fresh
  mushrooms
2 cans (about 14 ounces
  each) beef broth
3 ounces (1 cup) fresh snow
  peas, cut diagonally into
  1-inch pieces
1½ cups hot cooked thin egg
  noodles (2 ounces
  uncooked)
1 green onion, cut
  diagonally into thin
  slices
1 teaspoon dark sesame oil
  (optional)
  Red bell pepper strips for
  garnish
  Easy Wonton Chips
  (page 29, optional)

BEEF SOUP WITH NOODLES

Makes 4 main-dish or 6 appetizer servings

1. Combine soy sauce, ginger and crushed red pepper in small bowl. Spread mixture evenly over both sides of steak. Marinate at room temperature 15 minutes.

2. Heat deep skillet over medium-high heat. Add peanut oil; heat until hot. Drain steak; reserve soy sauce mixture. (There will only be a small amount of mixture.) Add steak to skillet; cook 4 to 5 minutes per side.* Let stand on cutting board 10 minutes.

3. Add mushrooms to skillet; stir-fry 2 minutes. Add broth, snow peas and reserved soy sauce mixture; bring to a boil, scraping up browned meat bits. Reduce heat to medium-low. Stir in noodles.

4. Cut steak across the grain into ⅛-inch slices; cut each slice into 1-inch pieces. Stir into soup; heat through. Stir in green onion and sesame oil, if desired. Ladle into soup bowls. Garnish with bell pepper strips. Serve with Easy Wonton Chips, if desired.

Cooking time is for medium-rare doneness. Adjust time for desired doneness.

1 small onion, chopped
1 tablespoon minced fresh
   ginger
1 teaspoon olive oil
1½ teaspoons curry powder
½ teaspoon ground cumin
2 cans (about 14 ounces
   each) reduced-sodium
   chicken broth, divided
1 pound peeled baby
   carrots
1 tablespoon sugar
¼ teaspoon ground
   cinnamon
   Pinch ground red pepper
2 teaspoons fresh lime juice
3 tablespoons chopped
   cilantro
¼ cup plain nonfat yogurt

Indian Carrot Soup

Makes 4 servings

1. Spray large saucepan with nonstick cooking spray; heat over medium heat. Add onion and ginger; reduce heat to low. Cover; cook 3 to 4 minutes or until onion is transparent and crisp-tender, stirring occasionally. Add oil; cook and stir, uncovered 3 to 4 minutes or until onion just turns golden. Add curry powder and cumin; cook and stir 30 seconds, until fragrant. Add 1 can chicken broth and carrots; bring to a boil over high heat. Reduce heat to low; simmer, covered, 15 minutes or until carrots are tender.

2. Ladle carrot mixture into food processor; process until smooth. Return to saucepan; stir in remaining 1 can chicken broth, sugar, cinnamon and red pepper; bring to a boil over medium heat. Remove from heat; stir in lime juice. Ladle into bowls; sprinkle with cilantro. Top each serving with 1 tablespoon yogurt.

INDIAN CARROT SOUP

1 lemon
1 lime
1 pound medium shrimp
1 tablespoon vegetable oil
1 green jalapeño pepper,*
   seeded and cut into
   slivers
1 tablespoon paprika
¼ teaspoon ground red
   pepper
4 cans (about 14 ounces
   each) reduced-sodium
   chicken broth
1 can (15 ounces) peeled
   straw mushrooms,
   drained
2 tablespoons reduced-
   sodium soy sauce
1 red Thai chili pepper or
   red jalapeño pepper,*
   seeded and cut into
   slivers
¼ cup cilantro leaves

*Chili peppers can sting and irritate
the skin; wear rubber gloves when
handling peppers and do not touch
eyes. Wash hands after handling.

SPICY THAI SHRIMP SOUP

Makes 8 appetizer or 4 main-dish servings

Remove ½-inch-wide strips of peel from lemon and lime with vegetable peeler; set aside. (Remove colored portion of skin only; white pith has bitter taste.) Extract juices from lemon and lime. Set aside. Peel shrimp, leaving legs attached to shell. Reserve shells. Devein shrimp.

Heat wok over medium-high heat 1 minute or until hot. Drizzle oil into wok and heat 30 seconds. Add shrimp and green jalapeño slivers; cook and stir 1 minute. Add paprika and ground red pepper. Stir-fry 1 minute or until shrimp turn pink and opaque. Remove shrimp mixture to bowl; set aside.

Add shrimp shells to wok and stir-fry 30 seconds. Add broth and lemon and lime peels; bring to a boil. Cover; reduce heat to low. Simmer 15 minutes. Remove shells and peels with slotted spoon; discard. Add mushrooms and shrimp mixture to broth; bring to a boil. Stir in lemon and lime juices, soy sauce and red chili pepper slivers. Ladle soup into bowls. Sprinkle with cilantro.

SPICY THAI SHRIMP SOUP

½ cup finely chopped
cabbage
8 ounces lean ground pork
4 ounces deveined peeled
shrimp, finely chopped
3 green onions with tops,
finely chopped
1 egg, lightly beaten
1½ tablespoons cornstarch
2 teaspoons soy sauce
2 teaspoons sesame oil,
divided
1 teaspoon oyster sauce
48 wonton wrappers (about
1 pound)
1 egg white, lightly beaten
¾ pound bok choy or napa
cabbage
6 cups chicken broth
1 cup thinly sliced
Barbecued Pork*
(page 30)
3 green onions with tops,
thinly sliced
Edible flowers for garnish

*Leftover grilled or roasted pork
may be substituted.*

WONTON SOUP

Makes 6 servings

For filling, squeeze cabbage to remove as much moisture as possible. Place cabbage in large bowl. Add pork, shrimp, chopped green onions, whole egg, cornstarch, soy sauce, 1½ teaspoons sesame oil and oyster sauce; mix well.

For wontons, work with about twelve wrappers at a time, keeping remaining wrappers covered with plastic wrap. Place one wonton wrapper on work surface with one point facing edge of counter. Place 1 teaspoon filling in bottom corner; fold bottom corner over filling. Moisten side corners of wonton wrapper with egg white. Bring side corners together, overlapping slightly; pinch together firmly to seal. Repeat with remaining wonton wrappers and filling. Cover finished wontons with plastic wrap while filling remaining wontons. (Cook immediately, refrigerate up to 8 hours or freeze in resealable plastic bag.)

Cut bok choy stems into 1-inch slices; cut leaves in half crosswise. Set aside. Add wontons to large pot of boiling water; cook until filling is no longer pink, about 4 minutes (6 minutes if frozen); drain. Place in bowl of cold water to prevent wontons from sticking together.

Bring chicken broth to a boil in large saucepan. Add bok choy and remaining ½ teaspoon sesame oil; simmer 2 minutes. Drain wontons; add to hot broth. Add slices of Barbecued Pork and sliced green onions; heat through. Ladle into soup bowls. Garnish, if desired.

WONTON SOUP

DELICIOUS SIDE DISHES

1 tablespoon vegetable oil,
  divided
1 egg, beaten
1 box (10 ounces)
  BIRDS EYE® frozen
  **Chinese or Japanese
  Stir-Fry Vegetables**
2 cups cooked rice
2 tablespoons soy sauce

ORIENTAL FRIED RICE

Makes about 4 side-dish servings

■ Heat 1 teaspoon oil in large skillet over high heat. Add egg; let spread in pan to form flat pancake shape. Cook 30 seconds. Turn egg over (egg pancake may break apart); cook 30 seconds more. Remove from skillet; cut into thin strips.

■ Remove seasoning pouch from vegetables. Add remaining 2 teaspoons oil to skillet; stir in rice and vegetables. Reduce heat to medium-high; cover and cook 5 minutes, stirring twice.

■ Add contents of seasoning pouch, soy sauce and cooked egg to skillet; mix well. Cook, uncovered, 2 minutes or until heated through.

PREP TIME: 5 minutes
COOK TIME: 10 minutes

ORIENTAL FRIED RICE

10 to 12 dried shiitake
    mushrooms (about
    1 ounce)
1/3 cup fresh basil leaves or
    chopped cilantro
3/4 cup water, divided
3 tablespoons oyster sauce
1 tablespoon cornstarch
4 cloves garlic, minced
1/8 teaspoon crushed red
    pepper
1 tablespoon vegetable oil
3/4 to 1 pound fresh green
    beans, ends trimmed
2 green onions, thinly sliced
1/3 cup roasted peanuts
    (optional)

GREEN BEANS AND SHIITAKE MUSHROOMS

Makes 4 to 6 servings

Place mushrooms in bowl; cover with hot water. Let stand 30 minutes or until caps are soft. Drain mushrooms; squeeze out excess water. Remove and discard stems. Slice caps into thin strips.

Meanwhile, remove stems from basil. Cut leaves into thin strips. Combine 1/4 cup water, oyster sauce, cornstarch, garlic and crushed red pepper in small bowl; mix well. Set aside.

Heat wok or medium skillet over medium-high heat. Add oil and swirl to coat surface. Add mushrooms, beans and remaining 1/2 cup water; cook and stir until water boils. Reduce heat to medium-low; cover and cook 8 to 10 minutes or until beans are crisp-tender, stirring occasionally. Stir cornstarch mixture; add to wok. Cook and stir until sauce thickens and coats beans. (If cooking water has evaporated, add enough water to form thick sauce.)

Stir in green onions, basil and peanuts, if desired; mix well. Transfer to serving platter. Garnish as desired.

GREEN BEANS AND SHIITAKE MUSHROOMS

1 teaspoon canola oil
1 teaspoon curry powder
1 teaspoon ground cumin
⅛ teaspoon crushed red
    pepper
1½ teaspoons finely chopped,
    seeded jalapeño pepper*
2 cloves garlic, minced
¾ cup chopped red bell
    pepper
¾ cup thinly sliced carrots
3 cups cauliflower florets
½ cup water, divided
½ teaspoon salt
2 teaspoons finely chopped
    cilantro (optional)

Jalapeños can sting and irritate the skin; wear rubber gloves when handling peppers and do not touch eyes. Wash hands after handling.

INDIAN-STYLE VEGETABLE STIR-FRY

Makes 6 servings

1. Heat oil in large nonstick skillet over medium-high heat. Add curry powder, cumin and crushed red pepper; cook and stir about 30 seconds.

2. Stir in jalapeño pepper and garlic. Add bell pepper and carrots; mix well to coat with spices. Add cauliflower; reduce heat to medium.

3. Stir in ¼ cup water; cook and stir until water evaporates. Add remaining ¼ cup water; cover and cook about 8 to 10 minutes or until vegetables are crisp-tender, stirring occasionally.

4. Add salt; mix well. Sprinkle with cilantro and garnish with mizuna and additional red bell pepper, if desired.

INDIAN-STYLE VEGETABLE STIR-FRY

½ cup chopped onion
2 teaspoons chopped
crystallized ginger
1 teaspoon margarine
1 carton (8 ounces) low-fat
lemon yogurt
Grated peel of 1 fresh
tangerine
2 California-Arizona
tangerines, peeled,
segmented and seeded
1½ pounds broccoli, trimmed
or 2 packages
(10 ounces each) frozen
broccoli spears, cooked
and drained

BROCCOLI WITH TANGERINE GINGER SAUCE

Makes 6 servings

In small nonstick skillet over low heat, cook and stir onion and ginger in margarine until onion is very tender. Stir in yogurt, tangerine peel and segments. Cook and stir over low heat until heated through. *Do not boil.* Serve sauce over hot cooked broccoli. Garnish with additional grated tangerine peel, if desired.

Favorite recipe from SUNKIST GROWERS

---

2 teaspoons minced fresh
ginger
1 clove garlic, minced
¼ teaspoon crushed red
pepper or crushed
Szechuan peppercorns
1 pound zucchini, cut into
¼-inch slices
2 teaspoons sugar
1 teaspoon cornstarch
2 tablespoons red wine
vinegar
2 tablespoons soy sauce
1 tablespoon peanut or
vegetable oil
1 teaspoon dark sesame oil

HOT AND SOUR ZUCCHINI

Makes 4 servings

1. Combine ginger, garlic and crushed red pepper in small bowl. Toss zucchini with ginger mixture.

2. Combine sugar and cornstarch in small bowl. Blend in vinegar and soy sauce until smooth.

3. Heat large nonstick skillet over medium-high heat. Add peanut oil; heat until hot. Add zucchini mixture; stir-fry 4 to 5 minutes until zucchini is crisp-tender.

4. Stir cornstarch mixture and add to skillet. Stir-fry 15 seconds or until sauce boils and thickens. Stir in sesame oil.

2 tablespoons vegetable oil
1 medium-size head
   cabbage, coarsely
   chopped (about 3
   quarts)
6 stalks celery, cut into
   ¼-inch slices
6 scallions, chopped
3 large yellow onions, sliced
   and slices cut in half
¼ cup lemon juice
2 tablespoons brown sugar
2 tablespoons soy sauce
1 teaspoon MCCORMICK®/
   SCHILLING® California
   Style Garlic Salt
½ teaspoon MCCORMICK®/
   SCHILLING® Ground
   Ginger
¼ teaspoon MCCORMICK®/
   SCHILLING® Hot Shot!
   Pepper Blend
1 large green bell pepper,
   cut into thin strips

ORIENTAL CABBAGE

Makes 12 servings (¾ cup each)

1. Heat oil in wok or large skillet over high heat. Add cabbage, celery, scallions, and onions. Stir to coat with oil.

2. Sprinkle lemon juice, sugar, soy sauce, garlic salt, ginger, and pepper blend over vegetables. Mix well.

3. Cook over high heat 7 minutes, stirring frequently, or until cabbage is crisp-tender.

4. Add bell pepper strips and cook, stirring, 3 minutes until pepper strips are crisp-tender.

4 dried Chinese black
   mushrooms
½ cup reduced-sodium
   chicken broth
2 tablespoons ketchup
2 teaspoons dry sherry
1 teaspoon red wine vinegar
1 teaspoon reduced-sodium
   soy sauce
¼ teaspoon sugar
1½ teaspoons vegetable oil,
   divided
1 teaspoon minced fresh
   ginger
1 clove garlic, minced
1 large tomato, peeled,
   seeded and chopped
1 green onion, finely
   chopped
4 tablespoons water,
   divided
1 teaspoon cornstarch
1 pound zucchini (about
   3 medium), diagonally
   cut into 1-inch pieces
½ small yellow onion, cut
   into wedges and
   separated

ZUCCHINI SHANGHAI STYLE

Makes 4 servings

1. Soak mushrooms in warm water 20 minutes. Drain, reserving ¼ cup liquid. Squeeze out excess water. Discard stems; slice caps. Combine reserved ¼ cup mushroom liquid, chicken broth, ketchup, sherry, vinegar, soy sauce and sugar in small bowl. Set aside.

2. Heat 1 teaspoon oil in large saucepan over medium heat. Add ginger and garlic; stir-fry 10 seconds. Add mushrooms, tomato and green onion; stir-fry 1 minute. Add chicken broth mixture; bring to a boil over high heat. Reduce heat to medium; simmer 10 minutes.

3. Combine 1 tablespoon water and cornstarch in small bowl; set aside. Heat remaining ½ teaspoon oil in large nonstick skillet over medium heat. Add zucchini and yellow onion; stir-fry 30 seconds. Add remaining 3 tablespoons water. Cover and cook 3 to 4 minutes until vegetables are crisp-tender, stirring occasionally. Add tomato mixture to skillet. Stir cornstarch mixture and add to skillet. Cook until sauce boils and thickens.

ZUCCHINI SHANGHAI STYLE

THREE HAPPINESS MUSHROOMS

Makes 4 servings

1 package (1 ounce) dried black Chinese mushrooms
2 tablespoons peanut or vegetable oil
1 small yellow onion, cut into thin wedges
2 cloves garlic, minced
2 cups sliced fresh mushrooms
1 jar (7 ounces) straw mushrooms, drained
1 cup firmly packed fresh spinach leaves
3 tablespoons stir-fry sauce

1. Place dried mushrooms in small bowl; cover with warm water. Soak 20 minutes to soften. Drain; squeeze out excess water. Discard stems; slice caps.

2. Heat wok or large skillet over medium-high heat. Add oil; heat until hot. Add onion and garlic; stir-fry 6 minutes or until limp. Add dried, fresh and straw mushrooms; stir-fry 4 minutes.

3. Stir in spinach and stir-fry sauce; stir-fry 1 minute or until spinach is wilted and sauce is heated through.

BOMBAY POTATOES

Makes 12 servings ($\frac{1}{2}$ cup each)

3 pounds potatoes, peeled and cut into 1-inch cubes
$\frac{1}{3}$ cup vegetable oil
3 tomatoes, chopped
$\frac{3}{4}$ cup chopped onion
3 tablespoons mango chutney
2 to 3 teaspoons MCCORMICK®/ SCHILLING® Indian Curry Powder
$\frac{1}{2}$ cup water
$\frac{3}{4}$ teaspoon salt

1. Place potatoes in 2-quart saucepan with small amount of water and boil until tender. Drain and set aside.

2. Heat oil in large skillet over medium heat.

3. Add tomatoes, onion, chutney, and curry powder. Cook over low heat 2 to 3 minutes. Add potatoes, $\frac{1}{2}$ cup water, and salt. Cook 5 minutes to heat thoroughly.

SAUCE

1 ½ cups chicken broth
3 tablespoons reduced-
   sodium soy sauce
1 ½ tablespoons rice wine or
   sake
1 tablespoon sugar
1 tablespoon cornstarch
1 teaspoon sesame oil

2 tablespoons sesame oil
3 dried red chili peppers
½ cup sliced green onions
1 tablespoon minced garlic
2 peeled carrots, thinly
   sliced into coins
2 cups small broccoli florets
1 red bell pepper, cut into
   thin strips
2 cups shredded napa
   cabbage
1 cup canned baby corn
1 can (8 ounces) sliced
   water chestnuts, drained
Hot cooked rice (optional)

BUDDHA'S DELIGHTFUL VEGETABLES

Makes 8 servings

Combine sauce ingredients in medium bowl and blend well. Set aside.

Heat wok; add 2 tablespoons sesame oil and heat until very hot. Add chili peppers and stir-fry until darkened. Add green onions and garlic; stir-fry 1 minute. Add carrots; stir-fry 4 minutes. Add broccoli and bell pepper; stir-fry 1 minute. Add cabbage and stir-fry 1 minute. Add baby corn and water chestnuts; stir-fry 30 seconds. Stir sauce; add to vegetables and mix well. Cover wok; cook until vegetables are crisp-tender. Serve over rice, if desired.

Favorite recipe from **THE SUGAR ASSOCIATION, INC.**

ASIAN-STYLE VEGETABLE STIR-FRY

¼ cup honey
¼ cup prepared stir-fry sauce
¼ to ½ teaspoon crushed red pepper flakes
4 teaspoons peanut or vegetable oil
2 cups small broccoli florets
2 cups small mushrooms
1 small onion, cut into wedges and separated into 1-inch strips
1 medium carrot, cut diagonally into ⅓-inch slices

Makes 4 servings

Combine honey, stir-fry sauce and pepper flakes in small bowl; set aside. Heat oil in wok or large skillet over medium-high heat. Add vegetables; cook and stir vegetables 2 to 3 minutes or until tender. Add honey mixture; cook and stir about 1 minute or until vegetables are glazed and sauce is bubbly. Serve vegetables over steamed rice or noodles.

Favorite recipe from **NATIONAL HONEY BOARD**

ALMOND BROCCOLI STIR-FRY

1 bunch (about 1 pound) broccoli
¾ cup BLUE DIAMOND® Chopped Natural Almonds
3 tablespoons vegetable oil
3 cloves garlic, thinly sliced
2 tablespoons soy sauce
1 tablespoon sugar
1 teaspoon grated fresh ginger *or* ¼ teaspoon ground ginger
1 teaspoon lemon juice

Makes 4 servings

Cut broccoli into florets. Trim and peel stalks; cut on diagonal into thin slices and reserve. In large skillet or wok cook and stir almonds in oil 1 minute. Add broccoli and stir-fry until barely tender, about 2 minutes. Add garlic and stir-fry until just tender, about 1 minute. Stir in soy sauce, sugar, and ginger. Continue stir-frying until sugar dissolves, about 1 minute. Add lemon juice.

ASIAN-STYLE VEGETABLE STIR-FRY

1 pound fresh broccoli
1½ teaspoons vegetable oil
2 medium yellow onions,
   cut into wedges and
   separated
4½ teaspoons minced fresh
   ginger
2 cloves garlic, minced
8 ounces fresh spinach,
   coarsely chopped
8 ounces fresh snow peas
   or 1 package (6 ounces)
   thawed frozen snow
   peas
4 stalks celery, diagonally
   cut into ½-inch pieces
4 medium carrots, sliced
8 green onions, diagonally
   cut into thin slices
¾ cup reduced-sodium
   chicken broth
1 tablespoon reduced-
   sodium soy sauce

CHINESE VEGETABLES

Makes 4 servings

Cut broccoli tops into florets. Cut stalks into 2×¼-inch strips. Heat oil in wok or large nonstick skillet over high heat. Add broccoli stalks, yellow onions, ginger and garlic; stir-fry 1 minute. Add broccoli florets, spinach, snow peas, celery, carrots and green onions; toss gently. Add broth and soy sauce to vegetables; toss to coat. Bring to a boil; cover and cook 2 to 3 minutes until vegetables are crisp-tender.

CHINESE VEGETABLES

1 tablespoon peanut or
vegetable oil
1 teaspoon finely chopped
garlic
¼ cup peanut butter
1 teaspoon soy sauce
2¼ cups water
1 package LIPTON® Noodles
& Sauce—Chicken
Flavor
½ cup sliced green onions
2 tablespoons sesame
seeds, toasted, divided
(optional)

SESAME PEANUT NOODLES WITH GREEN ONIONS

Makes about 4 servings

In medium saucepan, heat oil over medium heat and cook garlic 30 seconds. Stir in peanut butter and soy sauce and cook until melted. Add water and bring to a boil. Stir in noodles & sauce—chicken flavor, then simmer, stirring frequently, 10 minutes or until noodles are tender. Stir in green onions and 1 tablespoon sesame seeds. To serve, sprinkle with remaining 1 tablespoon sesame seeds.

Microwave Directions: In 1½-quart microwave-safe casserole, microwave oil with garlic, uncovered, at HIGH (Full Power) 20 seconds. Stir in peanut butter and soy sauce and microwave 30 seconds or until melted; stir. Add water and noodles & sauce—chicken flavor and microwave 12 minutes or until noodles are tender. Stir in green onions and 1 tablespoon sesame seeds. Sprinkle with remaining 1 tablespoon sesame seeds and serve immediately.

3 cups cooked brown rice, cold
½ cup slivered cooked roast pork
½ cup finely chopped celery
½ cup fresh bean sprouts,* rinsed and drained
⅓ cup sliced green onions
1 egg, beaten
Nonstick cooking spray
2 tablespoons soy sauce
¼ teaspoon black pepper

Substitute canned bean sprouts, rinsed and drained, for fresh, if desired.

ORIENTAL FRIED RICE

Makes 6 servings

Combine rice, pork, celery, bean sprouts, green onions, and egg in large skillet coated with nonstick cooking spray. Cook, stirring, 3 minutes over high heat until heated through and egg is set. Add soy sauce and pepper. Cook, stirring, 1 minute longer.

Microwave Directions: Combine rice, pork, celery, bean sprouts and green onions in shallow 2-quart microwave-proof baking dish coated with nonstick cooking spray. Cook at HIGH (100% power) 2 to 3 minutes. Add egg, soy sauce and pepper. Cook at HIGH 1 to 2 minutes or until egg is set, stirring to separate rice grains.

Tip: When preparing fried rice always begin with cold rice. The grains separate better if cold and it's a great way to use leftover rice.

Favorite recipe from **USA RICE FEDERATION**

3½ ounces dried Chinese rice
  sticks or rice noodles
⅓ cup chicken broth
3 tablespoons soy sauce
2 tablespoons tomato paste
1 tablespoon peanut or
  vegetable oil
1 medium green bell
  pepper, cut into thin
  strips
1 medium red bell pepper,
  cut into thin strips
1 medium onion, cut into
  thin wedges
2 cloves garlic, minced

RICE NOODLES WITH PEPPERS

Makes 6 servings

1. Place rice sticks in bowl; cover with warm water. Soak 15 minutes to soften. Drain; cut into 3-inch pieces.

2. Combine broth, soy sauce and tomato paste in cup.

3. Heat wok or large skillet over medium-high heat. Add oil; heat until hot. Add bell peppers, onion and garlic; stir-fry 4 to 5 minutes until vegetables are crisp-tender.

4. Stir in broth mixture; heat through. Add noodles; stir-fry 3 minutes or until heated through.

4 ounces vermicelli or
  Chinese egg noodles
1 tablespoon soy sauce
1 tablespoon peanut or
  vegetable oil
½ teaspoon dark sesame oil

SESAME NOODLE CAKE

Makes 4 servings

1. Cook vermicelli according to package directions; drain well. Place in large bowl. Toss with soy sauce until sauce is absorbed.

2. Heat 10- or 11-inch nonstick skillet over medium heat. Add peanut oil; heat until hot. Add vermicelli mixture; pat into an even layer with spatula.

3. Cook, uncovered, 6 minutes or until bottom is lightly browned. Invert onto plate, then slide back into skillet, browned side up. Cook 4 minutes or until bottom is well browned. Drizzle with sesame oil. Transfer to serving platter and cut into quarters.

RICE NOODLES WITH PEPPERS

SAUCE
- ¼ cup chicken broth
- 1½ tablespoons LA CHOY® Soy Sauce
- 1½ tablespoons cornstarch
- ¼ teaspoon Oriental sesame oil

VEGETABLES
- ¼ cup WESSON® Oil
- ½ teaspoon minced fresh garlic
- ½ teaspoon minced gingerroot
- 1½ cups sliced fresh mushrooms
- 1 cup julienne-cut carrots
- 1 (8-ounce) can LA CHOY® Sliced Water Chestnuts, drained
- 1 (8-ounce) can LA CHOY® Bamboo Shoots, drained
- 1 (6-ounce) package frozen pea pods, thawed and drained
- 6 green onions, cut into 1½-inch pieces
- 1 (2-ounce) package slivered almonds, toasted

VEGETABLE DELIGHT

Makes 4 to 6 servings

In small bowl, combine *sauce* ingredients; set aside. In large nonstick skillet or wok, heat Wesson Oil over medium-high heat. Add garlic and ginger; cook and stir 1 minute. Increase heat to high. Add mushrooms and carrots; stir-fry 1 to 2 minutes or until crisp-tender. Add water chestnuts, bamboo shoots, pea pods and green onions; heat thoroughly, stirring occasionally. Stir sauce; add to vegetables. Reduce heat to low. Heat, stirring constantly, until sauce is thick and bubbly. Sprinkle with almonds just before serving. Garnish, if desired.

Note: Add drained La Choy Sliced or Whole Water Chestnuts to your favorite steamed or stir-fried vegetables for extra crunch.

VEGETABLE DELIGHT

8 ounces vermicelli, broken
    in half, or Chinese egg
    noodles
3 tablespoons rice vinegar
3 tablespoons soy sauce
2 tablespoons peanut or
    vegetable oil
1 large clove garlic, minced
1 teaspoon minced fresh
    ginger
1 teaspoon Oriental sesame
    oil (optional)
½ teaspoon crushed
    Szechuan peppercorns
    or crushed red pepper
½ cup coarsely chopped
    cilantro (optional)
¼ cup chopped peanuts

SZECHUAN COLD NOODLES

Makes 4 servings

1. Cook vermicelli according to package directions; drain.

2. Combine vinegar, soy sauce, peanut oil, garlic, ginger, sesame oil, if desired, and peppercorns in large bowl. Add hot vermicelli; toss to coat. Sprinkle with cilantro and peanuts. Serve at room temperature or chilled.

Variation: For Szechuan Vegetable Noodles, add 1 cup chopped peeled cucumber, ½ cup each chopped red bell pepper and sliced green onions and an additional 1 tablespoon soy sauce.

2 cups water
1 tablespoon butter or
    margarine
1 package LIPTON® Rice &
    Sauce—Beef Flavor
½ cup sliced water chestnuts
¼ cup sliced green onions
½ cup unsalted cashews

PEKING CASHEW RICE

Makes about 4 servings

In medium saucepan, bring water, butter and rice & sauce—beef flavor to a boil; stir in remaining ingredients, except nuts. Reduce heat and simmer covered, stirring occasionally, 10 minutes or until rice is tender. Stir in nuts.

2 egg whites

1 egg

3 tablespoons soy sauce, divided

3 teaspoons toasted sesame seeds,* divided

1 tablespoon peanut or vegetable oil

½ cup chicken broth

1 teaspoon minced fresh ginger

1 teaspoon dark sesame oil

6 ounces Chinese egg noodles or vermicelli, cooked and well drained

⅓ cup sliced green onions

To toast sesame seeds, spread seeds in small skillet. Shake skillet over medium heat 2 minutes or until seeds begin to pop and turn golden.

GINGER NOODLES WITH SESAME EGG STRIPS

Makes 4 servings

1. Beat together egg whites, egg, 1 tablespoon soy sauce and 1 teaspoon sesame seeds in small bowl.

2. Heat large nonstick skillet over medium-high heat. Add peanut oil; heat until hot. Pour egg mixture into skillet; cook 1½ to 2 minutes or until bottom of omelet is set. Turn omelet over; cook 30 seconds to 1 minute. Slide out onto plate; cool and cut into ½-inch strips.

3. Add broth, remaining 2 tablespoons soy sauce, ginger and sesame oil to skillet. Bring to a boil; reduce heat. Add noodles; heat through. Add omelet strips and onions; heat through. Sprinkle with remaining 2 teaspoons sesame seeds.

1 pound fresh green beans
4 ounces lean ground pork
   or turkey
2 tablespoons plus
   1 teaspoon light soy
   sauce, divided
2 tablespoons plus
   1 teaspoon rice wine or
   dry sherry, divided
½ teaspoon dark sesame oil
2 tablespoons water
1 teaspoon sugar
3 cups vegetable oil
1 tablespoon sliced green
   onion (white part only)
Carrot flowers for garnish

DRY-COOKED GREEN BEANS

Makes 4 servings

1. Cut each bean diagonally in half or into 2-inch lengths. Set aside.

2. Combine pork, 1 teaspoon soy sauce, 1 teaspoon rice wine and sesame oil in medium bowl; mix well. Set aside.

3. Combine water, sugar, remaining 2 tablespoons soy sauce and 2 tablespoons rice wine in small bowl; mix well. Set aside.

4. Heat vegetable oil in wok over medium-high heat until oil registers 375°F on deep-fry thermometer. Carefully add half of beans* and fry 2 to 3 minutes until beans blister and are crisp-tender. Remove beans with slotted spoon to paper towels; drain. Reheat oil and repeat with remaining beans.

5. Pour off oil; heat wok over medium-high heat 30 seconds. Add pork mixture and stir-fry about 2 minutes or until well browned. Add beans and water mixture; toss until heated through. Transfer to serving dish. Sprinkle with green onion. Garnish, if desired.

Use long-handled spoon since oil may splatter.

DRY-COOKED GREEN BEANS

PICKLING LIQUID
- 3 cups sugar
- 3 cups distilled white vinegar
- 1½ cups water
- 1½ teaspoons salt

VEGETABLES
- 1 large Chinese white radish (about 1 pound)
- 3 large carrots
- 1 large cucumber, seeded
- 4 stalks celery, diagonally cut into ½-inch pieces
- 8 green onions, diagonally cut into ¼-inch pieces
- 1 large red bell pepper, cut into ½-inch pieces
- 1 large green bell pepper, cut into ½-inch pieces
- 4 ounces fresh ginger, peeled and thinly sliced
- Green Onion Curls for garnish (page 30)

CHINESE MIXED PICKLED VEGETABLES

Makes 1½ to 2 quarts

Combine all pickling liquid ingredients in 3-quart saucepan. Bring to a boil over medium heat, stirring occasionally. Cool.

Cut radish into matchstick pieces. Repeat with carrots and cucumber. Fill 5-quart stockpot or Dutch oven ½ full with water. Bring to a boil. Add all vegetables and ginger. Remove from heat. Let stand 2 minutes. Drain vegetables in large colander. Spread vegetables out onto clean towels; allow to dry 2 to 3 hours.

Pack vegetables firmly into clean jars with tight-fitting lids. Pour Pickling Liquid into jars to cover vegetables. Seal jars tightly. Store in refrigerator at least 1 week before using. Serve garnished, if desired.

CHINESE MIXED PICKLED VEGETABLES

1 pound whole green beans, trimmed
2 tablespoons chopped green onion
2 tablespoons dry sherry or chicken broth
1½ tablespoons reduced-sodium soy sauce
1 teaspoon Chinese chili sauce with garlic
1 teaspoon dark sesame oil
1 clove garlic, minced

Spicy Oriental Green Beans

Makes 4 servings

1. Fill Dutch oven with water to depth of ½ inch. Bring water to a boil. Place green beans in steamer basket; place basket in Dutch oven. Water should not touch bottom of steamer basket. Cover and steam beans about 5 minutes or just until crisp-tender. Drain and set aside.

2. Combine green onion, sherry, soy sauce, chili sauce, sesame oil and garlic in small bowl.

3. Spray large skillet with nonstick cooking spray; heat over medium heat. Add green beans; pour soy sauce mixture over beans. Toss well to coat. Cook 3 to 5 minutes, stirring constantly until heated through. Garnish with edible flowers, such as pansies, violets or nasturtiums, if desired.

---

1 bag (16 ounces) BIRDS EYE® frozen Broccoli Cuts
1 tablespoon sesame seeds
1 tablespoon oil
Dash soy sauce (optional)

Sesame Broccoli

Makes 4 to 6 servings

■ Cook broccoli according to package directions.

■ Cook sesame seeds in oil 1 to 2 minutes or until golden brown, stirring frequently.

■ Toss broccoli with sesame seed mixture. Add soy sauce, salt and pepper to taste.

PREP TIME: 1 minute
COOK TIME: 8 to 9 minutes

SPICY ORIENTAL GREEN BEANS

1 tablespoon vegetable oil
1 tablespoon
    MCCORMICK®/
    SCHILLING® Chinese
    Five Spice
¼ cup chopped green bell
    pepper
¼ cup chopped red bell
    pepper
¼ cup chopped onion
1 tablespoon chopped
    scallion, white part only
2 cups long grain rice
4 cups water
1 tablespoon
    MCCORMICK®/
    SCHILLING® Chicken
    Flavor Base
1 tablespoon chopped
    scallion, green part only
1 tablespoon chopped
    unsalted dry-roasted
    peanuts

THAI RICE

Makes 12 servings (½ cup each)

1. Heat oil and Chinese five spice in 4-quart saucepan over medium heat. Add green and red bell peppers, onion, and white portion of scallion. Sauté, stirring occasionally, until onion is transparent.

2. Stir in rice and cook, stirring occasionally, 5 minutes. Add water and flavor base.

3. Heat to a boil; reduce heat, cover, and simmer 25 to 30 minutes or until all water has been absorbed.

4. Fluff with fork and spoon into serving dish. Sprinkle with green portion of scallion and peanuts.

1 tablespoon olive oil
1 cup (about 2 ounces) sliced fresh shiitake mushrooms
1 cup asparagus spears cut into 1-inch pieces
1 clove garlic, minced
3 cups cooked brown rice
¼ cup pine nuts, toasted*
¼ cup sliced green onions
1 tablespoon grated lemon peel
½ teaspoon salt
½ teaspoon ground black pepper
Baked chicken (optional)

*To toast nuts, place on baking sheet. Bake at 350°F 5 to 7 minutes or until lightly browned.

BROWN RICE AND SHIITAKE PILAF

Makes 6 servings

Heat oil in large skillet over medium-high heat until hot. Add mushrooms, asparagus and garlic; cook and stir 1 to 2 minutes or until tender. Add rice, nuts, green onions, lemon peel, salt and pepper. Stir until well blended; heat thoroughly. Serve with chicken.

Favorite recipe from **USA RICE FEDERATION**

2 cups chilled cooked white rice
⅓ cup chopped red bell pepper
¼ cup thinly sliced green onions
2 egg whites, slightly beaten
1 egg, slightly beaten
2 tablespoons soy sauce
3 tablespoons peanut or vegetable oil, divided

CANTONESE RICE CAKE PATTIES

Makes about 6 servings (about 9 patties)

1. Mix rice, bell pepper, green onions, egg whites, egg and soy sauce in medium bowl.

2. Heat large nonstick skillet over medium heat. Add 1 tablespoon oil; heat until hot. For each patty, spoon ⅓ cup rice mixture into skillet; flatten patties slightly with back of spatula. Cook patties, 3 at a time, 3 to 4 minutes until bottoms are golden brown. Turn patties over; cook 3 minutes or until golden brown and egg is cooked. Keep patties warm in 200°F oven. Repeat with remaining oil and rice mixture.

6 ounces uncooked dry
   soba (buckwheat)
   noodles
2 teaspoons dark sesame
   oil
1 tablespoon sesame seeds
½ cup reduced-sodium
   chicken broth
1 tablespoon creamy peanut
   butter
4 teaspoons reduced-
   sodium soy sauce
½ cup thinly sliced green
   onions
½ cup minced red bell
   pepper
1½ teaspoons finely chopped
   seeded jalapeño pepper
1 clove garlic, minced
¼ teaspoon crushed red
   pepper

SPICY SESAME NOODLES

Makes 6 servings

1. Cook noodles according to package directions. (*Do not overcook.*) Rinse noodles thoroughly with cold water to stop cooking; drain. Place noodles in large bowl; toss with sesame oil.

2. Place sesame seeds in small skillet. Cook over medium heat about 3 minutes or until seeds begin to pop and turn golden brown, stirring frequently. Remove from heat; set aside.

3. Combine chicken broth and peanut butter in small bowl with wire whisk until blended. (Mixture may look curdled.) Stir in soy sauce, green onions, bell pepper, jalapeño pepper, garlic and crushed red pepper.

4. Pour mixture over noodles; toss to coat. Cover and let stand 30 minutes at room temperature or refrigerate up to 24 hours. Sprinkle with toasted sesame seeds before serving. Garnish, if desired.

SPICY SESAME NOODLES

TURMERIC POTATOES

Makes 6 to 8 servings

3 cups water
1½ pounds small boiling potatoes, unpeeled and scrubbed
¾ teaspoon salt
½ teaspoon ground turmeric
⅛ teaspoon ground red pepper
3 tablespoons vegetable oil

1. Heat water in small saucepan over high heat to boiling. Add potatoes. Reduce heat to medium-low; cook, covered, just until firm-tender when pierced with knife, about 20 minutes. Drain potatoes; rinse under cold running water. Let cool completely, at least 2 hours.

2. Peel potatoes; cut into 1-inch wedge-shaped pieces. Mix salt, turmeric and red pepper in small bowl; sprinkle over potatoes in large bowl and toss to coat.

3. Heat oil in large skillet over medium-high heat until hot; add potatoes. Cook, stirring gently and turning frequently, until potatoes are golden brown and crusty, 7 to 10 minutes.

ORIENTAL MUSTARD BARBECUE SAUCE

Makes 2 cups

1 bottle (10.5 ounces) PLOCHMAN'S® Mild Yellow Mustard (about 1 cup)
½ cup barbecue sauce
¼ cup packed brown sugar
¼ cup hoisin sauce
¼ cup soy sauce
2 tablespoons sesame oil
2 tablespoons Chinese rice wine
1 tablespoon minced fresh ginger
1 clove garlic, minced

Mix together all ingredients. Use as a condiment, or brush on chicken, seafood or steak during the last 15 minutes of cooking.

PREPARATION TIME: 5 minutes

½ cup dry white wine
½ cup honey
½ cup soy sauce
2 green onions, chopped
2 tablespoons Oriental
   sesame oil
1 tablespoon grated fresh
   gingerroot
1 clove garlic, minced

KOREAN-STYLE HONEY MARINADE

Makes about 1½ cups

Combine all ingredients in small bowl; mix thoroughly. Use to marinate steak or chicken.

Favorite recipe from **NATIONAL HONEY BOARD**

1 tablespoon reduced-
   sodium soy sauce
1 tablespoon rice vinegar
1 tablespoon Dijon mustard
1 tablespoon honey
1 tablespoon chopped fresh
   cilantro
¼ teaspoon salt
¼ teaspoon ground black
   pepper
1 tablespoon dark sesame
   oil
2 carrots, cut into julienned
   strips
1 cup fresh snow peas, cut
   diagonally in half
4 green onions, sliced
1 clove garlic, minced
3 cups cooked rice
1 tablespoon sesame seeds,
   toasted*
Grilled chicken (optional)

To toast sesame seeds, place in small skillet. Cook over medium-high heat 1 to 3 minutes or until lightly browned, stirring constantly.

ASIAN SESAME RICE

Makes 6 servings

Combine soy sauce, vinegar, mustard, honey, cilantro, salt and pepper in small bowl; set aside. Heat oil in large skillet over medium-high heat until hot. Add carrots, peas, onions and garlic; cook and stir 3 to 5 minutes or until carrots are crisp-tender. Add rice and soy sauce mixture. Stir until well blended; heat thoroughly. Sprinkle with sesame seeds. Serve with chicken.

Favorite recipe from **USA RICE FEDERATION**

LEAN DELIGHTS

6 ounces fresh uncooked
Chinese egg noodles
¼ cup plum preserves or
jam
3 tablespoons rice wine
vinegar
3 tablespoons reduced-
sodium soy sauce
1 tablespoon cornstarch
3 teaspoons oil, divided
1 small red onion, thinly
sliced
2 cups fresh snow peas,
diagonally sliced
12 ounces boneless skinless
chicken breasts, cut into
thin strips
4 medium plums or
apricots, pitted and
sliced

PLUM CHICKEN

Makes 4 servings

1. Cook noodles according to package directions, omitting salt. Drain and keep warm. Stir together plum preserves, vinegar, soy sauce and cornstarch; set aside.

2. Heat 2 teaspoons oil in wok. Add onion; stir-fry 2 minutes or until slightly soft. Add snow peas; stir-fry 3 minutes. Remove vegetables.

3. Heat remaining 1 teaspoon oil in wok. Add chicken; stir-fry over medium-high heat 2 to 3 minutes or until no longer pink. Push chicken to one side of skillet.

4. Stir preserves mixture; add to wok. Cook and stir until bubbly. Stir in vegetables, plums and chicken. Cook until hot. Toss with noodles.

NUTRIENTS PER SERVING:
Calories: 415, Total Fat: 5 g, Cholesterol: 43 mg, Sodium: 307 mg

PLUM CHICKEN

⅓ cup reduced-sodium soy sauce

2 tablespoons water

2 tablespoons fresh lime juice

2 teaspoons hot chili oil*

2 cloves garlic, minced

1 teaspoon minced fresh ginger

12 ounces well-trimmed pork tenderloin

1 red or yellow bell pepper, cut into ½-inch chunks

1 red or sweet onion, cut into ½-inch chunks

2 cups hot cooked rice

If hot chili oil is not available, combine 2 teaspoons vegetable oil and ½ teaspoon crushed red pepper in small microwavable cup. Microwave at HIGH 1 minute. Let stand 5 minutes to infuse flavor.

THAI-STYLE PORK KABOBS

Makes 4 servings

1. Combine soy sauce, water, lime juice, chili oil, garlic and ginger in medium bowl; reserve ⅓ cup mixture for dipping sauce. Set aside.

2. Cut pork tenderloin lengthwise in half; cut crosswise into 4-inch slices. Cut slices into ½-inch strips. Add to bowl with soy sauce mixture; toss to coat. Cover; refrigerate at least 30 minutes or up to 2 hours, turning once.

3. To prevent sticking, spray grid with nonstick cooking spray. Prepare coals for grilling.

4. Remove pork from marinade; discard marinade. Alternately weave pork strips and thread bell pepper and onion chunks onto eight 8- to 10-inch metal skewers.

5. Grill, covered, over medium-hot coals 6 to 8 minutes or until pork is no longer pink in center, turning halfway through grilling time. Serve with rice and reserved dipping sauce.

NUTRIENTS PER SERVING:
Calories: 248, Total Fat: 4 g, Cholesterol: 49 mg, Sodium: 271 mg

THAI-STYLE PORK KABOBS

4 ounces lean ground pork
½ cup reduced-fat ricotta cheese
½ tablespoon minced fresh cilantro
½ teaspoon black pepper
⅛ teaspoon Chinese 5-spice powder
20 wonton skins
1 teaspoon vegetable oil
⅓ cup chopped red bell pepper
1 teaspoon grated fresh ginger
2 cans (14½ ounces each) fat-free reduced-sodium chicken broth
2 teaspoons reduced-sodium soy sauce
4 ounces fresh snow peas
1 can (8¾ ounces) baby corn, rinsed and drained
2 green onions, thinly sliced

GINGER WONTON SOUP

Makes 4 (1½-cup) servings

1. Cook pork in small nonstick skillet over medium-high heat 4 minutes or until no longer pink. Cool slightly; stir in ricotta cheese, cilantro, black pepper and 5-spice powder.

2. Place 1 teaspoon filling in center of each wonton skin. Fold top corner of wonton over filling. Lightly brush remaining corners with water. Fold left and right corners over filling. Tightly roll filled end toward remaining corner in jelly-roll fashion. Moisten edges with water to seal. Cover and set aside.

3. Heat oil in large saucepan. Add bell pepper and ginger; cook 1 minute. Add chicken broth and soy sauce; bring to a boil. Add snow peas, baby corn and wontons. Reduce heat to medium-low and simmer 4 to 5 minutes or until wontons are tender. Sprinkle with green onions.

NUTRIENTS PER SERVING:
Calories: 259, Total Fat: 5 g, Cholesterol: 53 mg, Sodium: 261 mg

GINGER WONTON SOUP

1 tablespoon dark sesame oil
1 pound chicken tenders, cut into 1-inch pieces
2 cups broccoli florets
1 small red bell pepper, sliced
½ cup onion slices
½ cup snow peas
1 can (8 ounces) water chestnuts, sliced and drained
2 cloves garlic, minced
1 teaspoon Chinese 5-spice powder
1 cup fat-free reduced-sodium chicken broth
2 teaspoons cornstarch
2 tablespoons cold water
2 cups hot cooked rice

SESAME CHICKEN AND VEGETABLE STIR-FRY

Makes 4 servings

1. Heat oil in wok over medium heat until hot. Add chicken; stir-fry about 8 minutes or until chicken is no longer pink in center. Remove from wok.

2. Add broccoli, bell pepper, onion, snow peas, water chestnuts and garlic to wok; stir-fry 5 to 8 minutes or until vegetables are crisp-tender. Sprinkle with 5-spice powder; cook and stir 1 minute.

3. Return chicken to wok. Add chicken broth; heat to a boil. Combine cornstarch and water in small bowl until smooth; stir into broth mixture. Boil 1 to 2 minutes, stirring constantly. Serve over rice.

NUTRIENTS PER SERVING:
Calories: 354, Total Fat: 7 g, Cholesterol: 59 mg, Sodium: 83 mg

---

1 pound lean boneless pork loin
1 tablespoon vinegar
1 tablespoon soy sauce
1 teaspoon sesame oil
1 clove garlic, minced
½ teaspoon ground ginger
1 teaspoon vegetable oil
1 (10-ounce) package frozen stir-fry vegetables, unthawed
1 tablespoon chicken broth or water
Hot cooked rice (optional)
1 tablespoon toasted sesame seeds (optional)

SAVORY PORK STIR-FRY

Makes 4 servings

Slice pork across grain into ⅛-inch strips. Marinate in vinegar, soy sauce, sesame oil, garlic and ginger for 10 minutes. Heat vegetable oil in nonstick pan until hot. Add pork and stir-fry for 3 to 5 minutes, until pork is no longer pink. Add vegetables and chicken broth. Stir mixture, cover and steam until vegetables are crisp-tender. Serve over hot cooked rice and sprinkle with toasted sesame seeds, if desired.

PREPARATION TIME: 20 minutes

NUTRIENTS PER SERVING:
Calories: 233, Total Fat: 8 g, Cholesterol: 66 mg, Sodium: 713 mg

Favorite recipe from **NATIONAL PORK PRODUCERS COUNCIL**

SESAME CHICKEN AND VEGETABLE STIR-FRY

Garam Masala (recipe
follows)
1½ pounds chicken thighs,
skin removed
1 small onion, coarsely
chopped
⅓ cup plain nonfat yogurt
1 tablespoon tomato paste
2 large cloves garlic,
coarsely chopped
2 teaspoons chopped fresh
ginger
½ jalapeño pepper,* seeded
1 teaspoon paprika
Peel of ½ lemon, coarsely
chopped
Cucumber Raita (recipe
follows)
6 whole wheat pita breads

*Jalapeños can sting and irritate the
skin; wear rubber gloves when
handling peppers and do not touch
eyes. Wash hands after handling.*

TANDOORI-STYLE CHICKEN WITH CUCUMBER RAITA

Makes 6 servings

1. Prepare Garam Masala; set aside.

2. Lightly score each chicken thigh twice with sharp knife; place in large heavy-duty resealable plastic food storage bag.

3. Place onion, yogurt, tomato paste, garlic, ginger, jalapeño pepper, 1 teaspoon Garam Masala, paprika and lemon peel in food processor or blender; process until smooth. Add to chicken pieces in plastic bag; seal bag tightly and turn to coat chicken thoroughly. Refrigerate 4 hours or overnight.

4. Prepare Cucumber Raita; refrigerate.

5. Remove chicken from bag and discard marinade. Grill chicken on covered grill over medium coals 20 to 25 minutes or until chicken is no longer pink in center and juices run clear, turning once. Serve with Cucumber Raita and pitas. Garnish as desired.

GARAM MASALA*

- 2 teaspoons cumin seeds
- 2 teaspoons whole black peppercorns
- 1 ½ teaspoons coriander seeds
- 1 teaspoon fennel seeds
- ¾ teaspoon whole cloves
- ½ teaspoon whole cardamom seeds, pods removed
- 1 cinnamon stick, broken into several pieces

Prepared Garam Masala can also be purchased at large supermarkets in the specialty foods aisle or in Indian markets.

Preheat oven to 250°F. Combine all ingredients and spread on baking sheet; bake 30 minutes, stirring occasionally. Grind warm spices in spice mill or clean coffee grinder. Store in refrigerator in tightly covered glass jar.   *Makes about 3 tablespoons*

CUCUMBER RAITA

- 1 cup plain nonfat yogurt
- ½ cup finely chopped cucumber
- 1 tablespoon minced fresh mint leaves
- 1 clove garlic, minced
- ¼ teaspoon salt

Combine all ingredients in small bowl. Cover and refrigerate until ready to use.   *Makes 6 servings*

NUTRIENTS PER SERVING:
Calories: 218, Total Fat: 6 g, Cholesterol: 47 mg, Sodium: 344 mg

8 ounces uncooked rice
noodles, ⅛ inch wide
2 tablespoons rice wine
vinegar
1½ tablespoons fish sauce
1 to 2 tablespoons fresh
lemon juice
1 tablespoon ketchup
2 teaspoons sugar
¼ teaspoon crushed red
pepper
1 tablespoon vegetable oil
4 ounces boneless skinless
chicken breast, finely
chopped
2 green onions, thinly sliced
2 cloves garlic, minced
3 ounces small shrimp,
peeled
2 cups fresh bean sprouts,
rinsed and drained
1 medium carrot, shredded
3 tablespoons minced fresh
cilantro
2 tablespoons chopped
unsalted dry-roasted
peanuts

PAD THAI

Makes 5 (1-cup) servings

1. Place noodles in medium bowl. Cover with lukewarm water and let stand 30 minutes or until soft. Drain and set aside. Whisk together vinegar, fish sauce, lemon juice, ketchup, sugar and crushed red pepper in small bowl; set aside.

2. Heat oil in wok or large nonstick skillet over medium-high heat. Add chicken, green onions and garlic. Cook and stir until chicken is no longer pink. Stir in noodles; cook 1 minute. Add shrimp and bean sprouts; cook just until shrimp turn opaque, about 3 minutes. Stir in fish sauce mixture; toss to coat evenly. Cook until heated through, about 2 minutes.

3. Arrange noodle mixture on platter; sprinkle with carrot, cilantro and peanuts. Garnish with lemon wedges, tomato wedges and fresh cilantro, if desired.

NUTRIENTS PER SERVING:
Calories: 265, Total Fat: 6 g, Cholesterol: 38 mg, Sodium: 798 mg

PAD THAI

1 pound boneless skinless chicken breast halves, cut into ¾-inch strips
2 tablespoons sherry or canned pineapple juice
2 tablespoons reduced-sodium soy sauce
1 tablespoon sugar
1 tablespoon peanut oil
½ teaspoon minced garlic
½ teaspoon minced ginger
5 ounces red pearl onions
½ fresh pineapple, cut into 1-inch wedges

JAPANESE YAKITORI

Makes 6 servings

1. Place chicken in large heavy-duty resealable plastic food storage bag. Combine sherry, soy sauce, sugar, oil, garlic and ginger in small bowl; mix thoroughly to dissolve sugar. Pour into plastic bag with chicken; seal bag and turn to coat thoroughly. Refrigerate 30 minutes or up to 2 hours, turning occasionally. (If using wooden or bamboo skewers, prepare by soaking skewers in water 20 to 30 minutes to prevent them from burning.)

2. Meanwhile, place onions in boiling water for 4 minutes; drain and cool in ice water to stop cooking. Cut off root ends and slip off outer skins; set aside.

3. Drain chicken, reserving marinade. Weave chicken accordion-style onto skewers, alternating onions and pineapple with chicken. Brush with reserved marinade; discard remaining marinade.

4. Grill on uncovered grill over medium-hot coals 6 to 8 minutes or until chicken is no longer pink in center, turning once.

NUTRIENTS PER SERVING:
Calories: 124, Total Fat: 3 g, Cholesterol: 46 mg, Sodium: 99 mg

JAPANESE YAKITORI

PLUM-GOOD PORK

Makes 4 servings

1 pound boneless pork loin, cut into thin strips
2 teaspoons vegetable oil, divided
1 tablespoon grated fresh ginger
½ red bell pepper, cut into 1-inch squares
½ green bell pepper, cut into 1-inch squares
1 cup fresh mushrooms, sliced
6 fresh plums, pitted and halved
1 cup peach nectar
⅓ cup lime juice
2 tablespoons soy sauce
1 tablespoon cornstarch
1 teaspoon grated fresh orange peel
½ teaspoon dry mustard
¼ teaspoon cinnamon

Heat 1 teaspoon oil over high heat in nonstick skillet; stir-fry pork strips and ginger about 3 minutes. Remove from skillet. Heat remaining oil in skillet, stir-fry bell peppers and mushrooms for 3 minutes. Add plums and stir-fry for 2 minutes. Combine remaining ingredients; add to skillet with pork. Cook and stir until sauce bubbles and thickens.

PREPARATION TIME: 15 minutes

NUTRIENTS PER SERVING:
Calories: 300, Total Fat: 9 g, Cholesterol: 66 mg, Sodium: 579 mg

Favorite recipe from **NATIONAL PORK PRODUCERS COUNCIL**

PORK TENDERLOIN STIR-FRY

Makes 4 servings

1 pound pork tenderloin
1 tablespoon vegetable oil
½ teaspoon salt
1 small onion, sliced and separated into rings
3 small zucchini, cut into thin slices
1 medium green bell pepper, cut into thin strips
3 medium carrots, cut into thin slices
1 tablespoon soy sauce
1 clove garlic, minced

Cut pork tenderloin into ¼-inch-thick slices. Quickly brown pork slices, half at a time, in hot oil in wok or large skillet, stirring constantly. Remove from wok. Sprinkle pork with salt. Reduce heat; add onion, zucchini, bell pepper, carrots, soy sauce and garlic; mix well. Cook over medium heat 5 to 6 minutes, stirring occasionally. Return pork to wok and heat thoroughly.

PREPARATION TIME: 15 minutes

NUTRIENTS PER SERVING:
Calories: 217, Total Fat: 7 g, Cholesterol: 67 mg, Sodium: 603 mg

Favorite recipe from **NATIONAL PORK PRODUCERS COUNCIL**

2 cups rice
1 can (14½ ounces)
    vegetable broth, divided
3 tablespoons cornstarch
1 tablespoon reduced-
    sodium soy sauce
½ teaspoon sugar
¼ teaspoon dark sesame oil
1 package (16 ounces)
    extra-firm tofu
1 teaspoon peanut oil
1 tablespoon minced fresh
    ginger
3 cloves garlic, minced
3 cups broccoli florets
2 cups sliced mushrooms
½ cup chopped green onions
1 large red bell pepper, cut
    into strips
    Prepared Szechuan sauce
    (optional)

BROCCOLI-TOFU STIR-FRY

Makes 6 servings

1. Cook rice according to package directions. Combine ¼ cup vegetable broth, cornstarch, soy sauce, sugar and sesame oil in small bowl until well blended. Drain tofu; cut into 1-inch cubes.

2. Heat peanut oil in large nonstick wok or skillet over medium heat until hot. Add ginger and garlic. Cook and stir 5 minutes. Add remaining vegetable broth, broccoli, mushrooms, green onions and bell pepper. Cook and stir over medium-high heat 5 minutes or until vegetables are crisp-tender. Add tofu; cook 2 minutes, stirring occasionally. Stir cornstarch mixture; add to vegetable mixture. Cook and stir until sauce thickens. Serve over rice with Szechuan sauce, if desired. Garnish as desired.

NUTRIENTS PER SERVING:
Calories: 410, Total Fat: 8 g, Cholesterol: 0 mg, Sodium: 316 mg

1 package (5 ounces)
    Chinese-style rice
    noodles
1 pound boneless skinless
    chicken breasts, cut into
    2×½-inch pieces
3 cups snow peas
2 cups small broccoli florets
2 cups matchstick-size
    carrot strips
2 cups sliced mushrooms
¼ cup plus 2 tablespoons
    water, divided
1 teaspoon cornstarch
3 tablespoons reduced-
    sodium soy sauce
3 to 4 teaspoons rice wine
    vinegar
1 tablespoon sesame oil
1 tablespoon Szechuan
    sauce
½ teaspoon Chinese 5-spice
    powder
3 cups coarsely chopped
    napa cabbage

SZECHUAN CHICKEN SALAD

Makes 6 servings

1. Cook noodles according to package directions; cool to room temperature.

2. Spray wok or large nonstick skillet with cooking spray; heat over medium-high heat until hot. Add chicken; stir-fry 5 to 7 minutes or until browned and no longer pink in center. Remove chicken from wok.

3. Add snow peas, broccoli, carrots, mushrooms and 2 tablespoons water to wok; cook, covered, 2 minutes. Uncover; stir-fry about 5 minutes or until vegetables are crisp-tender. Remove vegetables from wok.

4. Combine remaining ¼ cup water and cornstarch in small bowl; stir in soy sauce, vinegar, oil, Szechuan sauce and 5-spice powder. Add to wok; heat to a boil. Cook 1 minute, stirring constantly. Return chicken and vegetables to wok; toss to coat with cornstarch mixture.

5. Divide cabbage among 6 serving plates; arrange noodles over cabbage. Top with warm chicken mixture. Serve immediately.

NUTRIENTS PER SERVING:
Calories: 261, Total Fat: 4 g, Cholesterol: 37 mg, Sodium: 377 mg

SZECHUAN CHICKEN SALAD

3/4 pound lean beef round steak
2 tablespoons reduced-sodium soy sauce
1 tablespoon rice wine
2 teaspoons sugar
Korean-Style Dressing (recipe follows)
2 cups thinly sliced napa cabbage
1 3/4 cups thinly sliced yellow bell peppers
1/2 cup thinly sliced radishes
1 medium carrot, shredded
1 green onions, thinly sliced
1 package (about 7 ounces) rice noodles

KOREAN-STYLE BEEF AND PASTA

Makes 8 (1-cup) servings

1. Freeze beef until partially firm; cut into very thin slices. Combine soy sauce, rice wine and sugar in small nonmetallic bowl. Add beef slices; toss to coat evenly. Cover and refrigerate 8 hours or overnight.

2. Drain and discard marinade. Grill beef over medium-hot coals 2 to 3 minutes or until desired doneness.

3. Meanwhile, prepare Korean-Style Dressing; set aside.

4. Combine cabbage, bell peppers, radishes, carrot, green onions and beef in medium bowl. Add Korean-Style Dressing; toss to coat evenly. Serve over noodles. Garnish, if desired.

KOREAN-STYLE DRESSING

2 teaspoons sesame seeds
1/3 cup orange juice
2 tablespoons rice wine
2 teaspoons reduced-sodium soy sauce
1 teaspoon sugar
1 teaspoon grated fresh ginger
1 teaspoon dark sesame oil
1 clove garlic, minced
1/8 teaspoon crushed red pepper

1. Place sesame seeds in small nonstick skillet. Cook and stir over medium heat until lightly browned and toasted, about 5 minutes. Cool completely.

2. Crush sesame seeds using mortar and pestle or with wooden spoon; transfer to small bowl. Add remaining ingredients; blend well.

NUTRIENTS PER SERVING:
Calories: 194, Total Fat: 4 g, Cholesterol: 29 mg, Sodium: 668 mg

KOREAN-STYLE BEEF AND PASTA

½ cup A.1.® Steak Sauce
¼ cup soy sauce
2 cloves garlic, crushed
1 pound top round steak, thinly sliced
1 (16-ounce) bag frozen broccoli, red bell peppers, bamboo shoots and mushrooms, thawed*
Hot cooked rice (optional)

*1 (16-ounce) package frozen broccoli cuts, thawed, may be substituted.

BEEF 'N' BROCCOLI

Makes 4 servings

In small bowl, combine steak sauce, soy sauce and garlic. Pour marinade over steak in nonmetal dish. Cover; refrigerate 1 hour, stirring occasionally.

Remove steak from marinade; reserve marinade. In large lightly oiled skillet over medium-high heat, stir-fry steak 3 to 4 minutes or until steak is no longer pink. Remove steak with slotted spoon; keep warm.

In same skillet, heat vegetables and reserved marinade to a boil; reduce heat to low. Cover; simmer for 2 to 3 minutes. Stir in steak. Serve over rice, if desired.

NUTRIENTS PER SERVING:
Calories: 209, Total Fat: 4 g, Cholesterol: 65 mg, Sodium: 1669 mg

---

8 ounces beef flank steak
¼ cup reduced-sodium soy sauce
2 jalapeño peppers,* finely chopped
2 tablespoons packed brown sugar
1 clove garlic, minced
½ cup lime juice
6 green onions, thinly sliced
4 carrots, diagonally cut into thin slices
½ cup finely chopped fresh cilantro
6 romaine lettuce leaves

*Jalapeños can sting and irritate the skin; wear rubber gloves when handling peppers and do not touch eyes. Wash hands after handling.

THAI BEEF SALAD

Makes 4 servings

1. Place flank steak in resealable plastic food storage bag. Combine soy sauce, jalapeño peppers, brown sugar and garlic in small bowl; mix well. Pour mixture over flank steak. Close bag securely; turn to coat steak. Marinate in refrigerator 2 hours.

2. Preheat broiler. Drain steak; place on broiler pan. Broil 4 inches from heat about 4 minutes per side until desired doneness. Remove from heat; let rest 15 minutes.

3. Thinly slice steak across grain. Toss with lime juice, green onions, carrots and cilantro in large bowl. Serve salad immediately on lettuce leaves. Garnish with chives and radish flowers, if desired.

NUTRIENTS PER SERVING:
Calories: 141, Total Fat: 4 g, Cholesterol: 27 mg, Sodium: 238 mg

¾ pound boneless lean beef, such as sirloin or round steak

3 cups water

1 can (about 14 ounces) beef broth

1 can (10½ ounces) condensed consomme

2 tablespoons minced fresh ginger

2 tablespoons reduced-sodium soy sauce

1 cinnamon stick (3 inches long)

4 ounces rice noodles (rice sticks), about ⅛ inch wide

½ cup thinly sliced carrot or matchstick-size carrot strips

2 cups fresh mung bean sprouts, rinsed and drained

1 small red onion, halved and thinly sliced

½ cup chopped fresh cilantro

½ cup fresh basil leaves, chopped

2 jalapeño peppers,* stemmed, seeded and minced *or* 1 to 3 teaspoons Chinese chili sauce or paste

Jalapeños can sting and irritate the skin; wear rubber gloves when handling peppers and do not touch eyes. Wash hands after handling.

VIETNAMESE BEEF SOUP

Makes 6 servings

1. Place beef in freezer 45 minutes or until firm. Meanwhile, combine water, beef broth, consomme, ginger, soy sauce and cinnamon stick in large saucepan; bring to a boil over high heat. Reduce heat to low; simmer, covered, 20 to 30 minutes. Remove cinnamon stick; discard. Meanwhile, place rice noodles in large bowl and cover with warm water; let stand until pliable, about 20 minutes.

2. Slice beef across grain into very thin strips. Drain noodles. Place noodles and carrots in simmering broth; cook 2 to 3 minutes or until noodles are tender. Add beef and bean sprouts; cook 1 minute or until beef is no longer pink.

3. Remove from heat; stir in red onion, cilantro, basil and jalapeño peppers. To serve, lift noodles from soup with fork and place in bowls. Ladle remaining ingredients and broth over noodles.

NUTRIENTS PER SERVING:
Calories: 180, Total Fat: 3 g, Cholesterol: 32 mg, Sodium: 800 mg

4 boneless skinless chicken
    breast halves (1 pound)
⅛ teaspoon salt
⅛ teaspoon black pepper
½ cup finely chopped onion
    (1 small)
½ cup orange juice
2 teaspoons minced fresh
    ginger
1 teaspoon sugar
2 teaspoons cornstarch
¼ cup cold water
1 can (11 ounces) mandarin
    orange segments,
    drained
2 to 3 tablespoons finely
    chopped cilantro
2 cups hot cooked rice,
    prepared with unsalted
    water

Mandarin Orange Chicken

Makes 4 servings

1. Pound chicken slightly between 2 pieces of plastic wrap to ¼-inch thickness using flat side of meat mallet or rolling pin. Broil chicken, 6 inches from heat source, 7 to 8 minutes on each side until chicken is no longer pink in center. Or, grill chicken, on covered grill over medium-hot coals, 10 minutes on each side or until chicken is no longer pink in center. Sprinkle with salt and pepper.

2. Spray medium nonstick saucepan with nonstick cooking spray; heat over medium heat until hot. Add onion; cook and stir about 5 minutes or until tender. Add orange juice, ginger and sugar. Heat to a boil.

3. Combine cornstarch and water in small bowl; add to juice mixture, stirring until thickened. Boil 1 minute, stirring constantly. Stir in orange segments and cilantro. Serve chicken over rice; top with sauce. Garnish as desired.

NUTRIENTS PER SERVING:
Calories: 310, Total Fat: 3 g, Cholesterol: 58 mg, Sodium: 122 mg

MANDARIN ORANGE CHICKEN

1 cup rice-flour noodles
1 can (6 ounces) mandarin orange segments, chilled
1/3 cup honey
2 tablespoons rice vinegar
2 tablespoons reduced-sodium soy sauce
1 can (8 ounces) sliced water chestnuts, drained
4 cups shredded napa cabbage
1 cup shredded red cabbage
1/2 cup sliced radishes
4 thin slices red onion, cut in half and separated
3 boneless skinless chicken breast halves (about 12 ounces), cooked and cut into strips

MANDARIN CHICKEN SALAD

Makes 4 servings

1. Place rice-flour noodles in medium bowl; cover with water. Let stand 10 minutes; drain. Drain mandarin orange segments, reserving 1/3 cup liquid. Whisk together reserved liquid, honey, vinegar and soy sauce in small bowl. Add water chestnuts.

2. Divide napa and red cabbages, radishes and onion evenly among four serving plates. Top with chicken and orange segments. Remove water chestnuts from dressing and arrange on salads. Serve with rice-flour noodles; drizzle with remaining dressing.

PREP AND COOK TIME: 20 minutes

NUTRIENTS PER SERVING:
Calories: 258, Total Fat: 2 g, Cholesterol: 34 mg, Sodium: 318 mg

---

4 fresh California plums, sliced
2 tablespoons sugar
1 1/2 teaspoons minced fresh ginger *or* 1/2 teaspoon ground ginger
2 chicken breast halves, skinned and boned
1/2 teaspoon paprika
1/2 teaspoon black pepper

CHINESE PLUM-GLAZED CHICKEN

Makes 2 servings

To Microwave: Combine plums with sugar and ginger in microwave-safe dish. Sprinkle chicken breast halves with paprika and pepper. Arrange on top of plums. Cover dish with plastic wrap, turning back 1 edge about 1/2 inch to form steam vent. Microwave at MEDIUM (50% power) 5 minutes. Baste chicken with juices and rotate dish 1/4 turn. Microwave at MEDIUM 5 to 7 minutes more. Let stand, covered, 2 to 3 minutes. To serve, arrange chicken on 2 plates; serve with plum sauce.

NUTRIENTS PER SERVING:
Calories: 261, Total Fat: 4 g, Cholesterol: 71 mg, Sodium: 65 mg

Favorite recipe from **CALIFORNIA TREE FRUIT AGREEMENT**

MANDARIN CHICKEN SALAD

1 package (8½ ounces)
  Japanese udon noodles
1 teaspoon vegetable oil
1 medium red bell pepper,
  cut into thin strips
1 medium carrot, diagonally
  sliced
2 green onions, thinly sliced
2 cans (14½ ounces each)
  fat-free reduced-sodium
  beef broth
1 cup water
1 teaspoon reduced-sodium
  soy sauce
½ teaspoon grated fresh
  ginger
½ teaspoon black pepper
2 cups thinly sliced fresh
  shiitake mushrooms,
  stems removed
4 ounces daikon (Japanese
  radish), peeled and cut
  into thin strips
4 ounces firm tofu, drained
  and cut into ½-inch
  cubes

JAPANESE NOODLE SOUP

Makes 6 (1½-cup) servings

1. Cook noodles according to package directions, omitting salt. Drain and rinse; set aside.

2. Heat oil in large nonstick saucepan. Add bell pepper, carrot and green onions; cook until slightly softened, about 3 minutes. Stir in beef broth, water, soy sauce, ginger and black pepper. Bring to a boil. Add mushrooms, daikon and tofu. Reduce heat and simmer gently 5 minutes or until heated through.

3. Place noodles in soup tureen or individual bowls. Ladle soup over noodles. Serve immediately.

NUTRIENTS PER SERVING:
Calories: 144, Total Fat: 3 g, Cholesterol: 0 mg, Sodium: 107 mg

JAPANESE NOODLE SOUP

SPICY ORANGE ORIENTAL CHICKEN BREAST

Makes 6 servings

¼ cup CRISCO® Vegetable Oil
1 orange, juiced (about ⅓ cup)
1 tablespoon orange marmalade
1 teaspoon minced fresh ginger *or* ½ teaspoon ground ginger
1 teaspoon grated orange peel
1 teaspoon soy sauce
  Dash salt and pepper
6 boneless, skinless chicken breast halves (about 1½ pounds)

1. Combine Crisco® Oil, orange juice, marmalade, ginger, orange peel, soy sauce, salt and pepper in shallow baking dish. Stir well. Add chicken. Turn to coat. Refrigerate 30 to 45 minutes, turning once.

2. Prepare grill or heat broiler.

3. Remove chicken from orange juice marinade; discard marinade. Grill or broil 3 to 5 minutes per side or until chicken is no longer pink in center.

NUTRIENTS PER SERVING:
Calories: 165, Total Fat: 4 g, Cholesterol: 65 mg, Sodium: 95 mg

CHICKEN CURRY BOMBAY

Makes 4 servings

1 medium onion, cut into wedges
2 cloves garlic, minced
2 teaspoons curry powder
1 tablespoon olive oil
2 boneless chicken breast halves, skinned and sliced ¼-inch thick
1 can (14½ ounces) DEL MONTE® Original Style Stewed Tomatoes
⅓ cup seedless raisins
1 can (14½ ounces) DEL MONTE® FreshCut™ Whole New Potatoes, drained and cut into chunks
1 can (14½ ounces) DEL MONTE® FreshCut™ Cut Green Beans, drained

In large skillet, cook onion, garlic and curry in oil over medium-high heat until onion is tender, stirring occasionally. Stir in chicken, tomatoes with juice and raisins; bring to a boil. Reduce heat to low. Cover and simmer over medium heat 8 minutes. Add potatoes and green beans. Cook, uncovered, 5 minutes, stirring occasionally. Season to taste with salt and pepper, if desired.

PREP TIME: 10 minutes
COOK TIME: 18 minutes

NUTRIENTS PER SERVING:
Calories: 233, Total Fat: 5 g, Cholesterol: 34 mg, Sodium: 643 mg

6 ounces uncooked fresh
  Chinese egg noodles
  Nonstick cooking spray
½ cup fat-free reduced-
  sodium chicken broth
2 tablespoons reduced-
  sodium soy sauce
1½ teaspoons cornstarch
½ teaspoon dark sesame oil
½ teaspoon black pepper
⅛ teaspoon Chinese 5-spice
  powder
6 ounces boneless skinless
  chicken breasts,
  coarsely chopped
2 green onions, sliced
2 cups thinly sliced bok
  choy
1½ cups mixed frozen
  vegetables, thawed and
  drained
1 can (8 ounces) sliced
  water chestnuts, rinsed
  and drained
1 cup fresh bean sprouts,
  rinsed and drained

CHICKEN CHOW MEIN

Makes 4 servings

1. Preheat oven to 400°F. Cook noodles according to package directions, omitting salt. Drain and rinse well under cold water until pasta is cool; drain well. Lightly spray 9-inch cake pan with nonstick cooking spray. Spread noodles in pan, pressing firmly. Lightly spray top of noodles with nonstick cooking spray. Bake 10 minutes.

2. Invert noodles onto baking sheet or large plate. Carefully slide noodle cake back into cake pan. Bake 10 to 15 minutes or until top is crisp and lightly browned. Transfer to serving platter. Whisk together chicken broth, soy sauce, cornstarch, sesame oil, pepper and 5-spice powder in small bowl until cornstarch is dissolved; set aside.

3. Spray large nonstick skillet with nonstick cooking spray. Add chicken and green onions. Stir-fry over medium-high heat until chicken is no longer pink, about 5 minutes. Stir in bok choy, mixed vegetables and water chestnuts. Cook 3 minutes or until vegetables are crisp-tender. Push vegetables to one side of skillet; stir in broth mixture. Cook and stir until thickened, about 2 minutes. Stir in bean sprouts. Spoon over noodle cake.

NUTRIENTS PER SERVING:
Calories: 284, Total Fat: 2 g, Cholesterol: 22 mg, Sodium: 322 mg

1 can (about 14 ounces)
     fat-free reduced-sodium
     chicken broth, divided
2 tablespoons cornstarch
2 tablespoons reduced-
     sodium soy sauce
1 tablespoon grated orange
     peel
1 pork tenderloin (about
     10 ounces)
2 tablespoons peanut oil,
     divided
1 tablespoon sesame seeds
2 cloves garlic, minced
2 cups broccoli florets
2 cups sliced carrots
1 teaspoon Szechuan
     seasoning
6 cups hot cooked rice,
     prepared with unsalted
     water

Spicy Pork Stir-Fry

Makes 6 servings

1. Combine 1½ cups chicken broth, cornstarch, soy sauce and orange peel in medium bowl. Cut pork lengthwise, then cut crosswise into ¼-inch slices.

2. Heat 1 tablespoon oil in wok over high heat until hot. Add pork, sesame seeds and garlic. Stir-fry 3 minutes or until pork is barely pink in center. Remove from wok.

3. Heat remaining 1 tablespoon oil in wok until hot. Add broccoli, carrots, Szechuan seasoning and remaining chicken broth. Cook and stir 5 minutes or until vegetables are crisp-tender. Add pork. Stir chicken broth mixture and add to wok. Cook and stir over medium heat until sauce is thickened. Serve over rice.

PREP AND COOK TIME: 30 minutes

NUTRIENTS PER SERVING:
Calories: 415, Total Fat: 8 g, Cholesterol: 34 mg, Sodium: 266 mg

---

1 pound boneless pork loin,
     cut into thin strips
1 teaspoon vegetable oil
2 cloves garlic, minced
1 (10-ounce) package
     frozen cut green beans,
     thawed
2 teaspoons sugar
2 teaspoons soy sauce
½ teaspoon crushed red
     pepper
½ teaspoon ground ginger
1 teaspoon sesame oil
1 teaspoon vinegar
2 cups hot cooked rice
     (optional)

Pork and Bean Stir-Fry

Makes 4 servings

Heat vegetable oil in nonstick skillet; add pork strips and garlic and stir-fry until lightly browned. Add green beans; stir-fry until beans and pork are tender, about 5 minutes. Push meat and beans to one side of skillet. Add sugar, soy sauce, red pepper and ginger; stir to dissolve sugar. Add sesame oil and vinegar. Stir to coat. Serve immediately with cooked rice, if desired.

PREPARATION TIME: 15 minutes

NUTRIENTS PER SERVING:
Calories: 212, Total Fat: 9 g, Cholesterol: 66 mg, Sodium: 241 mg

Favorite recipe from **NATIONAL PORK PRODUCERS COUNCIL**

SPICY PORK STIR-FRY

4 ounces uncooked linguine
½ pound boneless skinless chicken breasts, cut into 2×½-inch pieces
2 cups broccoli florets
⅔ cup chopped red bell pepper
6 green onions, sliced diagonally into 1-inch pieces
¼ cup reduced-fat creamy peanut butter
2 tablespoons reduced-sodium soy sauce
2 teaspoons dark sesame oil
½ teaspoon crushed red pepper
⅛ teaspoon garlic powder
¼ cup unsalted peanuts, chopped

THAI CHICKEN BROCCOLI SALAD

Makes 4 servings

1. Cook pasta according to package directions, omitting salt. Drain.

2. Spray large nonstick skillet with nonstick cooking spray; heat over medium-high heat until hot. Add chicken; stir-fry 5 minutes or until chicken is no longer pink. Remove chicken from skillet.

3. Add broccoli and 2 tablespoons cold water to skillet. Cook, covered, 2 minutes. Uncover; cook and stir 2 minutes or until broccoli is crisp-tender. Remove broccoli from skillet. Combine pasta, chicken, broccoli, bell pepper and green onions in large bowl.

4. Combine peanut butter, 2 tablespoons hot water, soy sauce, oil, crushed red pepper and garlic powder in small bowl until well blended. Drizzle over pasta mixture; toss to coat. Top with peanuts before serving.

NUTRIENTS PER SERVING:
Calories: 275, Total Fat: 9 g, Cholesterol: 29 mg, Sodium: 14 mg

THAI CHICKEN BROCCOLI SALAD

1 stalk lemongrass, outer leaves removed and upper stalk trimmed
1 tablespoon sugar
1 tablespoon fish sauce
1 teaspoon minced garlic
½ to 1 teaspoon hot chili oil
2 (8-ounce) boneless beef top loin steaks, about 1 inch thick
1 can (about 8¾ ounces) whole baby corn (about 8 cobs), rinsed and drained
1 can (about 15 ounces) black beans, rinsed and drained
1 cup diced mango
½ green bell pepper, cut into strips
2 tablespoons chopped red onion
1 jalapeño pepper,* seeded and sliced (optional)
Juice of ½ lemon
½ teaspoon vegetable oil
½ teaspoon honey
⅛ teaspoon salt

*Jalapeños can sting and irritate the skin; wear rubber gloves when handling peppers and do not touch eyes. Wash hands after handling.

VIETNAMESE LOIN STEAKS WITH BLACK BEAN RELISH

Makes 4 servings

1. Flatten lemongrass with meat mallet and mince. Combine with sugar, fish sauce, garlic and chili oil in baking dish. Cut each steak lengthwise into 2 strips. Place in dish with marinade, coating both sides. Cover; refrigerate 1 hour, turning once.

2. To make Black Bean Relish, halve corn cobs diagonally; combine with beans, mango, bell pepper, onion and jalapeño pepper, if desired, in large bowl. Combine lemon juice, vegetable oil, honey and salt in small bowl; stir into bean mixture.

3. Grill steaks on covered grill over medium-hot coals 10 minutes for medium-rare or until desired doneness is reached, turning once. Serve with relish.

NUTRIENTS PER SERVING:
Calories: 353, Total Fat: 8 g, Cholesterol: 65 mg, Sodium: 877 mg

VIETNAMESE LOIN STEAK WITH BLACK BEAN RELISH

3 tablespoons soy sauce
1 tablespoon finely chopped green onion
2 teaspoons dark sesame oil
1 teaspoon minced fresh ginger
1 clove garlic, minced
¼ teaspoon crushed red pepper
1 pound red snapper, scrod or cod fillets

BROILED HUNAN FISH FILLETS

Makes 4 servings

1. Combine soy sauce, green onion, sesame oil, ginger, garlic and crushed red pepper in cup.

2. Spray rack of broiler pan with nonstick cooking spray. Place fish on rack; brush with soy sauce mixture.

3. Broil 4 to 5 inches from heat 10 minutes or until fish flakes easily when tested with fork.

NUTRIENTS PER SERVING:
Calories: 143, Total Fat: 4 g, Cholesterol: 42 mg, Sodium: 446 mg

---

¾ cup fat-free reduced-sodium chicken broth
1 tablespoon oyster sauce
1 teaspoon rice vinegar
1 tablespoon cornstarch
½ teaspoon sugar
2 teaspoons peanut oil
1 small red onion, cut into thin wedges
1 teaspoon minced fresh ginger
1 clove garlic, minced
½ pound medium shrimp, peeled and deveined
2 cups snow peas, cut diagonally into 1-inch pieces
3 cups hot cooked white rice, prepared with unsalted water

STIR-FRY SHRIMP AND SNOW PEAS

Makes 4 servings

1. Blend chicken broth, oyster sauce and rice vinegar into cornstarch and sugar in small bowl until smooth.

2. Heat oil in wok or large nonstick skillet over medium heat until hot. Add onion, ginger and garlic; stir-fry 2 minutes. Add shrimp and snow peas. Stir-fry 3 minutes or until shrimp is opaque.

3. Stir chicken broth mixture and add to wok. Cook 1 minute or until sauce comes to a boil and thickens. Serve over rice.

PREP AND COOK TIME: 25 minutes

NUTRIENTS PER SERVING:
Calories: 287, Total Fat: 3 g, Cholesterol: 88 mg, Sodium: 251 mg

¼ cup CRISCO® Canola Oil
¼ cup dry white wine
¼ cup reduced-sodium soy
   sauce
1½ teaspoons sesame seeds
1 teaspoon sugar
½ teaspoon ground ginger
1 pound Dover sole fillets
12 green onions
½ teaspoon black pepper
   (optional)

BROILED ORIENTAL FISH

Makes 4 servings

1. Heat broiler. Combine Crisco® Canola Oil, wine, soy sauce, sesame seeds, sugar and ginger in shallow baking dish. Stir until blended.

2. Place fillets in marinade. Turn to coat. Marinate 20 minutes; turn fillets occasionally.

3. Wash green onions. Trim tops so onions are 5 to 6 inches in length. Make 3-inch lengthwise slices in onion tops to give onions feathered look.

4. Place onions in marinade for last 10 minutes of marinating time.

5. Remove fish and onions from marinade. Place on broiler pan. Sprinkle with pepper, if desired. Place pan in oven 4 to 5 inches from heat.

6. Broil 3 minutes. Turn fish and onions carefully using pancake turner and broil 3 minutes more or until fish flakes easily when tested with fork.

To Microwave: Prepare and marinate fish and green onions as above. Remove fish and onions from marinade. Place in 12×8-inch microwave-safe dish. Sprinkle with pepper, if desired. Cover with vented plastic wrap. Microwave at HIGH (100% power) 2 minutes. Rotate dish. Microwave at HIGH 1½ minutes or until fish flakes easily when tested with fork. Let stand, covered, 1 minute.

NUTRIENTS PER SERVING:
Calories: 190, Total Fat: 9 g, Cholesterol: 75 mg, Sodium: 180 mg

3 tablespoons orange juice
1 tablespoon reduced-sodium soy sauce
1 clove garlic, minced
1 pound bay scallops or halved sea scallops
1 tablespoon cornstarch
1 teaspoon vegetable oil, divided
1 green bell pepper, cut into short, thin strips
1 can (8 ounces) sliced water chestnuts, rinsed and drained
3 tablespoons toasted blanched almonds
3 cups hot cooked white rice
½ teaspoon finely grated orange peel

ORANGE ALMOND SCALLOPS

Makes 4 servings

1. Combine orange juice, soy sauce and garlic in medium bowl. Add scallops; toss to coat. Marinate at room temperature 15 minutes or cover and refrigerate up to 1 hour.

2. Drain scallops; reserve marinade. Blend marinade into cornstarch in small bowl until smooth.

3. Heat ½ teaspoon oil in wok or large nonstick skillet over medium heat. Add scallops; stir-fry 2 minutes or until scallops are opaque. Remove and reserve.

4. Add remaining ½ teaspoon oil to wok. Add bell pepper and water chestnuts. Stir-fry 3 minutes.

5. Return scallops along with any accumulated juices to wok. Stir reserved marinade mixture and add to wok. Stir-fry 1 minute or until sauce boils and thickens. Stir in almonds. Serve over rice. Sprinkle with orange peel. Garnish with orange peel strips and fresh herbs, if desired.

NUTRIENTS PER SERVING:
Calories: 427, Total Fat: 7 g, Cholesterol: 60 mg, Sodium: 442 mg

ORANGE ALMOND SCALLOPS

4 boneless skinless chicken breast halves (about 12 ounces)
1 tablespoon lemon juice
¼ cup plain nonfat yogurt
2 large cloves garlic, minced
1 ½ teaspoons finely chopped fresh ginger
¼ teaspoon ground cardamom
¼ teaspoon ground red pepper
    Yogurt Sauce (recipe follows)
2 whole wheat pitas, cut into halves
½ cup grated carrot
½ cup finely shredded red cabbage
½ cup finely chopped red bell pepper

TANDOORI CHICKEN BREAST SANDWICHES WITH YOGURT SAUCE

Makes 4 servings

1. Score chicken breast halves 3 or 4 times. Place in medium bowl; sprinkle with lemon juice and toss to coat.

2. Combine yogurt, garlic, ginger, cardamom and ground red pepper in small bowl; add to chicken. Coat all pieces well with marinade; cover and refrigerate at least 1 hour or overnight.

3. Remove chicken from refrigerator 15 minutes before cooking. Preheat broiler. Prepare Yogurt Sauce; set aside.

4. Line broiler pan with foil. Arrange chicken on foil (do not let pieces touch) and brush with any remaining marinade. Broil 3 inches from heat about 5 to 6 minutes per side or until chicken is no longer pink in center.

5. Place one chicken breast half in each pita half with 2 tablespoons each of carrot, cabbage and bell pepper. Drizzle sandwiches with Yogurt Sauce. Garnish, if desired.

YOGURT SAUCE
    ½ cup plain nonfat yogurt
    2 teaspoons minced red onion
    1 teaspoon minced cilantro
    ¼ teaspoon ground cumin
    ¼ teaspoon salt
       Dash ground red pepper

Blend all ingredients well in small bowl. Cover and refrigerate until ready to use.   *Makes about ½ cup*

NUTRIENTS PER SERVING:
Calories: 211, Total Fat: 3 g, Cholesterol: 44 mg, Sodium: 380 mg

TANDOORI CHICKEN BREAST SANDWICH WITH YOGURT SAUCE

2 Florida oranges
1 ¼ pounds top round steak, trimmed
½ cup Florida orange juice, divided
2 tablespoons low-sodium soy sauce
1 tablespoon plus
    1 teaspoon cornstarch, divided
2 teaspoons brown sugar, divided
½ cup low-sodium chicken broth
1 tablespoon dark sesame oil
1 teaspoon finely minced gingerroot
1 clove garlic, minced
4 cups broccoli flowerets
4 medium scallions, cut into 2-inch pieces
1 can (8 ounces) sliced water chestnuts, rinsed and drained
3 tablespoons chopped fresh cilantro

STIR-FRIED ORANGE BEEF

Makes 6 servings

Remove thin strips of rind from oranges with paring knife or zester; set aside. Section oranges; set aside. Cut steak along grain into 2-inch-wide strips. Cut steak across grain into ¼-inch-thick slices.

Combine steak, 2 tablespoons orange juice, soy sauce, 1 tablespoon cornstarch and 1 teaspoon brown sugar; stir to combine. Set aside.

Combine chicken broth, remaining 6 tablespoons orange juice, 1 teaspoon cornstarch and 1 teaspoon brown sugar in small bowl until well blended. Heat sesame oil in large nonstick skillet over medium-high heat until hot, but not smoking. Add reserved steak; stir-fry 3 to 4 minutes until steak is browned. Remove from skillet. Add ginger, garlic, reserved orange rind, broccoli, scallions, water chestnuts and chicken broth mixture. Stir-fry 2 to 3 minutes until vegetables begin to soften. Add cilantro and reserved steak (with juices); cook and stir until sauce has thickened slightly. Stir in orange sections and serve immediately.

NUTRIENTS PER SERVING:
Calories: 252, Total Fat: 7 g, Cholesterol: 66 mg, Sodium: 248 mg

Favorite recipe from **FLORIDA DEPARTMENT OF CITRUS**

1 cup chopped red onions
2 tablespoons vegetable oil
¾ pound medium shrimp, shelled and deveined
¼ cup chicken broth
1 tablespoon curry powder
4 cups cooked long-grain rice
2 cups frozen mixed carrots and peas, thawed
1 tablespoon soy sauce
3 medium, firm DOLE® Bananas, sliced
½ cup flaked coconut, toasted

CURRY COCONUT FRIED RICE

Makes 6 servings

■ **Cook** and stir onions in hot oil in large skillet over medium-high heat until tender-crisp.

■ **Add** shrimp, broth and curry powder; cook and stir until shrimp is pink. Add rice, and carrots and peas; cook and stir 3 to 5 minutes or until heated through.

■ **Stir** in soy sauce. Add bananas; cook and stir 1 minute or until heated through. Sprinkle with coconut, before serving.

PREP TIME: 25 minutes
COOK TIME: 20 minutes

NUTRIENTS PER SERVING:
Calories: 325, Total Fat: 7 g, Cholesterol: 86 mg, Sodium: 669 mg

8 ounces fresh or steamed Chinese egg noodles

¼ cup fat-free reduced-sodium chicken broth

2 tablespoons rice wine vinegar

2 tablespoons reduced-sodium soy sauce

1 tablespoon rice wine or dry sherry

1 teaspoon sugar

½ teaspoon crushed red pepper

1 tablespoon vegetable oil, divided

1½ cups fresh snow peas, sliced diagonally

1 cup thinly sliced green or red bell pepper

1 clove garlic, minced

1 pound boneless skinless chicken breasts, cut into ½-inch pieces

1 cup thinly sliced red or green cabbage

2 green onions, thinly sliced

HOT CHINESE CHICKEN SALAD

Makes 6 (1⅓-cup) servings

1. Cook noodles in boiling water 4 to 5 minutes or until tender. Drain and set aside.

2. Combine chicken broth, vinegar, soy sauce, rice wine, sugar and crushed red pepper in small bowl; set aside.

3. Heat 1 teaspoon oil in large nonstick skillet or wok. Add snow peas, bell pepper and garlic; cook 1 to 2 minutes or until vegetables are crisp-tender. Set aside.

4. Heat remaining 2 teaspoons oil in skillet. Add chicken and cook 3 to 4 minutes or until chicken is no longer pink. Add cabbage, cooked vegetables and noodles. Stir in broth mixture; toss to coat evenly. Cook and stir 1 to 2 minutes or until heated through. Sprinkle with green onions before serving.

NUTRIENTS PER SERVING:
Calories: 164, Total Fat: 6 g, Cholesterol: 45 mg, Sodium: 353 mg

HOT CHINESE CHICKEN SALAD

1¼ pounds large shrimp
1 large onion, chopped
½ cup canned light coconut
   milk
2 tablespoons finely
   chopped fresh ginger
3 cloves garlic, minced
2 to 3 teaspoons hot curry
   powder
¼ teaspoon salt
1 can (14½ ounces) diced
   tomatoes
1 teaspoon cornstarch
2 tablespoons chopped
   fresh cilantro
3 cups hot cooked rice,
   prepared with unsalted
   water

SHRIMP CURRY

Makes 6 servings

1. Peel shrimp, leaving tails attached and reserving shells. Place shells in large saucepan; cover with water. Bring to a boil over high heat. Reduce heat to low; simmer 15 to 20 minutes. Strain shrimp stock and set aside. Discard shells.

2. Spray large skillet with nonstick cooking spray; heat over medium heat. Add onion; cover and cook 5 minutes. Add coconut milk, ginger, garlic, curry powder, salt and ½ cup shrimp stock; bring to a boil. Reduce heat to low and simmer 10 to 15 minutes or until onion is tender.

3. Add shrimp and tomatoes to skillet; return mixture to a simmer. Cook 3 minutes.

4. Stir cornstarch into 1 tablespoon cooled shrimp stock until dissolved. Add mixture to skillet with cilantro; simmer 1 to 2 minutes or just until slightly thickened, stirring occasionally. Serve over rice. Garnish with carrot and lime slices, if desired.

NUTRIENTS PER SERVING:
Calories: 219, Total Fat: 2 g, Cholesterol: 145 mg, Sodium: 369 mg

SHRIMP CURRY

2 egg whites, slightly beaten
¾ cup fresh bread crumbs
2 tablespoons sesame seeds (optional)
¾ teaspoon salt
¼ teaspoon black pepper
4 boneless skinless chicken breast halves (about 1¼ pounds)
2 tablespoons all-purpose flour
¾ cup fat-free reduced-sodium chicken broth
4 teaspoons cornstarch
¼ cup fresh lemon juice
2 tablespoons brown sugar
1 tablespoon honey
2 tablespoons vegetable oil
4 cups thinly sliced napa cabbage or romaine lettuce

LIGHT-STYLE LEMON CHICKEN

Makes 4 servings

1. Place egg whites in shallow dish. Combine bread crumbs, sesame seeds, salt and pepper in another shallow dish.

2. Dust chicken with flour; dip into egg whites. Roll in crumb mixture.

3. Blend broth into cornstarch in small bowl until smooth. Stir in lemon juice, brown sugar and honey.

4. Heat oil in large nonstick skillet over medium heat. Add chicken; cook 5 minutes. Turn chicken over; cook 5 to 6 minutes until browned and juices run clear. Transfer to cutting board; keep warm.

5. Wipe skillet clean with paper towel. Stir broth mixture and add to skillet. Cook and stir 3 to 4 minutes until sauce boils and thickens.

6. Place cabbage on serving dish. Cut chicken crosswise into ½-inch slices; place over cabbage. Pour sauce over chicken. Garnish with lemon slices and fresh herbs, if desired.

NUTRIENTS PER SERVING:
Calories: 292, Total Fat: 10 g, Cholesterol: 57 mg, Sodium: 541 mg

LIGHT-STYLE LEMON CHICKEN

⅓ cup teriyaki sauce
2 cloves garlic, minced
¾ pound pork tenderloin
2 tablespoons peanut or
   vegetable oil, divided
1 small red onion, cut into
   thin wedges
1 small yellow onion, cut
   into thin wedges
1 teaspoon sugar
1 teaspoon cornstarch
2 green onions, cut into
   1-inch pieces
Fried bean threads*
   (optional)

*To fry bean threads, follow
package directions.

PORK WITH THREE ONIONS

Makes 4 servings

1. Combine teriyaki sauce and garlic in shallow bowl. Cut pork across the grain into ¼-inch slices; cut each slice in half. Toss pork with teriyaki mixture. Marinate at room temperature 10 minutes.

2. Heat large skillet over medium-high heat. Add 1 tablespoon oil; heat until hot. Drain pork; reserve marinade. Stir-fry pork 3 minutes or until no longer pink. Remove and set aside.

3. Heat remaining 1 tablespoon oil in skillet; add red and yellow onions. Reduce heat to medium. Cook 4 to 5 minutes until onions are softened, stirring occasionally. Sprinkle with sugar; cook 1 minute more.

4. Blend reserved marinade into cornstarch in cup until smooth. Stir into skillet. Stir-fry 1 minute or until sauce boils and thickens.

5. Return pork along with any accumulated juices to skillet; heat through. Stir in green onions. Serve over bean threads, if desired.

NUTRIENTS PER SERVING:
Calories: 217, Total Fat: 10 g, Cholesterol: 61 mg, Sodium: 958 mg

ACKNOWLEDGMENTS

A.1.® Steak Sauce
Alpine Lace Brands, Inc.
Birds Eye®
Blue Diamond Growers®
California Tree Fruit Agreement
Christopher Ranch Garlic
Delmarva Poultry Industry, Inc.
Del Monte Corporation
Diamond Walnut Growers, Inc.
Dole Food Company, Inc.
Florida Department of Agriculture
    and Consumer Services, Bureau
    of Seafood and Aquaculture
Florida Department of Citrus
GREY POUPON® Mustard
Heinz U.S.A.
Hunt-Wesson, Inc.
Jones Dairy Farm
Kikkoman International Inc.
The Kingsford Products Company
Lawry's® Foods, Inc.
Lee Kum Kee (USA) Inc.
Lipton™
McCormick®/Schilling®
McIlhenny Company

MOTT'S® Inc., a division of Cadbury
    Beverages
National Broiler Council
National Cattlemen's Beef Association
National Honey Board
National Onion Association
National Pork Producers Council
National Turkey Federation
North Dakota Beef Commission
Perdue Farms Incorporated
PLANTERS® Peanuts
Plochman, Inc.
The Procter & Gamble Company
The Quaker® Kitchens
Reckitt & Colman, Inc.
Riviana Foods, Inc.
The J.M. Smucker Company
StarKist® Seafood Company
The Sugar Association, Inc.
Sunkist Growers
Surimi Seafood Education Center
Texas Peanut Producers Board
USA Rice Federation
Walnut Marketing Board
Washington Apple Commission

INDEX

A

Almonds
Almond Broccoli Stir-Fry, 300
Almond Chicken, 136
Almond Chicken Salad Shanghai, 260
Lamb Meatballs in Spicy Gravy, 72
Orange Almond Scallops, 362
Pork Chops with Almond Plum Sauce, 112

Apples
Chicken Curry, 158, 168
Crispy Duck, 174
Golden Pork Stir-Fry, 100

Apricot
Apricot-Chicken Pot Stickers, 22
Curried Apricot Glazed Shrimp and Beef, 206
Aromatic Asian Beef Stew, 51
Asian Drums, 14
Asian Ginger Glazed Pork, 98
Asian Noodle Soup, 268
Asian Sesame Rice, 323
Asian-Style Vegetable Stir-Fry, 300
Asian Swordfish, 218

Asparagus
Asparagus Chicken with Black Bean Sauce, 155
Brown Rice and Shiitake Pilaf, 319
Stir-Fried Pork and Veggies, 119
August Moon Korean Ribs, 118

B

Baked Chicken Bombay, 140
Baked Fish with Thai Pesto, 224
Bananas: Curry Coconut Fried Rice, 367
Barbecued Pork, 30
Barbecued Pork Tenderloin, 37
Barbecued Ribs, 86

Basil
Baked Fish with Thai Pesto, 224
Pineapple Basil Chicken Supreme, 146
Thai Shrimp Curry, 222
Vietnamese Beef Soup, 345
Bean Curd with Oyster Sauce, 202
Bean Threads with Tofu and Vegetables, 180

Beef *(see also pages 38–83)*
Beef 'n' Broccoli, 344
Beef Soup with Noodles, 281
Curried Apricot Glazed Shrimp and Beef, 206
Egg Rolls, 15
Hot to Go Thai Salad, 246
Korean-Style Beef and Pasta, 342
Oriental Beef Salad, 261
Oriental Shrimp & Steak Kabobs, 226
Stir-Fried Beef & Eggplant Salad, 249
Stir-Fried Orange Beef, 366
Stir-Fry Beef & Vegetable Soup, 278
Thai Beef Salad, 248, 344

Beef *(continued)*
Thai Grilled Beef Salad, 258
Vietnamese Beef Soup, 345
Vietnamese Loin Steaks with Black Bean Relish, 358
Beef and Broccoli, 56
Beef & Broccoli Stir-Fry, 38
Beef & Napa with Noodles, 82
Beef Benihana, 74
Beef with Bean Threads and Cabbage, 66
Beef with Snow Peas & Baby Corn, 60
Beefy Bean & Walnut Stir-Fry, 82
Black Bean Garlic Fish, 218

Bok Choy
Almond Chicken, 136
Chicken Chow Mein, 353
Ground Turkey Spring Rolls, 28
Wonton Soup, 286
Bombay Potatoes, 298
Braised Cornish Hens, 144
Braised Lion's Head, 90
Braised Shrimp with Vegetables, 236

Broccoli
Almond Broccoli Stir-Fry, 300
Asian-Style Vegetable Stir-Fry, 300
Beef and Broccoli, 56
Beef 'n' Broccoli, 344
Beef & Broccoli Stir-Fry, 38
Braised Shrimp with Vegetables, 236
Broccoli-Tofu Stir-Fry, 339

Broccoli (continued)
Broccoli with Tangerine Ginger Sauce, 294
Buddha's Delightful Vegetables, 299
Chicken Thai Stir-Fry, 134
Chinese Vegetables, 302
Crispy Orange Vegetables and Tofu, 203
Ginger Beef & Noodle Stir-Fry, 56
Golden Pork Stir-Fry, 100
Hoisin Chicken, 128
Indian Vegetable Curry, 176
Ma Po Tofu, 196
Seafood Stir-Fry with Indonesian Rice, 228
Sesame Broccoli, 316
Sesame Chicken and Vegetable Stir-Fry, 330
Smucker's® Mandarin Shrimp and Vegetable Stir-Fry, 219
Spicy Beef and Broccoli Stir-Fry, 74
Spicy Pork Stir-Fry, 354
Stir-Fried Orange Beef, 366
Stir-Fried Turkey with Broccoli, 138
Sweet & Sour Mustard Pork, 104
Szechuan Chicken Salad, 340
Szechuan Vegetable Stir-Fry, 182
Teriyaki Beef, 48
Teriyaki Steak Strip Kabobs, 70
Teriyaki Stir-Fry Chicken Dinner, 143
Thai Chicken Broccoli Salad, 356
Tofu Stir-Fry, 188
Broiled Hunan Fish Fillets, 360
Broiled Oriental Fish, 361
Brown Rice and Shiitake Pilaf, 319
Buddha's Delightful Vegetables, 299

C

Cabbage
Apricot-Chicken Pot Stickers, 22
Beef & Napa with Noodles, 82
Beef with Bean Threads and Cabbage, 66
Braised Lion's Head, 90
Buddha's Delightful Vegetables, 299

Cabbage (continued)
Chinese Chicken Salad, 264
Egg Rolls, 15
Gingered Chicken Pot Stickers, 18
Golden Pork Stir-Fry, 100
Hot 'n Crunchy Thai Pork Salad with Spicy Peanut Dressing, 266
Hot Chinese Chicken Salad, 368
Indonesian Vegetable Salad, 254
Jones® Ham Stir-Fry Pasta Salad, 250
Korean-Style Beef and Pasta, 342
Light-Style Lemon Chicken, 372
Long Soup, 270
Mandarin Chicken Salad, 348
Mongolian Lamb, 58
Mu Shu Pork, 122
Mu Shu Vegetables, 186
Oriental Cabbage, 295
Pad Thai, 210
Soba Stir-Fry, 204
Spring Rolls, 24
Szechuan Chicken Salad, 340
Tender-ness Turkey Stir-Fry Salad, 252
Thai Pork Burritos, 113
Thai-Style Salad with Shredded Glazed Chicken, 262
Cantonese Rice Cake Patties, 319
Canton Pork Stew, 110
Caramelized Lemongrass Chicken, 160

Cashews
Honey Nut Stir-Fry, 114
Lemon Cashew Chicken Stir-Fry, 126
Peking Cashew Rice, 310
Pineapple Basil Chicken Supreme, 146

Cauliflower
Indian-Style Vegetable Stir-Fry, 292
Indian Vegetable Curry, 176
Lentil Rice Curry, 198

Chicken (see also pages 126–175)
Almond Chicken Salad Shanghai, 260
Apricot-Chicken Pot Stickers, 22

Chicken (continued)
Asian Drums, 14
Chicken and Cucumber Salad, 257
Chicken Chow Mein, 353
Chicken Curry Bombay, 352
Chicken Satay with Peanut Sauce, 10
Chicken Sesame with Oriental Crème, 8
Chinese Chicken Noodle Soup, 276
Chinese Chicken Salad, 264
Chinese Plum-Glazed Chicken, 348
Gingered Chicken Pot Stickers, 18
Hot Chinese Chicken Salad, 368
Japanese Yakitori, 336
Light-Style Lemon Chicken, 372
Mandarin Chicken Salad, 348
Mandarin Orange Chicken, 346
Pad Thai, 334
Plum Chicken, 324
Sesame Chicken and Vegetable Stir-Fry, 330
Soy-Braised Chicken Wings, 16
Spicy Orange Oriental Chicken Breasts, 352
Szechuan Chicken Salad, 340
Tandoori Chicken Breast Sandwiches with Yogurt Sauce, 364
Tandoori-Style Chicken with Cucumber Raita, 332
Thai Chicken Broccoli Salad, 356
Thai Noodle Soup, 270
Thai-Style Salad with Shredded Glazed Chicken, 262
Chicken Curry, 158, 168
Chicken Fried Rice, 167
Chicken Thai Stir-Fry, 134
Chili Garlic Prawns, 232
Chilled Shrimp in Chinese Mustard Sauce, 34
Chinatown Turkey Salad, 267
Chinese Chicken & Walnut Stir-Fry, 149
Chinese Chicken Noodle Soup, 276
Chinese Chicken Rolls, 166
Chinese Chicken Salad, 264

Chinese Mixed Pickled Vegetables, 314
Chinese Plum-Glazed Chicken, 348
Chinese Vegetables, 302
Cilantro
Baked Chicken Bombay, 140
Baked Fish with Thai Pesto, 224
Lamb Meatballs in Spicy Gravy, 72
Pad Thai, 210
Shrimp Java, 222
Thai Barbecued Chicken, 156
Thai Beef Salad, 344
Thai Fried Rice, 96
Thai Salad Rolls with Spicy Sweet & Sour Sauce, 26
Vietnamese Beef Soup, 345
Clarified Butter, 170
Coconut: Curry Coconut Fried Rice, 367
Coconut Milk
Coconut Ginger Rice, 208
Masaman Curry Beef, 46
Shrimp Curry, 370
Thai Shrimp Curry, 222
Cornish Hens: Braised Cornish Hens, 144
Crabmeat
Crab-Stuffed Shrimp, 214
Stir-Fried Crab, 236
Crispy Duck, 174
Crispy Orange Vegetables and Tofu, 203
Cucumbers
Chicken and Cucumber Salad, 257
Chinese Mixed Pickled Vegetables, 314
Cucumber Raita, 333
Glass Noodles with Peanut Sauce, 172
Hot and Sour Shrimp, 240
Hot to Go Thai Salad, 246
Indonesian Vegetable Salad, 254
Japanese Petal Salad, 250
Raita, 142
Sesame Noodles, 202
Thai Beef Salad, 248
Thai Grilled Beef Salad, 258

Cucumbers (continued)
Thai Salad Rolls with Spicy Sweet & Sour Sauce, 26
Thai-Style Salad with Shredded Glazed Chicken, 262
Curried Apricot Glazed Shrimp and Beef, 206
Curried Beef Kabobs, 73
Curried Pork Kabobs, 124
Curries
Chicken Curry, 158, 168
Chicken Curry Bombay, 352
Curried Shrimp with Coconut Ginger Rice, 208
Indian Vegetable Curry, 176
Lentil Rice Curry, 198
Masaman Curry Beef, 46
Shrimp Curry, 370
Thai Shrimp Curry, 222
Curry Coconut Fried Rice, 367

D
Dim Sum Pork Buns, 36
Dragon Tofu, 190
Dry-Cooked Green Beans, 312
Duck: Crispy Duck, 174

E
Easy Seafood Stir-Fry, 212
Easy Wonton Chips, 29
Egg Foo Yung, 197
Egg Roll, Wonton or Rice Paper Wrappers
Apricot-Chicken Pot Stickers, 22
Easy Wonton Chips, 29
Egg Rolls, 15
Gingered Chicken Pot Stickers, 18
Ginger Wonton Soup, 328
Vietnamese Summer Rolls, 12
Vietnamese Vegetarian Spring Rolls, 32
Wonton Soup, 286
Egg Rolls, 15

F
Fish
Asian Swordfish, 218
Baked Fish with Thai Pesto, 224
Black Bean Garlic Fish, 218
Broiled Hunan Fish Fillets, 360
Broiled Oriental Fish, 361

Fish (continued)
Grilled Chinese Salmon, 234
Grilled Swordfish with Hot Red Sauce, 242
Lemon Teriyaki Halibut, 226
Seared Salmon Teriyaki, 216
Shanghai Fish Packets, 230
Sweet and Sour Fish, 229
Thai-Style Tuna Fried Rice, 238
Tuna Teriyaki, 237
Fragrant Basmati Rice, 198

G
Garam Masala, 149, 333
Ginger Beef, 59
Ginger Beef & Noodle Stir-Fry, 56
Gingered Chicken Pot Stickers, 18
Gingered Chicken Thighs, 170
Ginger Noodles with Sesame Egg Strips, 311
Ginger Wonton Soup, 328
Glass Noodles with Peanut Sauce, 172
Glazed Pork and Pepper Kabobs, 88
Golden Pork Stir-Fry, 100
Green Beans and Shiitake Mushrooms, 290
Green Onion Curls, 30
Grilled Dishes
Asian Swordfish, 218
August Moon Korean Ribs, 118
Chicken Satay with Peanut Sauce, 10
Curried Apricot Glazed Shrimp and Beef, 206
Curried Beef Kabobs, 73
Curried Pork Kabobs, 124
Glazed Pork and Pepper Kabobs, 88
Grilled Chinese Salmon, 234
Grilled Swordfish with Hot Red Sauce, 242
Honey-Lime Glazed Chicken, 130
Japanese Yakitori, 336
Korean Beef Short Ribs, 54
Korean-Style Beef and Pasta, 342
Lemon Teriyaki Halibut, 226
Marinated Flank Steak with Pineapple, 44

Grilled Dishes (continued)
Oriental Flank Steak, 70
Oriental Glazed Tenderloins, 114
Oriental Grilled Chicken, 132
Oriental Shrimp & Steak
Kabobs, 226
Peanut Pork Tenderloin, 113
Pineapple Teriyaki Marinated
Steak, 60
Sesame-Garlic Flank Steak, 80
Shanghai Fish Packets, 230
Spicy Glazed Short Ribs, 45
Spicy Orange Oriental Chicken
Breasts, 352
Spicy Thai Chicken, 173
Sweet and Sour Chicken Breasts,
173
Szechuan Grilled Flank Steak,
40
Szechuan Wings, 167
Tandoori-Style Chicken with
Cucumber Raita, 332
Tandoori Turkey Kabobs, 142
Teriyaki Lamb Riblet Appetizers,
29
Teriyaki Plum Chicken, 152
Teriyaki Steak Strip Kabobs, 70
Thai Barbecued Chicken, 156
Thai Beef Salad, 248
Thai Grilled Beef Salad, 258
Thai Satay Chicken Skewers, 164
Thai-Style Pork Kabobs, 326
Vietnamese Grilled Steak Wraps,
76
Vietnamese Loin Steaks with
Black Bean Relish, 358
Ground Turkey Spring Rolls, 28

H
Ham
Jones® Ham Stir-Fry Pasta Salad,
250
Spring Rolls, 24
Steamed Pork and Ham, 108
Hearty Egg Drop Soup, 272
Hoisin Chicken, 128
Hoisin Peanut Dipping Sauce, 34
Honey
Crispy Duck, 174
Honey-Glazed Pork, 89
Honey-Glazed Spareribs, 120
Honey-Lime Dressing, 262

Honey (continued)
Honey-Lime Glazed Chicken,
130
Honey Nut Stir-Fry, 114
Honey Sesame Tenderloin, 125
Indian Pork with Honey, 107
Korean-Style Honey Marinade,
323
Hot 'n Crunchy Thai Pork Salad
with Spicy Peanut Dressing,
266
Hot and Sour Shrimp, 240
Hot and Sour Soup, 280
Hot and Sour Zucchini, 294
Hot and Spicy Onion Beef, 67
Hot Chinese Chicken Salad, 368
Hot to Go Thai Salad, 246
Hunan Chili Beef, 78
Hunan Stir-Fry with Tofu, 118

I
Indian Carrot Soup, 282
Indian Pork with Honey, 107
Indian-Style Vegetable Stir-Fry,
292
Indian Vegetable Curry, 176
Indonesian Vegetable Salad, 254
Ivory, Rubies and Jade, 92

J
Japanese Noodle Soup, 350
Japanese Petal Salad, 250
Japanese Yakitori, 336
Jen's Ginger-Garlic Chicken
Drummettes, 132
Jones® Ham Stir-Fry Pasta Salad,
250

K
Kabobs
Curried Apricot Glazed Shrimp
and Beef, 206
Curried Beef Kabobs, 73
Curried Pork Kabobs, 124
Glazed Pork and Pepper Kabobs,
88
Japanese Yakitori, 336
Oriental Shrimp & Steak
Kabobs, 226
Tandoori Turkey Kabobs, 142
Teriyaki Steak Strip Kabobs, 70
Thai-Style Pork Kabobs, 326

Korean Beef Short Ribs, 54
Korean-Style Beef and Pasta, 342
Korean-Style Dressing, 342
Korean-Style Honey Marinade, 323
Kung Pao Chicken, 154

L
Lamb
Lamb Meatballs in Spicy Gravy,
72
Mongolian Lamb, 58
Teriyaki Lamb Riblet Appetizers,
29
Lemon
Lemon Cashew Chicken Stir-Fry,
126
Lemon Chicken, 150
Lemon-Orange Glazed Ribs, 94
Lemon Sesame Scallops, 220
Lemon Teriyaki Halibut, 226
Light-Style Lemon Chicken, 372
Lentil Rice Curry, 198
Light Teriyaki Sauce, 253
Lime
Honey-Lime Dressing, 262
Honey-Lime Glazed Chicken,
130
Long Soup, 270

M
Malabar Shrimp, 232
Mandarin Chicken Salad, 348
Mandarin Orange Chicken, 346
Mango: Vietnamese Loin Steaks
with Black Bean Relish, 358
Ma Po Tofu, 196
Marinade: Korean-Style Honey
Marinade, 323
Marinated Flank Steak with
Pineapple, 44
Masaman Curry Beef, 46
Masaman Curry Paste, 48
Mint
Thai Beef Salad, 248
Thai Salad Rolls with Spicy
Sweet & Sour Sauce, 26
Mixed Vegetables with Noodles
and Beef, 64
Mogul-Style Fried Chicken, 148
Mongolian Lamb, 58
Moo Goo Gai Pan, 135
Mu Shu Pork, 122

Mu Shu Vegetables, 186
Mustard
Chilled Shrimp in Chinese
Mustard Sauce, 34
Oriental Mustard Barbecue
Sauce, 322
Sweet & Sour Mustard Pork, 104
Thai Peanut Noodle Stir-Fry, 181

N
Noodle Dishes
Bean Threads with Tofu and
Vegetables, 180
Beef & Napa with Noodles, 82
Beef with Bean Threads and
Cabbage, 66
Chicken Chow Mein, 353
Ginger Beef & Noodle Stir-Fry, 56
Ginger Noodles with Sesame
Egg Strips, 311
Glass Noodles with Peanut
Sauce, 172
Hot Chinese Chicken Salad, 368
Mixed Vegetables with Noodles
and Beef, 64
Oriental Beef & Noodle Toss, 67
Oriental Tofu Noodle Salad with
Spicy Peanut Sauce, 191
Pad Thai, 210, 334
Plum Chicken, 324
Rice Noodles with Peppers, 306
Sesame Noodle Cake, 306
Sesame Noodles, 202
Sesame Peanut Noodles with
Green Onions, 304
Soba Stir-Fry, 204
Spicy Sesame Noodles, 320
Stir-Fried Sirloin & Spinach with
Noodles, 50
Sweet & Sour Mustard Pork, 104
Szechuan Cold Noodles, 310
Tender-ness Turkey Stir-Fry
Salad, 252
Thai Beef and Noodle Toss, 42
Thai Chicken Broccoli Salad,
356
Thai Peanut Noodle Stir-Fry, 181
Thai-Style Warm Noodle Salad,
244
Vegetarian Rice Noodles, 194
Wok Sukiyaki, 52
Nutty Rice, 116

O
Orange
Chinatown Turkey Salad, 267
Crispy Orange Vegetables and
Tofu, 203
Honey Nut Stir-Fry, 114
Lemon-Orange Glazed Ribs, 94
Mandarin Chicken Salad, 348
Mandarin Orange Chicken, 346
Orange Almond Scallops, 362
Orange Beef, 68
Orange Chicken Stir-Fry, 130
Sesame Noodles, 202
Smucker's® Mandarin Shrimp
and Vegetable Stir-Fry, 219
Spicy Orange Chicken, 162
Spicy Orange Oriental Chicken
Breasts, 352
Stir-Fried Orange Beef, 366
Thai-Style Salad with Shredded
Glazed Chicken, 262
Oriental Beef & Noodle Toss, 67
Oriental Beef Salad, 261
Oriental Cabbage, 295
Oriental Flank Steak, 70
Oriental Fried Rice, 288, 305
Oriental Glazed Tenderloins, 114
Oriental Grilled Chicken, 132
Oriental Mustard Barbecue Sauce,
322
Oriental Shrimp & Steak Kabobs,
226
Oriental Tofu Noodle Salad with
Spicy Peanut Sauce, 191

P
Pad Thai, 210, 334
Pasta
Asian Noodle Soup, 268
Beef Soup with Noodles, 281
Chicken Thai Stir-Fry, 134
Chinese Chicken Noodle Soup,
276
Crispy Orange Vegetables and
Tofu, 203
Hoisin Chicken, 128
Japanese Noodle Soup, 350
Jones® Ham Stir-Fry Pasta Salad,
250
Korean-Style Beef and Pasta, 342
Lemon Sesame Scallops, 220
Long Soup, 270

Pasta *(continued)*
Mandarin Chicken Salad, 348
Szechuan Chicken Salad, 340
Thai Noodle Soup, 270
Thai Salad Rolls with Spicy
Sweet & Sour Sauce, 26
Vietnamese Beef Soup, 345
Peanut Butter
Chicken Satay with Peanut
Sauce, 10
Glass Noodles with Peanut
Sauce, 172
Hoisin Peanut Dipping Sauce, 34
Peanut Pork Tenderloin, 113
Peanut Sauce, 188
Sesame Noodles, 202
Sesame Peanut Noodles with
Green Onions, 304
Spicy Peanut Sauce, 191
Tangy Peanut Sauce, 256
Thai Peanut Noodle Stir-Fry, 181
Peanuts
Asian Drums, 14
Masaman Curry Beef, 46
Mu Shu Vegetables, 186
Pad Thai, 210
Sesame-Peanut Spaghetti
Squash, 184
Szechuan Vegetable Stir-Fry,
182
Thai-Style Tuna Fried Rice, 238
Pearl-Rice Balls, 20
Peking Cashew Rice, 310
Pepper Beef, 81
Pineapple
Curried Beef Kabobs, 73
Curried Shrimp with Coconut
Ginger Rice, 208
Japanese Yakitori, 336
Marinated Flank Steak with
Pineapple, 44
Pineapple Basil Chicken
Supreme, 146
Pineapple Teriyaki Marinated
Steak, 60
Shanghai Party Pleasers, 21
Sweet and Sour Fish, 229
Sweet & Sour Mustard Pork, 104
Sweet and Sour Pork, 84
Sweet & Sour Pork, 101
Teriyaki Steak Strip Kabobs, 70
Thai Shrimp Curry, 222

Plum
Chinese Plum-Glazed Chicken, 348
Plum Chicken, 324
Plum-Good Pork, 338
Plum Sauce, 37
Pork Chops with Almond Plum Sauce, 112
Tandoori Pork Sauté, 116
Teriyaki Plum Chicken, 152
Pork *(see also pages 84–125)*
Barbecued Pork, 30
Barbecued Pork Tenderloin, 37
Dim Sum Pork Buns, 36
Dry-Cooked Green Beans, 312
Ginger Wonton Soup, 328
Hearty Egg Drop Soup, 272
Hot 'n Crunchy Thai Pork Salad with Spicy Peanut Dressing, 266
Hot and Sour Soup, 280
Long Soup, 270
Pearl-Rice Balls, 20
Plum-Good Pork, 338
Pork and Bean Stir-Fry, 354
Pork Tenderloin Stir-Fry, 338
Pork with Three Onions, 374
Savory Pork Stir-Fry, 330
Spicy Pork Stir-Fry, 354
Thai-Style Pork Kabobs, 326
Wonton Soup, 286
Pork Chops with Almond Plum Sauce, 112

R
Raita, 142
Rice Dishes
Asian Sesame Rice, 323
Brown Rice and Shiitake Pilaf, 319
Cantonese Rice Cake Patties, 319
Chicken Fried Rice, 167
Coconut Ginger Rice, 208
Curried Shrimp with Coconut Ginger Rice, 208
Curry Coconut Fried Rice, 367
Fragrant Basmati Rice, 198
Hot to Go Thai Salad, 246
Lentil Rice Curry, 198
Nutty Rice, 116
Oriental Fried Rice, 288, 305

Rice Dishes *(continued)*
Pearl-Rice Balls, 20
Peking Cashew Rice, 310
Seafood Stir-Fry with Indonesian Rice, 228
Sizzling Rice Cakes with Mushrooms and Bell Peppers, 192
Tandoori Pork Sauté, 116
Thai Fried Rice, 96
Thai Rice, 318
Thai-Style Tuna Fried Rice, 238
Rice Noodles with Peppers, 306
Roasted Pork, 95

S
Salad Dressings
Honey-Lime Dressing, 262
Korean-Style Dressing, 342
Sesame Dressing, 250
Salads *(see also pages 244–267)*
Hot Chinese Chicken Salad, 368
Mandarin Chicken Salad, 348
Oriental Tofu Noodle Salad with Spicy Peanut Sauce, 191
Szechuan Chicken Salad, 340
Thai Beef Salad, 344
Thai Chicken Broccoli Salad, 356
Sandwiches
Tandoori Chicken Breast Sandwiches with Yogurt Sauce, 364
Tandoori-Style Chicken with Cucumber Raita, 332
Tandoori Turkey Kabobs, 142
Thai Chicken Satays, 152
Satays
Chicken Satay with Peanut Sauce, 10
Thai Chicken Satays, 152
Thai Satay Chicken Skewers, 164
Sauces
Cucumber Raita, 333
Hoisin Peanut Dipping Sauce, 34
Light Teriyaki Sauce, 253
Oriental Mustard Barbecue Sauce, 322
Peanut Sauce, 188
Plum Sauce, 37
Raita, 142
Spicy Peanut Sauce, 191

Sauces *(continued)*
Spicy Sweet & Sour Sauce, 24
Sweet and Sour Cooking Sauce, 100
Tangy Peanut Sauce, 256
Vietnamese Dipping Sauce, 12
Yogurt Sauce, 364
Savory Pork Stir-Fry, 330
Scallops
Easy Seafood Stir-Fry, 212
Lemon Sesame Scallops, 220
Orange Almond Scallops, 362
Seafood Stir-Fry with Indonesian Rice, 228
Seared Salmon Teriyaki, 216
Seoul Rolled Beef with Vegetables, 62
Sesame Chicken and Vegetable Stir-Fry, 330
Sesame Dressing, 250
Sesame-Garlic Flank Steak, 80
Sesame Noodle Cake, 306
Sesame Noodles, 202
Sesame Seeds
Asian Sesame Rice, 323
Chicken Sesame with Oriental Crème, 8
Ginger Noodles with Sesame Egg Strips, 311
Honey Sesame Tenderloin, 125
Lemon Sesame Scallops, 220
Sesame Broccoli, 316
Sesame Peanut Noodles with Green Onions, 304
Sesame-Peanut Spaghetti Squash, 184
Sesame Salt, 66, 242
Soy-Braised Chicken Wings, 16
Spicy Sesame Noodles, 320
Shanghai Fish Packets, 230
Shanghai Party Pleasers, 21
Shantung Twin Mushroom Soup, 273
Shrimp
Braised Lion's Head, 90
Braised Shrimp with Vegetables, 236
Chili Garlic Prawns, 232
Chilled Shrimp in Chinese Mustard Sauce, 34
Crab-Stuffed Shrimp, 214

Shrimp (continued)
Curried Apricot Glazed Shrimp and Beef, 206
Curried Shrimp with Coconut Ginger Rice, 208
Curry Coconut Fried Rice, 367
Easy Seafood Stir-Fry, 212
Hot and Sour Shrimp, 240
Japanese Petal Salad, 250
Malabar Shrimp, 232
Oriental Shrimp & Steak Kabobs, 226
Pad Thai, 210, 334
Shrimp, Mushroom and Omelet Soup, 274
Shrimp Curry, 370
Shrimp Java, 222
Shrimp Omelets, 213
Shrimp with Snow Peas, 234
Smucker's® Mandarin Shrimp and Vegetable Stir-Fry, 219
Spicy Honey Garlic Shrimp, 240
Spicy Thai Shrimp Soup, 284
Stir-Fried Shrimp Appetizers, 14
Stir-Fry Shrimp and Snow Peas, 360
Thai Salad Rolls with Spicy Sweet & Sour Sauce, 26
Thai Shrimp Curry, 222
Thai-Style Tuna Fried Rice, 238
Vietnamese Summer Rolls, 12
Wonton Soup, 286
Sizzling Five-Spice Beef, 45
Sizzling Rice Cakes with Mushrooms and Bell Peppers, 192
Smucker's® Mandarin Shrimp and Vegetable Stir-Fry, 219
Snow Peas
Asian Sesame Rice, 323
Beef Soup with Noodles, 281
Beef with Snow Peas & Baby Corn, 60
Braised Cornish Hens, 144
Chinatown Turkey Salad, 267
Chinese Chicken Noodle Soup, 276
Chinese Vegetables, 302
Curried Apricot Glazed Shrimp and Beef, 206
Easy Seafood Stir-Fry, 212
Ginger Wonton Soup, 328

Snow Peas (continued)
Hearty Egg Drop Soup, 272
Hot Chinese Chicken Salad, 368
Ivory, Rubies and Jade, 92
Jones® Ham Stir-Fry Pasta Salad, 250
Lemon Cashew Chicken Stir-Fry, 126
Lemon Sesame Scallops, 220
Oriental Beef Salad, 261
Plum Chicken, 324
Sesame-Peanut Spaghetti Squash, 184
Shrimp with Snow Peas, 234
Stir-Fried Crab, 236
Stir-Fried Pork and Vegetables, 106
Stir-Fried Tofu and Vegetables, 178
Stir-Fry Shrimp and Snow Peas, 360
Szechuan Chicken Salad, 340
Szechuan Vegetable Stir-Fry, 182
Szechwan Beef Stir-Fry, 54
Vegetable Delight, 308
Vegetarian Tofu Stir-Fry, 190
Soba Stir-Fry, 204
Soups (see also 268–287)
Ginger Wonton Soup, 328
Japanese Noodle Soup, 350
Vietnamese Beef Soup, 345
Soy-Braised Chicken Wings, 16
Spicy Beef and Broccoli Stir-Fry, 74
Spicy Glazed Short Ribs, 45
Spicy Honey Garlic Shrimp, 240
Spicy Orange Chicken, 162
Spicy Orange Oriental Chicken Breasts, 352
Spicy Oriental Green Beans, 316
Spicy Peanut Sauce, 191
Spicy Pork Stir-Fry, 354
Spicy Sesame Noodles, 320
Spicy Sweet & Sour Sauce, 24
Spicy Thai Chicken, 173
Spicy Thai Shrimp Soup, 284
Spring Rolls, 24
Steamed Pork and Ham, 108
Stews
Aromatic Asian Beef Stew, 51
Canton Pork Stew, 110

Stir-Fried Beef & Eggplant Salad, 249
Stir-Fried Crab, 236
Stir-Fried Orange Beef, 366
Stir-Fried Pork and Vegetables, 106
Stir-Fried Pork and Veggies, 119
Stir-Fried Shrimp Appetizers, 14
Stir-Fried Sirloin & Spinach with Noodles, 50
Stir-Fried Tofu and Vegetables, 178
Stir-Fried Turkey with Broccoli, 138
Stir-Fry Beef & Vegetable Soup, 278
Stir-Fry Shrimp and Snow Peas, 360
Sweet and Sour Chicken Breasts, 173
Sweet and Sour Cooking Sauce, 100
Sweet and Sour Fish, 229
Sweet & Sour Mustard Pork, 104
Sweet and Sour Pork, 84
Sweet & Sour Pork, 101
Szechuan Chicken Salad, 340
Szechuan Chicken Tenders, 166
Szechuan Cold Noodles, 310
Szechuan Grilled Flank Steak, 40
Szechuan Vegetable Stir-Fry, 182
Szechuan Wings, 167
Szechwan Beef Stir-Fry, 54

T
Tandoori Chicken Breast Sandwiches with Yogurt Sauce, 364
Tandoori Pork Sauté, 116
Tandoori-Style Chicken with Cucumber Raita, 332
Tandoori Turkey Kabobs, 142
Tangy Peanut Sauce, 256
Tender-ness Turkey Stir-Fry Salad, 252
Teriyaki Beef, 48
Teriyaki Lamb Riblet Appetizers, 29
Teriyaki Plum Chicken, 152
Teriyaki Pork Tenderloin, 124
Teriyaki Steak Strip Kabobs, 70
Teriyaki Stir-Fry Chicken Dinner, 143
Thai Barbecued Chicken, 156

Thai Beef and Noodle Toss, 42
Thai Beef Salad, 248, 344
Thai Chicken Broccoli Salad, 356
Thai Chicken Satays, 152
Thai Fried Rice, 96
Thai Grilled Beef Salad, 258
Thai Noodle Soup, 270
Thai Peanut Noodle Stir-Fry, 181
Thai Pork Burritos, 113
Thai Rice, 318
Thai Salad Rolls with Spicy Sweet
 & Sour Sauce, 26
Thai Satay Chicken Skewers, 164
Thai Shrimp Curry, 222
Thai-Style Pork Kabobs, 326
Thai-Style Salad with Shredded
 Glazed Chicken, 262
Thai-Style Tuna Fried Rice, 238
Thai-Style Warm Noodle Salad,
 244
Thick Coconut Milk Substitute, 10
Three Happiness Mushrooms, 298
Three-Pepper Steak, 68
Tofu
 Bean Curd with Oyster Sauce,
  202
 Bean Threads with Tofu and
  Vegetables, 180
 Broccoli-Tofu Stir-Fry, 339
 Crispy Orange Vegetables and
  Tofu, 203
 Dragon Tofu, 190
 Hot and Sour Soup, 280
 Hunan Stir-Fry with Tofu, 118
 Indonesian Vegetable Salad,
  254
 Japanese Noodle Soup, 350
 Ma Po Tofu, 196
 Mu Shu Vegetables, 186
 Oriental Tofu Noodle Salad with
  Spicy Peanut Sauce, 191
 Soba Stir-Fry, 204
 Stir-Fried Crab, 236
 Stir-Fried Tofu and Vegetables,
  178
 Szechuan Vegetable Stir-Fry,
  182
 Tofu Stir-Fry, 188
 Vegetable-Tofu Stir-Fry, 200
 Vegetarian Rice Noodles, 194
 Vegetarian Tofu Stir-Fry, 190
 Wok Sukiyaki, 52

Tomatoes
 Bombay Potatoes, 298
 Chicken Curry Bombay, 352
 Indian Vegetable Curry, 176
 Lamb Meatballs in Spicy Gravy,
  72
 Lentil Rice Curry, 198
 Oriental Shrimp & Steak
  Kabobs, 226
 Seafood Stir-Fry with Indonesian
  Rice, 228
 Seoul Rolled Beef with
  Vegetables, 62
 Shrimp Curry, 370
 Vegetarian Tofu Stir-Fry, 190
 Zucchini Shanghai Style, 296
Tortillas
 Mu Shu Pork, 122
 Mu Shu Vegetables, 186
 Spring Rolls, 24
 Thai Pork Burritos, 113
 Vietnamese Grilled Steak Wraps,
  76
Tuna Teriyaki, 237
Turkey
 Chinatown Turkey Salad, 267
 Ground Turkey Spring Rolls,
  28
 Shanghai Party Pleasers, 21
 Stir-Fried Turkey with Broccoli,
  138
 Tandoori Turkey Kabobs,
  142
 Tender-ness Turkey Stir-Fry
  Salad, 252
Turmeric Potatoes, 322
Two-Onion Pork Shreds, 102

V
Vegetable Delight, 308
Vegetable-Tofu Stir-Fry, 200
Vegetarian Rice Noodles, 194
Vegetarian Tofu Stir-Fry, 190
Vietnamese Beef Soup, 345
Vietnamese Dipping Sauce, 12
Vietnamese Grilled Steak Wraps,
 76
Vietnamese Loin Steaks with Black
 Bean Relish, 358
Vietnamese Summer Rolls, 12
Vietnamese Vegetarian Spring
 Rolls, 32

W
Walnuts
 Beefy Bean & Walnut Stir-Fry,
  82
 Chinese Chicken & Walnut Stir-
  Fry, 149
 Chinese Chicken Rolls, 166
Water Chestnuts
 Buddha's Delightful Vegetables,
  299
 Chicken Chow Mein, 353
 Chinatown Turkey Salad, 267
 Chinese Chicken Noodle Soup,
  276
 Hearty Egg Drop Soup, 272
 Ivory, Rubies and Jade, 92
 Mandarin Chicken Salad, 348
 Orange Almond Scallops, 362
 Sesame Chicken and Vegetable
  Stir-Fry, 330
 Shrimp with Snow Peas, 234
 Spicy Beef and Broccoli Stir-Fry,
  74
 Stir-Fried Orange Beef, 366
 Tender-ness Turkey Stir-Fry
  Salad, 252
 Teriyaki Beef, 48
 Teriyaki Stir-Fry Chicken Dinner,
  143
 Vegetable Delight, 308
Wok Sukiyaki, 52
Wonton Soup, 286

Y
Yogurt
 Baked Chicken Bombay, 140
 Broccoli with Tangerine Ginger
  Sauce, 294
 Chicken Curry, 168
 Cucumber Raita, 333
 Curried Pork Kabobs, 124
 Indian Pork with Honey, 107
 Lamb Meatballs in Spicy Gravy,
  72
 Mogul-Style Fried Chicken, 148
 Raita, 142
 Tandoori Pork Sauté, 116
 Thai Chicken Satays, 152
 Yogurt Sauce, 364

Z
Zucchini Shanghai Style, 296

METRIC CONVERSION CHART

VOLUME MEASUREMENTS (dry)

$1/8$ teaspoon = 0.5 mL
$1/4$ teaspoon = 1 mL
$1/2$ teaspoon = 2 mL
$3/4$ teaspoon = 4 mL
1 teaspoon = 5 mL
1 tablespoon = 15 mL
2 tablespoons = 30 mL
$1/4$ cup = 60 mL
$1/3$ cup = 75 mL
$1/2$ cup = 125 mL
$2/3$ cup = 150 mL
$3/4$ cup = 175 mL
1 cup = 250 mL
2 cups = 1 pint = 500 mL
3 cups = 750 mL
4 cups = 1 quart = 1 L

VOLUME MEASUREMENTS (fluid)

1 fluid ounce (2 tablespoons) = 30 mL
4 fluid ounces ($1/2$ cup) = 125 mL
8 fluid ounces (1 cup) = 250 mL
12 fluid ounces ($1\frac{1}{2}$ cups) = 375 mL
16 fluid ounces (2 cups) = 500 mL

WEIGHTS (mass)

$1/2$ ounce = 15 g
1 ounce = 30 g
3 ounces = 90 g
4 ounces = 120 g
8 ounces = 225 g
10 ounces = 285 g
12 ounces = 360 g
16 ounces = 1 pound = 450 g

DIMENSIONS

$1/16$ inch = 2 mm
$1/8$ inch = 3 mm
$1/4$ inch = 6 mm
$1/2$ inch = 1.5 cm
$3/4$ inch = 2 cm
1 inch = 2.5 cm

OVEN TEMPERATURES

250°F = 120°C
275°F = 140°C
300°F = 150°C
325°F = 160°C
350°F = 180°C
375°F = 190°C
400°F = 200°C
425°F = 220°C
450°F = 230°C

BAKING PAN SIZES

Utensil	Size in Inches/Quarts	Metric Volume	Size in Centimeters
Baking or Cake Pan (square or rectangular)	8×8×2	2 L	20×20×5
	9×9×2	2.5 L	23×23×5
	12×8×2	3 L	30×20×5
	13×9×2	3.5 L	33×23×5
Loaf Pan	8×4×3	1.5 L	20×10×7
	9×5×3	2 L	23×13×7
Round Layer Cake Pan	8×1½	1.2 L	20×4
	9×1½	1.5 L	23×4
Pie Plate	8×1¼	750 mL	20×3
	9×1¼	1 L	23×3
Baking Dish or Casserole	1 quart	1 L	—
	1½ quart	1.5 L	—
	2 quart	2 L	—